CAE Testbuilder
New edition

Amanda French

MACMILLAN

Macmillan Education
4 Crinan Street
London N1 9XW
A division of Macmillan Publishers Limited
Companies and representatives throughout the world

ISBN 978-0-230-72791-5 (+ key)

ISBN 978-0-230-72792-2 (- key)

Original design by eMC Desisgn Ltd.

Page layout by Xen

Illustrated by Paul Collicutt; Oxford Designers and Illustrators;
Gary Rees

Cover design by Jim Evoy

The author would like to thank Liam, Georgia and Joe Keane for
the joy they bring, and Louise Tester for her commitment and
contribution to this book.

The publishers would like to thank Peter Sunderland.

The author and publishers are grateful for permission to reprint
the following copyright material:

Extracts from 'The Girl's Guide to Writing and Wishing' by
Felicity Price, copyright Felicity Price 2008, first published in
North & South Magazine 2008, reprinted by permission of the
author; Material from 'How peach turned me into a blue cow'
by Mark Dapin, copyright © Mark Dapin 2002, first published
in The Observer 07.04.02, reprinted by permission of the author;
Information taken from Devonport Family Medicine Leaflet used
with permission; Material from Pacific Islands Development
Program/East-West Center – Feature 'Fiji Woman Keeps 'Masi'
Tradition Alive' by Ernest Heatley 2007, reprinted by permission
of Fiji Times Limited; Extracts from 'Not just a pretty face' by
Maureen Freely, copyright © Maureen Freely 2002, first published
in The Observer 01.09.02, reprinted by permission of the author;
Extracts from 'On the other hand…' by Robert Fulford, copyright
© Robert Fulford 2002, first published in National Post 25.06.02,
reprinted by permission of the author; Material from 'The Triumph
of the Airheads and the Retreat from Commonsense' by Shelley
Gare, copyright © Shelley Gare 2006, reprinted by permission
of the author; Extracts from 'What's the best way to climb Mont
Blanc?' by Alex Wade first published in The Independent on Sunday
11.08.02, reprinted by permission of the publisher; Extracts
from 'A Bundle of cash for writing jokes' by Veronica Lee first
published in The Independent 04.08.02, reprinted by permission of
the publisher; Extracts from 'Er, well, um…And now I have your
full attention' by Philip Hensher, copyright © Philip Hensher 2007,
first appeared in The Independent 25.09.07, reprinted by permission
of the publisher; Extracts from 'The languages of extinction: The
world's endangered tongues' by Claire Soares, copyright © Claire
Soares 2007, first appeared in The Independent 19.09.07, reprinted
by permission of the publisher; Extracts from 'Do elephants
really never forget? the truth about proverbs' by Geoff Rolls,
copyright © Geoff Rolls 2007, first appeared in The Independent
12.11.07, reprinted by permission of the publisher; Extracts
from 'Ghanaian fashion accessory is plastic fantastic' by Tristan
McConnell, copyright © Tristan McConnell 2008, first appeared in
The Independent 18.03.08, reprinted by permission of the publisher;
Extracts from 'Feeling stressed? pull yourself together' by Angela
Patmore, copyright © Angela Patmore 2008, first appeared in The
Independent 22.04.08, reprinted by permission of the publisher;
Extracts from 'The world's rubbish dump: a garbage tip that
stretches from Hawaii to Japan' by Kathy Marks and Daniel
Howden, copyright © Kathy Marks and Daniel Howden 2008,
first appeared in The Independent 05.02.08, reprinted by permission
of the publisher; Extracts from 'More than a breath of fresh air'
first published in New Zealand Wilderness Magazine September
2002, reprinted by permission of the publisher; Extracts from
'Let's Dance' by Rupert Mellor and friends copyright © News
International Newspaper Limited, London 2002, first published
in The Times 03.08.02, reprinted by permission of the publisher;
Extracts from 'What does every corporate boss need? Lego' by
David Rowan, copyright © David Rowan 2002, first published
in The Observer 01.09.02, reprinted by permission of the author;
Material taken from 'Taking Our Time Off' by Rana Foroohar and
William Underhill taken from Newsweek Issue 14.05.07, copyright
© Newsweek 2007. All Rights Reserved. Used by permission and
protected by Copyright Laws of the United States; Book reviews
of Earthshaking Science reviewed by Sue Bowler, Small Wonder
reviewed by Maggie McDonald, Zoo: A History of Zoological
Gardens In The West reviewed by Adrian Barnett and Solar Flair
reviewed by Ben Longstaff all taken from www.newscientist.
com/opbooks 04.07.02, reprinted by permission of the publisher;
Extracts from 'Lamb's Tales' by Stephanie Pain first published
in New Scientist Magazine 15.06.02, reprinted by permission of
the publisher; Extracts from 'Virtuous Nature' by Mark Bekoff
first published in New Scientist Magazine 13.07.02; Extracts from
'No dodo' by Stephanie Pain first published in New Scientist
01.06.02, reprinted by permission of the publisher; Extract from
'Peckish pilferers caught out by snack attack' by Anna Gosline,
first published in New Scientist 12.03.05, reprinted by permission
of the publisher; Extract from 'Babies are born liars – but lies are
vital for our survival' by Desmond Morris, copyright © Desmond
Morris 2007, first appeared in The Daily Mail 04.07.07, reprinted
by permission of the publisher; Extracts from 'The Brain Gain'
by Sharon Stephenson first published in She Magazine July 2002,
reprinted by permission of the author; Extract from 'Childhood
memories, how was your childhood? by Christopher Middleton,
copyright © Christopher Middleton 2008, first appeared in The
Daily Telegraph 17.05.08, reprinted by permission of the publisher;
Extracts from 'How will advertisers reach us?' by Jay Chiat first
published in Time New Zealand 26.06.00.

These materials may contain links for third party websites. We
have no control over, and are not responsible for, the contents of
such third party websites. Please use care when accessing them.

The author and publishers would like to thank Cambridge ESOL
for the sample answer sheets. Reproduced with the permission of
Cambridge ESOL.

The author and publishers would like to thank the following for
permission to reproduce their photographs:

Alamy/Ashley Cooper p148(m), Alamy/Deco Images II p154(m),
Alamy/Max Earey p144(b), Alamy/Imae Broker p154(b), Alamy/
Paolo Patrizi p154(rm), Alamy/Phototake p154(lm), Alamay/
Stock Connection Blue p144(m); **Ardea**/Adrian Warren p153(m);
Corbis pp152(br), 154(tr), Corbis/Gideon Mendel p152(tr),
Corbis/Les Stone/Zuma p145(t); **Getty**/Aurora p145(b), Garry
Buss p149(l,r), Getty/Ryan McVay p141(m), Getty/Popperfoto
p153(b), Getty/Zomi p154(tl); **Masterfile**/Pierre Arsenault
p144(t); **PA Photos**/Stephan Rousseau p141(b); **Photolibrary**/
AnamalsAnamals p153(t), Photolibrary/Corbis Flirt p145(m),
Photolibrary/Ted Harowitz p148(t), Photolibrary/Imagestate
p141(t), Photolibrary/Robery Llewellyn p148(b), Photolibrary/
Ryan McVay p152(l).

Printed and bound in Thailand

2016   2015   2014
12 11 10 9 8 7 6

With Answer Key
2016   2015   2014
14 13 12 11 10 9

CONTENTS

INTRODUCTION

The Certificate in Advanced English Testbuilder is more than a book of practice tests; it offers students 'tests that teach'. This teaching function is achieved in part through sections of further practice and guidance. These sections review the questions in the practice tests, helping students to reconsider their answers and increasing their chances of getting the answers correct. The tests are designed to reflect the actual CAE examination as closely as possible.

The edition with the answer key helps to further the learning process. Answers are often accompanied by an explanation of why they are correct, and why other options are wrong.

Using the Certificate in Advanced English Testbuilder

Either:
- Do each part of a Paper under 'exam conditions'. This means that you cannot use a dictionary and you limit the time you spend on it. Then check your answers or do the further practice and guidance section. When you have answered the questions in this section, you can reconsider your answers to the original questions in the test before checking the final answers.

Or:
- You may wish to do some of the further practice and guidance questions before answering the questions in the test that they relate to. Alternatively, teachers may wish to do the further practice and guidance pages as discussion or pairwork, or ask students to prepare them before class.

The Certificate in Advanced English

Paper 1 Reading (1 hour 15 minutes)

Part	Task Type	Number of questions	Task Format	Marks per question
1	Multiple choice	6	A set of three thematically-linked texts. Candidates choose the correct answer from two four-option multiple-choice questions for each text.	2
2	Gapped text	6	A long text from which paragraphs have been removed and mixed up. Candidates choose the correct paragraph to fill each of the six gaps.	2
3	Multiple choice	7	A single long text. Candidates choose the correct answer from seven four-option multiple-choice questions.	2
4	Multiple matching	15	A single long text clearly divided into sections or a set of short texts connected by a similar theme. Candidates match 15 prompts to specific information in the text.	1
				Total 53

Paper 2 Writing (1 hour 30 minutes)

Part	Question format	Writing tasks	Word length	Marks
1 One task. Candidates must answer it.	Candidates read a question which outlines their task, their reason for writing, and the intended reader. They also read one or more short texts, eg an email, notes, survey results, or an extract from a newspaper article. Candidates use the information in these texts to answer the task.	Candidates write either: a letter, an article, a report, a proposal.	180–220	Part 1 and Part 2 are worth equal marks. See assessment criteria on page 21.
2 Five tasks. Candidates choose one of them.	Questions 2–4 Candidates read a question which usually requires them to respond to two or three points. Question 5 Candidates can choose either task (a) or (b). The tasks are based on the set reading texts chosen by the University of Cambridge Examinations Syndicate (see www.cambridgeesol.org/exams/general-english/cae.html for details of current texts).	2–4 Candidates write either: an article, a letter, a report, an essay, a proposal, a competition entry, an information sheet, a character reference, a review, or a contribution to a longer piece. 5 Candidates write either: a review, an essay, an article, a report.	220–260	

Paper 3 Use of English (1 hour)

Part	Task type	Number of questions	Task Format	Marks per question
1	Multiple-choice cloze	12	A single short text with 12 gaps. Candidates choose from four options for each gap. The focus is on vocabulary.	1
2	Open cloze	15	A single short text with 15 gaps. Candidates use the surrounding context to work out what the missing word is. The focus is on grammatical structure and text cohesion.	1
3	Word formation	10	A single short text with 10 gaps, each of which corresponds to a missing word. Candidates change the words in bold beside the text to form the missing word.	1
4	Gapped sentences	5	Five sets of three sentences. Candidates complete each set with one word that is appropriate in all three sentences.	2
5	Key word transformations	8	Eight pairs of sentences. The second sentence in each pair is incomplete. Candidates use a key word in bold to complete the second sentence so that it accurately paraphrases the first sentence. Candidates use between three and six words, including the key word, to complete the sentence.	0–2
				Total 63

Paper 4 Listening (about 40 minutes)

Each part is heard twice. After candidates have heard the final recording, they have five minutes to transfer their answers to the separate answer sheet.

Part	Task type	Number of questions	Task format	Marks per question
1	Multiple choice	6	Three short unrelated extracts from conversations between two or three speakers. Candidates choose the correct answer from six three-option multiple-choice questions. There are two multiple-choice questions for each extract.	1
2	Sentence completion	8	A monologue eg a speech, a presentation, or a talk. Candidates write a word or short phrase to complete the sentences.	1
3	Multiple choice	6	A conversation between two or three speakers. Candidates choose the correct answer from six four-option multiple-choice questions.	1
4	Multiple matching	10	Five short monologues on a similar theme. Candidates match a set of eight options to each of the five monologues. There are two separate matching tasks.	1
				Total 30

Paper 5 Speaking (about 15 minutes)

Part	Task Type	Time	Task format	Marks
1	Social interaction	3 minutes	Candidates respond to examiner's questions by giving personal information.	See assessment criteria on page 45.
2	Individual long turn	4 minutes	Each candidate talks about a set of pictures for about 1 minute. Each candidate also comments on the other candidate's pictures for about 30 seconds.	
3	Collaborative task	4 minutes	Candidates do a problem-solving task together based on a set of visual and written prompts.	
4	Further discussion	4 minutes	Candidates express their views on a series of questions that the examiner asks. The questions will be based on the topic in Part 3.	

Marking the Practice Tests

In CAE all five papers are worth 20% of the total mark. You should aim to get 60–65% in each paper, but if you do not achieve 60% in one paper, and you do very well in another paper, you may still pass.

CAE TEST ONE

PAPER 1 READING 1 hour 15 minutes

Part 1

You are going to read three extracts which are all concerned in some way with communication. For questions **1–6**, choose the answer **(A, B, C** or **D)** which you think fits best according to the text.

THE SUNDAY STAR YOUNG WRITERS COMPETITION

This year sees the 7th anniversary of the Young Writers Competition. The general theme for this event is 'ISSUES FOR THE 21ST CENTURY', which allows entrants to choose from a broad range of contemporary subjects; anything from global warming to globalization. Whatever topic is selected, however, it must relate specifically to the impact it has on the young generation, and while we do not expect our writers to have first-hand knowledge of the issues they select, we would expect them to demonstrate sound research skills by accessing and acknowledging a variety of sources for their information. These could include interviews that were conducted by the writer, reputable journals and magazines, and authoritative Internet sites. We require an academic style, with an objective approach to the topic.

This is a nationwide competition but to be eligible for entry, writers must either be permanent residents of New Zealand or international students enrolled here on a course of minimum 12 months' duration. There is an entry fee of $5 for each article submitted and writers may submit multiple entries. The deadline for submission is July 15th, and articles must be between 3000 and 5000 words in length. Please include a stamped addressed envelope for notification of results. Please note that no entries will be returned. The winners are expected to attend the official awards ceremony at the end of August.

1 The articles which are submitted must

   A be based on the writer's own personal experience.

   B be presented in a factual rather than opinionated way.

   C have an emphasis on either a business or environmental theme.

   D focus on issues that only concern young people.

2 What are we told about the conditions of competition entry?

   A It is a requirement that winners accept prizes in person.

   B There is a restriction on the number of articles participants can send in.

   C Only the winners should expect to be informed of the results.

   D It is necessary for participants to be taking a programme of study.

Extract from a newspaper

Language isn't just meaning. Conversely, not all non-verbal communications are bodily; some come from the mouth, too. An interesting piece of academic research from Scotland has focused on those much-despised elements of speech, 'ums' and 'ers'. Technically known as 'fillers', they are strongly criticized by all teachers of public discourse as promoting an image of uncertainty and vagueness. The research, however, suggests that these fillers might serve a purpose, as sirens on the ambulances of significance.

The researchers invited volunteers to listen to a series of spoken sentences. Some sentences were interrupted by non-verbal fillers such as 'er' and 'um'; others were spoken without hesitation. The results were interesting. The inarticulate speaker registered much more powerfully in the minds of the listeners. An hour after listening, the volunteers got 62 per cent of the words correct in the stumbled-over sentence, compared to 55 per cent of those in the strictly enunciated and articulate performance. It seems as if the listener, therefore, alerted by stumbling to a speaker's struggling with a difficult concept, automatically pays more attention. They might want to help out; they might simply be alerted to complexities. Either way, it does seem as if the connection, between inarticulacy and profundity, is to some degree hardwired in our brains.

3 The writer compares fillers to 'sirens' in order to

   A suggest that they can interfere with clear communication.

   B show how they alert people to important information.

   C compare them to an irritating background noise.

   D emphasize the sense of urgency they convey.

4 What is the writer's main point in the second paragraph?

   A Most people have a tendency to use fillers in speech.

   B Frequent pauses in speech make it difficult for listeners to recall ideas.

   C It is impossible to express complex ideas without some rephrasing.

   D People instinctively listen more carefully when others hesitate.

THE LANGUAGES OF EXTINCTION

For the Nivkh people of eastern Siberia, counting is not a simple matter of 'one, two, three'. Depending on whether they are talking about skis, boats or batches of dried fish, there are different ways of counting. Twenty-six different ways in fact. Small wonder, then, that 90 per cent of Nivkhs prefer the option of communicating in Russian. While this no doubt makes interaction simpler, what it doesn't do is to save Nivkh
line 9 from the list of endangered languages. And it is not alone. Linguists believe half the languages in the world will be extinct by the end of the century. The 80 major languages are spoken by about 80 per cent of the global population, while the 3500 least spoken languages have just 0.2 per cent of the world keeping them alive. 'The pace of language extinction we're seeing is unprecedented,' said Dr David Harrison, author of the

book *When Languages Die*. 'And it's happening faster than the extinction of flora and fauna.' However, when dolphin or eagle species become extinct, it's an event that the public are made well aware of, and which tends to evoke sentimentality and mourning.

Globalization and migration are the main culprits. Economic pressures lead to the disappearance of rural communities as people move to the cities, where first and local languages are coming under threat from the lingua franca of the workplace. Today's children are also unwittingly affecting the potential survival of a language, such as a child growing up speaking Mayan and Spanish soon figuring out that Spanish is better because it's spoken in school and on television, meaning that the Mayan language is likely to die out.

5 What does the word 'it' in line 9 refer to?

   A the multiple ways of counting

   B a direct manner of communication

   C the decision to talk in Russian

   D the possibility that the Nivkh language will disappear

6 The writer refers to dolphins and eagles to make the point that

   A the death of a language tends to go unnoticed.

   B there is little time left to save certain languages.

   C some global issues deserve more attention than others.

   D it is impossible to avoid extinction in some cases.

Before you check your answers, go to page 9.

WHAT'S TESTED

The Reading Paper has four parts. The texts come from a variety of sources, for example, newspapers, magazines, brochures, journals and novels, and may deal with a range of general interest topics. You will need a high level of vocabulary to understand the texts so it is important that you read English language newspapers and magazines as often as possible. A range of reading skills are tested: in Parts 1 and 3, your ability to understand detail, opinion, tone, purpose, main idea, implication, attitude, and to recognize how certain text features show exemplification, comparison and reference. Part 2 tests your ability to deal with text structure, cohesion and coherence; in other words, you need to be able to recognize how a text fits together. In Part 4, you must be able to locate specific information, detail, opinion or attitude.

Part 1 and Part 3 Multiple choice

In Part 1, there are three short texts on a similar theme from a variety of sources. Each text has two four-option multiple-choice questions. In Part 3, there is a single long text and there are seven four-option questions. The order of the questions follows the same order as the corresponding information in the text. In Part 3, the final question may test your overall understanding of the text, for example, you may need to interpret the writer's purpose for writing the text, or their attitude or opinion towards the subject matter.

TIPS

- Read the text first to get a general understanding of the main points. (If you look at the questions first, you might choose an answer because you think it 'looks right' or is 'the most likely answer'. This doesn't always work!)

- After reading the text, highlight the key words in the questions and the four options. Carefully read the part of the text where you think the relevant information is contained. Make sure the option you choose paraphrases the information in the text exactly.

A DETAILED STUDY

The exercise below will help you to make sure you have chosen the correct options for the questions in Part 1.

Extract One

- Match options A–D with parts 1–4 of the text that they probably correspond to.

- Write a synonym or short explanation under each word in bold.

- Look back at the article 'Sunday Star Young Writers Competition' and underline parts 1–4 of the text and the surrounding language. Then decide which option matches which part of the text *exactly*.

First paragraph

A	be based on the writer's own personal experience.	1	a **broad** range of contemporary topics
B	be presented in a factual rather than **opinionated** way.	2	an **objective** approach
C	have an emphasis on either a business or environmental theme.	3	the **impact** it has on the young generation
D	focus on issues that only **concern** young people.	4	**first-hand knowledge** of the issues

Second paragraph

A   It is a requirement that winners accept prizes **in person**.

B   There is a **restriction** on the number of articles participants can send in.

C   Only the winners should expect to be informed of the results.

D   It is necessary for participants to be taking a programme of official study.

1   include a stamped addressed envelope for **notification** in person of results.

2   international students enrolled here on a course.

3   Writers may submit **multiple** entries.

4   The winners **are expected** to attend the awards ceremony.

Extract Two

First paragraph

Sirens can be used as a means of *communication* (option A), as a way of *alerting* (B) people and can also be *irritating* (C) and sound *urgent* (D). But which option A–D reflects the idea of *significance* (*sirens on the ambulances of significance*)?

Second paragraph

Match the explanations below to words in the text.

1 line 2 hesitation   **2** line 3 inarticulate   **3** line 5 articulate   **4** line 6 stumbling
5 line 6 concept   **7** line 8 profundity

a making mistakes in speaking   **b** clearly expressed   **c** wisdom/seriousness/importance
d stopping/pausing in speech   **e** not able to express clearly what you want to say   **f** idea

Extract Three

First paragraph

'*It*' refers back to '*this*' in the same sentence. What part of the text in the first paragraph does '*this*' correspond to?

Second paragraph

In the final sentence, what do '*to be made aware of*' and '*sentimentality and mourning*' mean?

What do the phrases above tell you about the public reaction to the extinction of dolphin and eagle species?

In general, what is the function of the conjunction '*However*'?

Now return to page 7 and use these exercises to help you answer the questions.

Now check your answers to Part 1 of the test.

Part 2

You are going to read an extract from a magazine article. Six paragraphs have been removed from the extract. Choose from the paragraphs **A–G** the one which fits each gap (**7–12**). There is one extra paragraph which you do not need to use.

The fight to save New Zealand's giant parrot

For the past 28 years Don Merton has battled to save the kakapo, New Zealand's extraordinary green parrot. In 1995, when numbers fell to 50, it looked like the end for this bird. But this year they staged a comeback. The last survivors of this unique species have produced 26 chicks – more than in the whole of the past two decades. Instead of having no future at all, the kakapo suddenly has prospects.

| 7 |

Males gather at an arena to compete for females. After mating, the females raise their young alone. 'The kakapo is important because it has combinations of features found in no other bird,' says Merton, the longest serving member of the National Kakapo team. Unfortunately, its peculiarities have also made it vulnerable. Before man arrived, their only enemies were predatory birds and the kakapo's green plumage provided perfect camouflage against the vegetation.

| 8 |

Then after years of searching, Merton and a team from the New Zealand Wildlife Service discovered a single bird in a valley in Fjordland in the far south. It was an old male. Search parties found 17 more – all old males. Three years later, Merton's team finally uncovered signs of kakapo in the south of New Zealand's Stewart Island. It turned out to be a colony of 200 birds and some were breeding. 'We thought the kakapo was safe then,' says Merton. They were wrong. Cats were killing them at an alarming rate.

| 9 |

Merton knew what he had to do. The birds had to breed before it was too late and nothing could jeopardize this. From now on, the team would manage almost every aspect of kakapo life. They laid traps for rats and watched nests 24 hours a day. If anything other than a kakapo entered the nest, a watcher set off a tiny explosive charge that made a small bang, enough to startle intruders. By 1999, all the kakapo had been successfully moved to two islands – Maud Island, and Codfish Island, both free of rats.

| 10 |

'The challenge was to work out a diet and persuade them to eat it,' says Merton. The team eventually found that kakapo were especially partial to nuts. The birds thrived on the extra food, but still wouldn't breed. They seemed to be waiting for some special cue. On Maud Island it wasn't clear what that cue was, but on Codfish island there was no doubt that the birds bred in response to some signal from the rimu tree that alerts them to a coming mast.

| 11 |

Armed with this new knowledge, the team was ready to swing into action as soon as they spotted signs of masting on Codfish Island. Last year, it became obvious that the rimu were going to produce a large crop of seeds the next autumn. Merton moved all the adult females to Codfish Island. As the breeding season drew nearer, the kakapo rescue team arrived with electronic monitoring equipment, and spent the next months watching nests throughout the long nights.

| 12 |

The result was a large batch of chicks, a remarkable breakthrough, but there are still only 86 kakapo in the world. Do they really have good prospects? Merton is confident they do. 'As long as we keep using the same techniques, the population will steadily rise,' he says. 'The kakapo won't be extinct in our lifetime.'

A   What followed was an intensive rescue operation. During the following 15 years all the kakapo were moved to islands free from cats, stoats or possums. 'We thought we'd put them out of reach of predators,' says Merton. Again they were mistaken. They hadn't realized how dangerous the rats were. Not only did they compete with kakapo for food, they also ate eggs and chicks. It finally came to the point where only 50 kakapo remained.

B   In September the team began to put out extra food. 'We provided enough so the birds could breed but not so much that they'd get fat,' says Merton. 'We wanted to keep their weight down to encourage them to produce female chicks.' In December the males began their booming noises, and the females trekked to the courtship areas to choose a mate, unaware that electronic eyes were watching them.

C   The kakapo is nocturnal, looks like an owl, smells sweet and makes some very odd noises – from growls to deep resonant booms. Kakapo can't fly, but they are excellent climbers. They live a very long time and are the world's biggest parrots. The kakapo also has a unique breeding system.

D   Persuading the birds to breed was the next harder step as this only occurs when certain plants produce large crops of fruit and seeds, an event known as masting. At other times, the birds manage on very little. It's enough to support their metabolism, but not enough to raise a family. In the past, the kakapo from Fjordland and Stewart Island bred in response to masting by a range of plants including rimu trees. The team hoped with extra food the birds might breed.

E   Merton estimates this could take at least 15 years, less if they can trick the birds into breeding more often. 'We're looking for whatever it is in rimu that triggers breeding. It's probably chemical,' says Merton. 'Or it might be nutritional.' The team is currently testing an improved food pellet to see if that works.

F   There was nothing the team could do but patiently wait for nature to take its course. They continued with the food programme to ensure the females were in top condition and monitored the males to keep an eye on their numbers. The population remained stable but the team recognized the fact that it was only the rimu tree that would turn things around.

G   Once man arrived, bringing with him not only his dogs but rats that could sniff out nests, it was a different story. The rats went for eggs, chicks and even adults. The decline in numbers accelerated once European settlers arrived. They cleared large areas of kakapo habitat and brought more predators – cats, rats, stoats, and possums. By the late 1960s the kakapo was feared extinct.

Part 3

You are going to read a magazine article. For questions **13–19**, choose the answer (**A**, **B**, **C** or **D**) which you think fits best according to the text.

How will advertisers reach us?

It's Superbowl live in 2020. Record-setting numbers of viewers are tuned in to watch the game by using handheld devices that allow them to project the transmissions on to any flat surface. And in 2020, not unlike today, viewers are interested in the game, but they're actually more absorbed by the advertising. The commercials on screen are far better than they are now. Directors make sure they are moving, exciting, entertaining and technicians make sure the effects are breathtaking. It's not the commercials on screen that are the most interesting part, though: the really crucial advertising is hiding in plain sight on the field. Brand names blaze from each player's shirt. The game is held at U-tech Stadium in U-tech town – formerly known as Philadelphia. Corporations will pay big money for the right to digitize logos on to the T-shirts of the fans in the stands. Logos of sponsors won't be painted on stadium signs or on the field any more. Thanks to technology that is already emerging, logos of sponsors will be digitally embedded in the image on your screen. The logos you see will be chosen depending on your personal interests and profile, and they'll be different from the ones aimed at your next-door neighbours.

Advertising will change profoundly over the next couple of decades, although there's a good chance you won't notice the difference, since the most meaningful changes won't be visible to the casual observer. It's the changes that are happening underground that will count, and they're the ones we should be aware of. Advertising in the future will be stealthily and eerily targeted, disturbingly omnipresent and inescapable. Technology, naturally, will be the engine. User-tracking software that records your TV and Internet viewing habits in minute detail – and crosses it with your purchasing history – will allow the advertiser to know that you have children, that you eat meat, that your native tongue is Spanish and that your dishwasher is however many years old. That way you will be shown commercials for mini-vans, cheeseburgers and replacement dishwashers, all in Spanish, and not for sports cars, tofu and replacement refrigerators, in English. In fact, this technology already exists. Refined with data that track what kinds of online ads you tend to click on – funny, sentimental, fact-laden – every commercial will hit home.

Say what you will, that's a nifty trick. In the future, people won't be bothered with advertising messages irrelevant to them. They'll tend to like advertising better because it's so carefully tailored to their tastes and will begin to feel less like an intrusion. This works for the advertiser too because fewer dollars will be wasted. While it's a little dispiriting to think we can be so predictably manipulated, maybe that's a fair price to pay to avoid the pollution of messages you don't care about.

Nevertheless, it seems clear that the advertising outlets that exist today – TV and radio commercials, prints ads, billboards and taxi tops – will be inadequate for accommodating all the commercial messages that are agitating to get out. Advertising will therefore inevitably slip beyond the boundaries of the 30-second commercial and the full-page ad and migrate to the rest of the world, including entertainment, journalism and art. You can glimpse the future now. Product placement in movies is an obvious instance of where advertising has slipped outside its traditional container into entertainment. The music channels which are an entertainment medium designed expressly to sell records are another classic example. Every time an artist mentions a brand in their lyrics, advertising slips into art. If you have a tattoo of your team's name, you're already there. If you wear a T-shirt with a logo on it, you're also there but with less pain. Eventually, every surface that can display a message will be appropriated for advertising. A backlash is inevitable. Perhaps people will pay a premium to live in advertising-free zones.

People get very nervous when they see the line blurring between advertising and other forms of content; they think advertising is some kind of infection that pollutes the purity of art, ruins objectivity and distracts from the pleasure of entertainment. Yet this is missing the point. Surely consumers are smart and perfectly aware when they're being sold something; surely people who go to company websites are happy to find worthwhile information there and are capable of distinguishing between a commercial message and an editorial one? In the main, art and journalism have long relied on direct subsidy from private sources. Don't think for a minute that commercial interests didn't enter into it.

The genuinely disturbing aspect of the ubiquity of advertising is that it has begun to take over what was formally the property of the community. Take, for example, the popular Boston Garden park, naturally named after the city. It is now known as the 'Fleet Centre', after the sponsoring bank. A little town in the Pacific Northwest just renamed itself after a dotcom company in return for a generous donation. I won't mention the name here, since I figure advertising should be paid for. That's when advertising has gone too far: when it's become something we are, rather than something we see.

13 According to the writer, the greatest difference about TV audiences in 2020 is that they will

   A buy products because they are impressed by special effects.

   B have the right to choose the kind of commercials they wish to receive.

   C be exposed to different mediums of advertising than are common today.

   D appreciate certain programmes to a lesser extent than current audiences.

14 The writer suggests that over the next couple of decades, viewers will probably

   A be unaware of the effect that advertising has on them.

   B fail to realize how advertisers are promoting products.

   C resent the lack of privacy they have in their own homes.

   D feel pressurized to consume more disposable products.

15 In the third paragraph, what does the writer feel about the consumer being 'predictably manipulated'?

   A He condemns it as a form of deception.

   B He believes people will be indignant at the removal of choice.

   C He suggests that this is a cost-effective approach for the consumer.

   D He states that consumers will appreciate the precision of this approach.

16 What does the writer state about the future of advertising in the fourth paragraph?

   A Current outlets will no longer be used for promotional purposes.

   B Advertisements will take on a globally similar style and approach.

   C Advertising will overtake the importance of artistic value in music.

   D People will feel resentful that they are surrounded by advertising.

17 What point is the writer making in the fifth paragraph?

   A Artists have always depended on the financial support of people aiming to make a profit.

   B Some consumers are not able to discriminate between truth and subjectivity.

   C It is not always clear what some commercials are advertising.

   D People should be more wary about the invasion of advertising into art.

18 What point is exemplified by the references to Boston Garden and the 'little town'?

   A The public are being denied access to certain places.

   B Companies are exploiting public places for advertising purposes.

   C It is essential to choose the right location to advertise successfully.

   D Companies are trying to find ways to advertise for free.

19 In writing this article, the writer's aim is to

   A highlight which consumers will be most vulnerable.

   B dispel unnecessary fear about the impact of advertising.

   C warn people against becoming part of an advertising culture.

   D attack certain companies for being unethical.

Before you check your answers, go to page 15.

A DETAILED STUDY

The questions below will help you to make sure that you have chosen the correct options for questions 13–19 on page 14. Use a dictionary to help you where necessary.

13 Look at the first paragraph.

A   Does it say that viewers in 2020 would be persuaded to buy products because of special effects?

B   Who will choose the advertisements? Think about the grammatical structure and meaning of *'the logos you see will be chosen depending on your personal interests and profile, and they'll be different from the ones aimed at your next-door neighbours'*.

C   What does the word *'medium'* mean? Can you find any *'mediums of advertising'* mentioned in the text?

D   Does the text mention some different types of programmes? Does it say that people are less interested in the Superbowl than before?

14 Look at the second paragraph.

A   What does *'there's a good chance you won't see the difference'* refer to? The effect of advertising or the way viewers are exposed to advertising?

B   What do you understand by the terms *'targeted'*, *'omnipresent'* and *'inescapable'*? What connection do these words have with the previous sentence in the text?

C   The text states that technology will allow advertisers to track or discover what kind of advertisements viewers prefer to watch. Does it mention how viewers will react to this?

D   The text mentions some disposable products: dishwashers and refrigerators. Does the text state anywhere that viewers will feel forced to buy them?

15 Look at the third paragraph.

A   What do you understand by the word *'condemn'*? What does *'nifty'* mean? Does each word have a positive or a negative connotation?

B   What does *'indignant'* mean? Are there any words in the text that show the attitude of the viewers?

C   What does *'cost-effective'* mean? Who will be saving money?

D   What does a *'tailor'* do? What does *'to tailor something to somebody's taste'* mean? If something was tailored exactly to your taste, would you appreciate or dislike it?

16 Look at the fourth paragraph.

A   Does the text say that advertisers will stop using current outlets, eg TV and radio commercials and taxi tops?

B   *'The rest of the world'* is used idiomatically here. What does it actually refer to?

C   Does the text say that advertising will become more important than musical creativity?

D   What does the phrase *'a backlash is inevitable'* mean?

17 Look at the fifth paragraph.

   A Can you find any words or phrases that reflect *'financial support'* and *'profit'*?

   B Does the writer contradict the idea that 'consumers are not able to discriminate between truth and subjectivity'?

   C What does *'blur'* mean? In the text, *'the line blurring'* is metaphorical. What is the *'line'* separating in this context?

   D Does the writer agree with people who think *'advertising is some kind of infection that pollutes … art'*?

18

   A Does the writer say that people are no longer allowed to enter the park?

   B What does *'disturbing'* mean? Does it have a positive or negative connotation? The Boston Park is now called the Fleet Centre. How did it get its new name?

   C Does the writer suggest that Boston Park or *'the little town'* were particularly good places for companies to advertise themselves?

   D Which word in the last paragraph shows that a payment was made to *'the little town'*?

19 This question covers the whole text.

   A What does *'vulnerable'* mean? Does the writer especially refer to any group he thinks will be at risk?

   B What does *'to dispel'* mean? Is the writer afraid of the impact of advertising in any way?

   C Which sentence in the final paragraph shows the writer's true feelings about the advertising culture?

   D Does the writer accuse any company of behaving in an unethical or dishonest way?

Now check your answers to Part 3 of the test.

Part 4

You are going to read a set of science book reviews. For questions **20–34**, choose from the reviews (**A–D**). The reviews may be chosen more than once.

In which review are the following mentioned?

the warning that the author does not always simplify the subject matter for the reader	20
an admission of past ignorance on the reviewer's part	21
the subject matter being dealt with in an impressive amount of detail	22
the book having both a narrative and simple academic approach	23
the depressing revelations the book makes about certain areas of its subject matter	24
the book's combination of established fact and doubt about the subject	25
the reviewer's sense of satisfaction concerning a personal achievement	26
a comparison between two very different causes of anxiety	27
praise for the author's clarity of thinking and enthusiasm for the subject	28
a mild criticism about some mistakes which occur in the book	29
the reviewer's implication that the subject matter deserves more consideration	30
the book's neutral approach to its subject matter	31
a warning that the conclusions the author draws may be frustrating	32
the fact that opinions on the subject were once based on guesswork	33
the suggestion that this book would be a good starting point for readers	34

This month's new science books

A   Maggie McDonald: *Small Wonder* by Barbara Kingsolver

White letters chalked on a blackboard in Sri Lanka are the first things I remember reading. The pleasure of deciphering that first word (C-A-T, of course) remains with me to this day. By age 11, I read a book a day, and at 14 I was being tested by an irritated teacher and school librarian who demanded proof that I was actually reading my library books. But there are only so many authors even the most avid of readers can digest, and some evaded me. Barbara Kingsolver was one. I had her filed in a 'sentimental nature-lover: must avoid' category. Friends kept recommending her and a few years ago, I read my first Kingsolver and ditched my ill-founded prejudice. She's a biologist by training and a wonderful writer. Possessed of an analytical mind, she's capable of putting it all down with real passion: a rare find. If you haven't tried her yet, do! *Small Wonder* is Kingsolver the essayist, elegant and insightful, and a great place to set out from before you tackle her backlist. Here you'll find the San Pedro river on the edge of survival, the energy bill behind the production of a five-calorie strawberry, and scientist Charles Darwin in all his complexity summed up in a mere four clear paragraphs.

B   Sue Bowler: *Earthshaking Science* by Susan Elizabeth Hough

Anyone who has ever driven an elderly, ailing car knows the feeling: it's going to break down, but who knows when, where and what part of the system will fail? Predicting earthquakes is much the same. Tidy forecasts of what, when, where and how much it will cost are as rare for quakes as for car repairs, and about as reliable. Have earthquake seismologists failed, then? Susan Elizabeth Hough says not, and *Earthshaking Science* sets out her case. This book gives us an excellent outline of how, why and where earthquakes happen together with a clear-eyed look at the subject's inherent uncertainties. This is not a book that proposes simplistic answers. It presents a real picture of a lively research field in all its gritty glory, written with a sharp eye for the absurdities of scientific life.

The focus on uncertainty has the paradoxical effect of highlighting the areas in which seismologists are confident, which makes it easier to deal with the ambiguities. Hough includes a careful and informative discussion of the earthquake risk across the US. Although her findings do not make easy reading, given the unexpected changes of intraplate quakes, it is an excellent analysis of what to worry about and where. Overall, this is an intelligent look at a broad field of science that affects many lives. Anyone heading for an earthquake area should buy a copy.

C   Adrian Barnett: *Zoo* by Eric Baratay

What's the attraction of gazing at captive animals? It's a good question and others have often sketched out an answer. But in *Zoo*, Eric Baratay gives us an unprecedented, in-depth answer. He explains why zoos lodge in the human psyche, their place in society, and how they developed over time. Placing them in their social and cultural context, *Zoo* traces the development of animal collections from medieval bear fights through the menagerie of the French king Louis XIV to modern captive breeding centres. Combining architectural analysis and political history, the author shows that the desire to display our domination over nature has long been a hidden feature of zoos.

The text has been translated from the French and in places, not very successfully. A trained biologist on the translation team might have weeded out appalling zoological errors such as describing the gannet as a 'rare and much sought after' bird, which it is definitely not. But these are forgivable oversights in a wonderful book that is acute at tracing themes of modern animal husbandry. While the book neither apologizes for nor criticizes the modern zoo, the extensive appendices tell a grim story. They contain a wealth of statistics on the death rate in collections, and the success rate of captive breeding. An absolute must for those interested in zoo history – or anyone fascinated by homosapiens' changing relationship with our fellow creatures.

D   Ben Longstaff: *Journey from the Center of the Sun* by Jack B. Zirker

Up, down, in or out. If that's about as much attention as you pay the Sun, you're ignoring something incredible. Did you know that it loses a million tonnes every second in the form of light alone? That's just for starters. In *Journey from the Center of the Sun*, Jack Zirker goes on a breakneck trip from its hellish core out into the realm of the planets, explaining as much as possible about our star on the way. His story-meets-textbook approach mainly avoids confusing scientific equations, but enables him to delve into lots of physics from massive sound waves to exploding pieces of sun the size of Asia.

Zirker's explanations are clear and sharp, although don't expect him to lead you by the hand. You do need to find the patience for a few serious pages of physics and daunting diagrams, but that's just great news if you want plenty of fascinating details as well as the grand overview. His informal style keeps things moving along swiftly, while balancing the latest findings with background on the pioneers of the field. He shows how solar research has progressed from inspired speculation into a flourishing science.

PAPER 2 WRITING 1 hour 30 minutes

Part 1

You **must** answer this question. Write your answer in **180–220** words in an appropriate style.

---

1 You recently had a meal at your friend David's restaurant, on the same evening that a food critic was there. The critic's review has since appeared in a local newspaper.

Read an extract from the review, and the notes you have made on it. Then, using the information appropriately, write a letter to the editor of the newspaper, giving reasons why you disagree with the review and explaining why you recommend the restaurant.

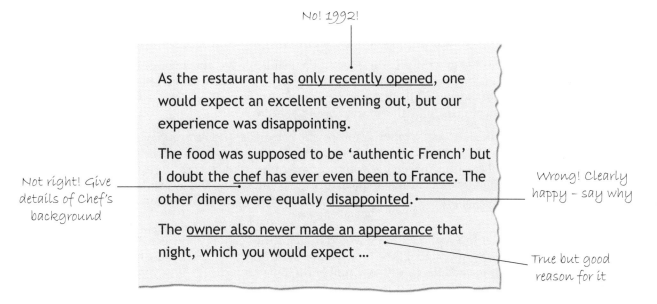

Write your **letter**. You do not need to include postal addresses. You should use your own words as far as possible.

Before you write your letter, go to page 21.

WHAT'S TESTED?

There are two parts in the Writing Paper: Part 1 (one compulsory question) and Part 2 (one question from a choice of five). You have 1 hour 30 minutes to do both questions. Each question carries equal marks. You need to write 180–220 words for Part 1, and 220–260 words for Part 2. You need to put the number of the question you are answering in the box at the top of the page of the answer sheet.

Part 1: Types of task

- **a letter:** you may be asked to write a letter to, for example, a friend, an editor, a school director or a possible employer. It is therefore important to think carefully who you are writing to as this will affect the style and register you use. In other words, you could use informal language to persuade a friend to come and study in your country, but you would need to use more polite, formal language to apply for a job. For some tasks, you can present your response as an email, but you must still use an opening salutation (eg Dear Mr Smith/Dear Jenny/To whom it may concern etc), and clear paragraphing and close your response with an appropriate phrase (eg Thank you for your attention/I look forward to hearing from you/Best wishes etc).

- **an article:** you may be asked to write an article for an English-language magazine or newspaper. Your target reader is somebody who has similar interests to you. An article should be informative and engaging, so you should: use a title that gets the reader's attention, use direct or indirect questions and then answer them, and give examples and anecdotes.

- **a report:** you may be asked to write a report for a specific person or specific group of people who already have some knowledge or interest in the subject you are writing about, either a superior (eg your manager or college principal etc) or your peer group (eg students in your class or colleagues etc). It is generally more formal than an article, so you should use a clear heading and subheadings, use a factual approach in presenting your information, and make clear suggestions and recommendations.

- **a proposal:** this is similar to a report in that it would need a clear heading and clearly separate paragraphs for each point. Although it is written in a formal way like a report, there may be more emphasis on trying to persuade the reader to accept or do something.

Part 2: Types of task

- **a letter** (also possibly including an application and a character reference), **an article**, **a report**, **a proposal**.

- **a review:** you may be asked to write a review for an English-language newspaper, magazine or website. In the review you should describe and give your personal opinion on something you have seen or used (eg a product, a film, a book, a television programme etc). You will usually be asked to say clearly whether or not you would recommend it, and give reasons.

- **an essay:** you may be asked to write an essay for a teacher, based on a class activity or project. You will usually be given a statement and asked to give your opinion on it. In your response, you can choose whether to agree or disagree with the statement or whether to discuss both sides. You are expected to structure your essay with an introduction, separate paragraphs which show the main points and reasons for your argument and a conclusion.

- **a contribution to a longer piece:** you may be asked to write part of a longer document (eg a guidebook or a college orientation pack etc). You will need to provide information and give your opinion, and organize your contribution under different headings. The style that you use depends on the longer document; for example, you might use a more colloquial style for a college orientation pack but use more factual and neutral language for a guidebook.

- **a competition entry:** you may be asked to enter a competition in which you either recommend yourself for selection (eg why you should be chosen to represent your school in a national competition) or you propose that someone else is chosen (eg why someone you know should be rewarded for their services to the community). You should be able to give your opinion and use the language of persuasion to convince the judges.

- **an information sheet:** you may be asked to provide information, advice or instruction to the target readers. The register of an information sheet is usually neutral and factual, and the content should be organized below headings.

- **set text:** you may be asked to write an article, an essay, a report or a review on the set text you have read. The style and format of your response will be similar to the other Part 2 questions. You will be required to give some description of the book (eg the plot, the personality of the characters, relationships between characters etc) and give your opinion on these.

What are the examiners looking for in your writing?

Marking criteria	What you need to consider when answering the tasks
1 Content	In Part 1, read the rubric and the input material carefully. Decide which points you must respond to in your answer and which information you can omit.
	In Part 2, there are usually two or three points you need to respond to in each task.
	Make sure you have included them all in your plan.
2 Organization and cohesion	Decide whether the task requires an introduction and a conclusion and/or headings. Organize your main points into clearly separate sections or paragraphs. Ask yourself if someone reading your report/essay/article would be able to see a logical order. Use linking words and phrases to show the connection between sentences, main points and ideas.
3 Range	Use a variety of grammatical structures and a good range of vocabulary. Avoid repeating the same words and phrases by using synonyms and paraphrasing instead.
4 Accuracy	Avoid making too many mistakes with basic English.
5 Appropriacy of register and format	Consider who you are writing to and the purpose for your writing. Choose a style that is appropriate – in other words, use informal language when writing to friends, neutral language for factual tasks, polite language when you are trying to persuade someone in authority.
6 Target reader	Consider what effect you want your document to have on the intended reader. As well as providing the reader with clear information, you need to use an appropriate tone.

For the General Impresion Mark Scheme go to page 128.

A DETAILED STUDY

Look again at Part 1 of the test on page 19 and answer the questions below.

Effect on target reader

a   Who is the reader?   b   Why are you writing to him?   c   What effect or result do you want your letter to have?

Content

What points need to be mentioned in your letter? Find them in the task outline, your notes and the review.

Now read the model answer below and find the answers to the questions above.

Dear Editor,

I am writing to take issue with the review of the Café Perigord, published in your newspaper 18/10/08. I was dining there on the same night as your critic, Mike Champion, and in my opinion his comments are completely unfair.

First of all, Mr Champion .... [**check**] his facts as the restaurant was established in 1992, and has not just 'recently opened'. The fact that it has been running for such a long time should show how popular it is.

Mr Champion's remarks on the food are also completely unjustified. If he .... [**ask**] to meet the chef, he .... [**find**] out that he is actually from Perigord and has won many awards.

Regarding the other customers, the people I observed were obviously satisfied, judging by the tips and the extremely positive comments they made to the waiters.

It is true that the owner David Vaylet was not at the restaurant that night, but again, if Mr Champion .... [**enquire**], he .... [**learn**] that David was off sick. In fact this was the first time I have ever known David to miss work.

I would absolutely recommend this restaurant to all your readers. I have been going there for many years and have always enjoyed truly excellent food and service.

Yours faithfully,

K. Wittner

Karen Wittner

Now answer the questions below.

Organization and cohesion

a   What is the purpose of paragraph 1?

b   What is the function of 'Regarding' (para 4)?

c   What is the function of 'actually' (para 3) and 'In fact' (para 5)?

Range

a   Explain the phrase 'to take issue with' something.

b   Find synonyms in the letter for 'comments' and 'unfair' (para 1), 'opened' (para 2) 'ask' (para 3).

c   Find five different adverbs that intensify an adjective or a verb.

d   Complete the missing parts of the letter using appropriate structures. The structures should show that you are criticizing Mike Champion for not doing something in the past.

Part 2

Write an answer to **one** of the questions **2–5** in this part. Write your answers in **220–260** words in an appropriate style.

2 You read the following announcement in an English-language newspaper that is published in your country.

FAMOUS CITIZENS COMPETITION

To celebrate our national holiday this year, we are planning a special edition of this newspaper. We will be focusing on citizens who have made some kind of positive contribution to our country. Which citizen would you nominate to be included in this edition? Write to us explaining in what way this person has contributed to our country and saying why you feel he or she should be included.

Write your **competition entry**.

3 Your class has recently been doing a project on people's attitudes to marriage in the twenty-first century. Your teacher has asked you to write an essay, giving your opinion on the following statement.

Marriage is a tradition that is unnecessary in modern society.

Write your **essay**.

Before you write your essay, go to page 24.

4 You see the following announcement on the website of a company that produces world guidebooks.

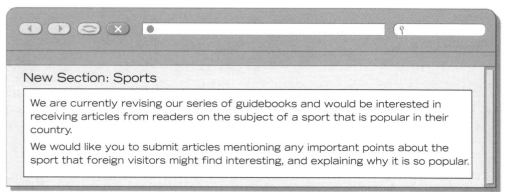

New Section: Sports

We are currently revising our series of guidebooks and would be interested in receiving articles from readers on the subject of a sport that is popular in their country.

We would like you to submit articles mentioning any important points about the sport that foreign visitors might find interesting, and explaining why it is so popular.

Write your **article**.

5 Answer **one** of the following two questions based on **one** of the [set books] below.

   a Your class has recently been doing a project on female characters in fiction. You have been asked by your teacher to write a report on one of the female characters in [the set book]. In the report, you should say what is known about the character and explain the contribution she makes to the development of the story.

   Write your **report**.

   b You have been asked to write a review of [the set book] by your college magazine. In your review, briefly outline the plot and explain what the author does to maintain the reader's interest to the end.

   Write your **review**.

A DETAILED STUDY – Essay

Essay: Marriage is a tradition that is unnecessary in modern society.

1   Read the sample answer below and decide whether the writer is:
   a   suggesting that marriage is unnecessary
   b   suggesting that marriage is still a good idea
   c   providing a balanced argument for and against marriage.

Over the last few decades there <u>has been</u> a considerable change in many people's attitudes towards the institution of marriage. **It** <u>used to</u> **be the case that** people had to get married in order to live together and raise a family but now more and more people <u>are choosing</u> to remain as 'partners'. **The question is whether** or not marriage still has a role to play in society today.

Central to this issue is the idea that marriage is an expression of commitment. **Advocates** of marriage believe that a wedding ceremony symbolizes the couple's serious intention to remain together no matter what difficulties they may face. However, the high rate of divorce does not support this theory. **It could be argued** that 'unmarried partners' also frequently break up, but this does nothing to support the theory that marriage is better .

There is also the subject of children **to consider**. There was a time when the children of unmarried parents were stigmatized but now a family is judged more on how they interact with one another; **in other words**, whether the parents spend enough time with their children and encourage them to think positively about themselves. **The point is that** a good home environment can be created by both married and unmarried parents, and it is their love and guidance that counts.

To conclude, for those people who are not religious, there seems to be no genuinely good reason to undergo a formal ceremony. Couples should be able to devote themselves to one another without the aid of a ring or formal document.

TIPS

1   Start your essay with some background information on the topic.

2   Rephrase the statement/essay title rather than just repeating it.

3   Separate your main points into different paragraphs (eg para 2 = the subject of commitment, para 3 = the subject of children).

4   Do not just write one or two sentences for each main point. Try to extend your ideas.

5   Make your final opinion clear without repeating the information from the paragraphs above.

2   **Range**

   Which underlined form in the first paragraph shows:
   a   a past situation/state that is no longer true.
   b   a trend that started recently and will probably continue into future.
   c   a situation/state that started in the past and is still true.

3   Which phrase or word in bold:
   a   means 'the most important thing about this subject'.
   b   could be rephrased as 'some people might say'.
   c   is used to show the writer's final opinion or decision.
   d   is used to introduce a new point.
   e   is followed by an explanation or rephrasing of what the previous sentence means.
   f   means 'it was true in the past'.
   g   is a synonym for 'supporters'.
   h   could be rephrased as 'we need to ask if'.
   i   is used to summarize one particular argument or the information in a particular paragraph.

PAPER 3 USE OF ENGLISH 1 hour

Part 1

For questions **1–12**, read the text below and decide which answer (**A, B, C** or **D**) best fits each gap. There is an example at the beginning (**0**).

Example:

0   **A** measure   **B consider**   **C** regard   **D** notice

---

Beauty is in the eye of the beholder

People have been debating the principles of beauty for thousands of years, but it still seems impossible to (**0**) ……………. it objectively. German philosopher Immanuel Kant (**1**) …………… whether something can possess an objective property that makes it beautiful. He concluded that although everyone accepts that beauty exists, no one has ever (**2**) …………….on the precise criteria by which beauty may be (**3**) ………… .

The ancient Greek philosopher Plato wrote of a scale called the 'golden proportion', (**4**) ……………..... to which the width of the face should be two-thirds of its length, preferably (**5**) …………… by a nose no longer than the distance between the eyes.

Symmetry has been proved to be attractive to the human (**6**) ……………, so a face may seem beautiful because of the (**7**) ………….. between its two sides. Babies spend more time looking at symmetrical faces than asymmetrical ones and symmetry is also (**8**) ………….... as more attractive by adults looking at photos. So although there seems to be no (**9**) …………… agreement or even national consensus on what (**10**) ………….. beauty, there is at least some agreement that facial symmetry is an important (**11**) ………….. .

In the meantime, if you look at your partner and (**12**) ……..……. them as beautiful, you can congratulate yourself with the thought that people generally end up with a partner of a comparable level of attractiveness as themselves.

1 **A** argued   **B** decided   **C** suggested   **D** questioned

2 **A** thought   **B** agreed   **C** fixed   **D** written

3 **A** judged   **B** appreciated   **C** awarded   **D** viewed

4 **A** corresponding   **B** according   **C** connecting   **D** relating

5 **A** accompanied   **B** escorted   **C** joined   **D** coupled

6 **A** appearance   **B** sight   **C** eye   **D** vision

7 **A** equality   **B** reflection   **C** opposition   **D** similarity

8 **A** voted   **B** rated   **C** selected   **D** valued

9 **A** world   **B** global   **C** community   **D** universal

10 **A** constitutes   **B** contains   **C** involves   **D** comprises

11 **A** reason   **B** cause   **C** role   **D** factor

12 **A** believe   **B** consider   **C** regard   **D** think

Part 2

For questions **13–27**, read the text below and think of the word which best fits each gap. Use only **one** word in each gap. There is an example at the beginning (**0**).

Example: 0   WHICH

On the other hand?

We left-handed people tend to lack pride (**0**) .... means that we rarely complain about having

to live in a 'right-handed' world. We make (**13**) .... demands and we avoid a fuss. I used to

say whenever someone watched me sign my name and remarked that he or she was also left-handed:

'You and me and Leonardo da Vinci!' That was a weak joke, (**14**) .... it contained my often

unconscious desire to belong to Left Pride, a social movement that (**15**) .... far doesn't exist

but I hope may one day come. There are many false stories about left-handed people (**16**) ....

circulation: for example, a few decades ago someone wrote that Picasso was left-handed, and others

kept repeating it, but the proof is all (**17**) .... the contrary. The great genius Einstein

(**18**) .... often still claimed as one of ours, also (**19**) .... proof. And sadly there is also

no truth (**20**) .... the myth that the left-handed tend to be smarter and more creative.

(**21**) .... the great amount of research that has been carried out, researchers in the field still

find it hard to decide precisely what we mean (**22**) .... left-handed. Apparently a third of

those (**23**) .... write with their left hand throw a ball with their right. (**24**) .... , those

using their right hand for writing rarely throw with their left. The skill of writing is one that becomes

crucial at a most impressionable age, and defines (**25**) .... you will call yourself. I have never

used scissors, baseball bat, hockey stick or computer mouse with anything but my right;

(**26**) .... so, I still regard myself as left-handed, as (**27**) .... everyone else.

Before you check your answers, go to page 28.

WHAT'S TESTED

Part 2 of the Use of English Paper is primarily a test of structural control, with many questions involving the completion of grammatical structures. Missing words can include articles, conjunctions, prepositions. Some questions may involve completing collocations and fixed phrases.

TIPS

- Always read through the text for general understanding before you begin to fill the gaps.
- Before you decide what the word should be, read the whole sentence including the sentences before and after it.

A DETAILED STUDY

1   Before you check your answers to Part 2 of Test 1, choose from the following:

	a		b		c		d	
13	a	some	b	few	c	little	d	any
14	a	yet	b	while	c	still	d	even
15	a	so	b	as	c	this	d	by
16	a	on	b	by	c	in	d	under
17	a	for	b	at	c	to	d	on
18	a	is	b	has	c	was	d	had
19	a	despite	b	without	c	lacking	d	beyond
20	a	with	b	from	c	in	d	for
21	a	Although	b	However	c	Nevertheless	d	Despite
22	a	as	b	for	c	by	d	with
23	a	can	b	people	c	types	d	who
24	a	However	b	Whereas	c	Despite	d	Unlike
25	a	what	b	how	c	this	d	which
26	a	more	b	yet	c	even	d	and
27	a	is	b	does	c	was	d	has

2   Now read the following information on conjunctions.

However

There are three ways to use *however*:

1   Jane doesn't have much money. **However**, she bought a new car last week.

- We can use *however* for the same subject: eg Jane.

2   Jane doesn't have much money. **However**, her sister, Mary, is quite rich.

- We can use *however* for two subjects: Jane + Mary.
- *However* starts the second sentence.
- Notice the position of the comma.

3   Jane doesn't have much money, **however**, she bought a new car last week.

- *however* can be placed between two clauses.
- Notice the position of the two commas.

Nevertheless

Jane doesn't have much money. **Nevertheless**, she bought a new car last week.

- We can use *nevertheless* for the same subject: eg Jane.
- *Nevertheless* starts the second sentence.
- Notice the position of the comma.

Despite/In spite of

There are four ways to use *despite* or *in spite of*:

1   Jane doesn't have much money. **Despite/In spite of** this, she bought a new car last week.

- *Despite/In spite of* + this

2   **Despite/In spite of** the fact that Jane doesn't have much money, she bought a new car last week.

- *Despite/In spite of the fact that ...*

3   **Despite/In spite of** her lack of money, Jane bought a new car last week.

- *Despite/In spite of* + noun phrase

4   **Despite/In spite of** not having much money, Jane bought a new car last week.

- *Despite/In spite of* + (not) -ing

Although/Even though/Though

1   **Although/Even though** Jane doesn't have much money, she bought a new car last week.

- *Although/Even though* + subj + verb.
- Notice the position of the comma.

2   Jane doesn't have much money. She bought a new car last week, **though**.

- *though* is informal and used in spoken English and in informal letters.

Whereas

There are two ways to use *whereas*:

1   **Whereas** Jane doesn't have much money, her sister is quite rich.

2   Jane doesn't have much money **whereas** her sister is quite rich.

- *Whereas* is used to contrast two subjects: Jane + her sister
- Notice the position of the comma in the first sentence.

3   Use the conjunctions to complete the sentences below. There may be more than one possible answer.

a   .... rising unemployment, the government still feel confident of winning the next election.

b   .... the position requires experience, we would consider hiring a graduate with excellent qualifications.

c   We were told that the price was all-inclusive. .... , we then found out we had to pay for meals.

d   .... some journalists are keen to expose the truth, others seem keener on making up lies.

e   A healthy diet can prolong life .... a diet of junk food can be harmful to your health.

f   It's said 'travel broadens the mind', ... , it might depend on how open-minded you are.

g   .... working longer hours, some workers are actually taking fewer holidays.

h   Learning Italian was a real challenge for me. .... , the lessons were interesting and useful.

i   .... the fact that I enjoy working for the company, I would love the chance to work abroad.

Now check your answers to Part 2 of the test.

Part 3

For questions **28–37**, read the text below. Use the word given in capitals at the end of some of the lines to form a word that fits in the gap **in the same line**. There is an example at the beginning (**0**).

Example: 0   EXHIBITION

Community Centre Summer Events

June 3rd sees the opening of an incredible (**0**) .... of photographs by professional   **EXHIBIT**

photographer and local (**28**) .... , John Taylor. In the 50 years that John has   **RESIDE**

been taking photographs, he has amassed a (**29**) .... fascinating record of   **VISION**

village life. The show is (**30**) .... *History Through The Lens* and includes   **TITLE**

nostalgic portraits of local people and hypnotic images of the landscape. There is

also a section on (**31**) .... important events which is equally fascinating.   **HISTORY**

Another upcoming event is a book reading by author Maria Treadway. You may

know Maria as a children's writer, but over the last three years she has

(**32**) .... into adult fiction. Her novels, all set in the 17th century, are   **DIVERSE**

both entertaining and highly (**33**) .... Maria has often admitted in the past   **INFORM**

to being a (**34**) .... and she carries out extensive research before she   **PERFECT**

writes. On June 9th, she will be reading from her latest novel *The Last Key*, which

is (**35**) .... her best work to date.   **ARGUE**

This is a really (**36**) .... evening so be sure to book well in advance.   **MISS**

(**37**) .... to both events is $10 for adults and free for pensioners.   **ADMIT**

Before you check your answers, go to page 31.

WHAT'S TESTED

Part 3 of the Use of English Paper is a test of your ability in word formation, for example, you may be given a noun and have to transform it into a verb, or produce an adjective from a noun. It is important that you know the meaning and functions of the many different prefixes (eg un/in/re-) and suffixes (eg ally/ion/ment) in the English language, and that you are familiar with compounds (eg worldwide, outcome, downsize).

TIPS

Carefully read the text to get an overview of the topic and to understand the main points of each paragraph or group of sentences. This will help you decide a) what class of word you need to produce b) how the word fits in to the context and c) whether you need to use a singular or plural form.

A DETAILED STUDY

Each set of words below can be formed from the words in bold on page 30. Write down the word class next to the word and then match it to the definition below.

A   **reside (v)**   **a** residential (…)   **b** resident (…)   **c** residence (…)

- someone who lives in a particular place
- (formal) a house or a place where someone lives
- describing an area in which most of the buildings are houses

B   **vision (n)**   **a** visually (…)   **b** visualize (…)   **c** visible (…)

- to form a picture of someone or something in your mind
- in a way that is related to the appearance of something
- clearly seen/obvious

C   **title (n)**   **a** titled (…)   **b** entitled (…)

- describing a person belonging to a high social class and who has a title eg Lord/Lady
- to give a title to a book/song etc

D   **history (n)**   **a** historian (…)   **b** historic (…)   **c** historically (…)

- describing a past event that was significant and had great consequences
- in a way that is connected with places, events or people from the past
- someone who studies or writes about events in history

E   **diverse (adj)**   **a** diversified (…)   **b** diversely (…)   **c** diversity (…)

- to develop into something different or to add to what you already do
- the existence of a variety of people or things within a group or place
- describing how something is treated or dealt with in different ways

E   **inform (v)**   **a** informed (…)   **b** misinform (…)   **c** informative (…)

- describing a person or thing that provides a lot of useful information
- describing a choice or decision made on good information
- to give someone the wrong/false information about something

F   perfect (adj)   a perfectly (…)   **b** perfectionist (…)   **c** perfection (…)

- a state in which someone or something is perfect or as good as they can be
- in a way that could not be better
- someone who always wants things to be done perfectly

G   argue (v)   a argumentative (…)   **b** argument (…)   **c** arguable (…)

- an angry disagreement between two or more people
- used to say you are not completely certain if something is true or right
- (negatively) describing a person who likes to argue

H   miss (v)   a unmissable (…)   **b** missing (…)

- used to describe someone who has disappeared and who others are looking for
- used to praise something and recommend that other people experience it

I   admit (v)   a admittedly (…)   **b** admission (…)   **c** admittance (…)

- the amount of money required to enter a place such as a gallery/museum etc
- (formal) permission to enter a place or join something
- used to say that you admit something is true, alhough it makes your argument weaker

Now decide which of these words best fit the gaps on page 30.

Part 4

For questions **38–42**, think of **one** word only which can be used appropriately in all three sentences. Here is an example (**0**).

Example:

0   Please explain to me the .... of having another meeting.

It was at that .... that most of the audience got up and left.

We lost a .... because one person in our team started the race too early.

Example: POINT

---

38   The bad weather is expected to .... by the afternoon.

It's time to .... out these cupboards and make some space.

The lawyer announced that he had new evidence that would .... the young man of murder.

39   If we .... prices any more we'll be making hardly any profit.

The censors insisted that some violent scenes were .... from the movie.

We were so poor that my mother was forced to .... up her old dresses to make new ones for us.

40   The company needs to .... this problem before it gets worse.

This glue will .... any material to any another surface.

Before we all leave, we should .... a date for the next meeting.

41   All the castle towers .... north across the entrance to the harbour.

It doesn't .... as if we'll have the chance to see the museum.

It'll take some time to .... through the report and make a decision.

42   The .... in the newspaper said the roadworks would begin on July 2nd.

It has come to my .... that staff are dissatisfied with the company cafeteria.

Both witnesses failed to .... the clothes the thief was wearing.

Part 5

For questions **43–50**, complete the second sentence so that it has a similar meaning to the first sentence, using the word given. **Do not change the word given**. You must use between **three** and **six** words, including the word given. Here is an example (0).

Example:

0   There is a strong possibility that this species of rhino will become extinct.

   DANGER

   This species of rhino is .... extinct.

Example: 0   IN DANGER OF BECOMING

---

43   I thought Sue's original plan was to move to Australia.

   IMPRESSION

   I .... was originally planning to move to Australia.

44   Mr Smith was well-known as a bad-tempered man, but he was also fair.

   REPUTATION

   Despite .... bad-tempered, Mr Smith was also fair.

45   Signing the contract without the director's approval is not allowed.

   CIRCUMSTANCES

   Under .... sign the contract without the director's approval.

46   It looks like you didn't sleep well last night.

   IF

   You look .... much sleep last night.

47   I don't believe that Jane ran that distance in only five minutes!

   POSSIBLY

   Jane .... that distance in only five minutes!

48   Simon doesn't agree with me about which slogan is best for the campaign.

   DIFFERENCE

   Simon .... opinion over which slogan is best for the campaign.

49   Jane's lawyer suggested that she ignored all the reporters.

   ATTENTION

   Jane's lawyer advised .... all the reporters.

50   I doubt that Simon will lend us the money.

   CHANCE

   I think .... Simon lending the money to us.

PAPER 4 LISTENING approximately 40 minutes

Part 1

You will hear three different extracts. For questions **1–6**, choose the answer (**A, B** or **C**) which fits best according to what you hear. There are two questions for each extract.

Extract One

You hear part of an interview with an environmental campaigner called Richard Frost.

1   Why did businessman Kwabena Osei Bonsu set up *Trashy Bags*?

    A   He wanted to solve a problem.

    B   He had seen similar projects overseas.

    C   He was given government funding.

2   What does Richard Frost recommend about plastic bags in Britain?

    A   Customers should be made to pay for them.

    B   They should be disallowed by the government.

    C   Supermarkets should offer other kinds of bag instead.

Extract Two

You hear two people on a radio programme talking about the subject of hypnotherapy.

3   What did the woman think about hypnotism before she visited a hypnotherapist?

    A   She doubted that it was effective.

    B   She believed it could treat psychological problems.

    C   She thought it worked for people who believed in it.

4   The two speakers agree that many people

    A   have a negative image of hypnotists.

    B   are not in control of themselves during hypnosis.

    C   are disappointed with the results of hypnotherapy.

Extract Three

You hear part of an interview with a woman called Fiona who works as a zoo tour guide.

5   What does Fiona say about visitors who go on zoo tours?

    A   They encounter some animals for the first time.

    B   They have strong preferences about which animals to see.

    C   They are unaware of the potential danger.

6   How did Fiona feel after the incident with the chimpanzee?

    A   She was reluctant to work with chimpanzees again.

    B   She realized that she needed to be more careful at work.

    C   She was uncertain why the incident had occurred.

Before you check your answers, go to page 36.

WHAT'S TESTED

For Part 1 of the Listening Paper, you will hear three short conversations. There are usually two speakers taking part in the conversation, but three are also possible. Each conversation is about a different topic or theme; for example, the first conversation might be about an exhibition both the speakers have seen, and the second one might be about one of the speaker's experience of preparing for a sports competition.

Part 1 tests your ability to identify the speakers' feelings, attitudes and opinions, as well as recognizing the function of the conversation, what decisions the speakers have made, and what they agree about.

A DETAILED STUDY

* Read through the tapescripts of the conversations below.
* Listen to the recording and write down the words you hear.
* Pause or stop the recording if you need time to write down the missing words.

Extract One

Int: Richard, can you give us an example of what people in other countries are doing in terms of recycling?

Richard: Absolutely. Erm, well, 60 tonnes of plastic packaging are dumped on the streets of Accra, the capital city of Ghana, every day. But recently a businessman called Kwabena Osei Bonsu set up a company called Trashy Bags to do something about it. He pays people to collect plastic bags and these are stitched together to make new ones. This kind of venture (1) .... sponsored by governments, and there are plenty of similar projects occurring in other countries (2) .... But Kwabena had decided he wasn't going to wait around. He says he wanted to come up with an idea that would (3) .... in his lifetime.

Int: I believe that in Britain, though, you'd like to stop the use of plastic bags completely?

Richard: Well yes – they are an absolute environmental disaster, but (4) .... our government going as far as banning them. I know that some supermarkets are charging customers 5 or 10 pence per bag, but such a small charge (5) .... Actually, you can get bags made of bamboo or other fabrics but only a minority of people are using them, so I'd say it's up to the supermarkets to start promoting them a bit more actively – so that customers know they're (6) .... instead.

Extract Two

Man: You've just had a few sessions of hypnotherapy, haven't you? I have to say, I didn't think you were into that kind of thing.

Woman: You thought I was the skeptical type? Well I've never been a believer in most alternative therapies but I've always been fairly (7) .... when it comes to hypnotherapy … at least when it came to dealing with psychological problems. I mean, before I experienced hypnotism for myself, I didn't think it would work for actual (8) ……………………….. symptoms. I went along because I wanted to quit smoking, but Dr Grey helped me overcome my back pain, too.

Man: I guess a lot of people see celebrity hypnotists on TV embarrassing people they've hypnotized – making them do ridiculous things. And I think the result of that is that people are (9) ………………………….. to see genuine hypnotherapists – because they think anyone who practises hypnotism is not (10) ……………………………… .

Woman: I think you're right, but people should know that hypnotherapy is a serious profession. And if the idea of being under someone else's control makes you nervous, I can tell you it's not like that. You're always (11) …………………………….. of what's going on.

Extract Three

Int: Erm, Fiona, how is it working with visitors to the zoo?

Fiona: The public? Generally they're fantastic. Maybe they're a little bit quiet to start with because they're not sure what they're (12) ……………………………. what they're going to do but soon after we've met the rhinos or we've starting doing the monkeys they normally open up and they're all 'Oh, this is fantastic'. They start asking questions and they know a lot about the animals anyway because they've been going to the zoo (13) ………………………….. . But the hardest thing for me is being constantly alert to the risks because even though you do (14) ………………………….. people about them, they just don't realize what could happen. I mean even the cheetahs look so docile and so cuddly.

Int: Have you ever had an incident yourself?

Fiona: No, not exactly, but I did get a bit too close to the bars of the chimpanzee enclosure once, and the chimps had branches with them to try and get food from beyond the bars, and one of the male chimps basically just reached through the bars with his branch and poked me in the ribs and it was basically a 'Get back! That's my food!' and from that moment on I've always been doubly (15) ………………………….. I am to an animal and what tools it has to get to me as well. He could have been a lot nastier, though, than he was. It was just (35) ……………………………. .

Use the words you wrote down to help you choose the correct answers to questions 1–6 on page 35.

Part 2

You will hear a museum curator called Frank Turner talking about a dinosaur exhibition.
For questions **7–14**, complete the sentences.

DINOSAUR EXHIBITION

Frank believes people want to be [_____ **7**] which is why they visit the

dinosaur exhibition.

According to Frank, children first look for the [_____ **8**] in the exhibition.

Frank thinks the exhibition helps develop children's [_____ **9**] .

Scientists rely on two [_____ **10**] fossilized skeletons of Tyrannosaurus Rex

to help them with research.

Dinosaurs are mainly found preserved in [_____ **11**] environments.

Frank refers to a huge [_____ **12**] in China which killed many dinosaurs.

The Chinese dinosaurs had feathers which were probably used for [_____ **13**]

purposes.

Frank says that the museum appreciates [_____ **14**] from visitors.

Part 3

You will hear part of a radio interview in which a naval officer called Peter Martin is talking about his experience. For questions **15–20**, choose the answer (**A, B, C** or **D**) which fits best according to what you hear.

15 What made Peter first decide to join the navy?

   A He liked the idea of being able to travel.

   B He thought it would impress people at home.

   C He believed he could get promoted more quickly.

   D He felt he had wasted his time when he was younger.

16 What effect did Peter's upbringing have on his suitability for the navy?

   A He found it difficult to take orders at first.

   B He was often too competitive during training sessions.

   C He experienced few problems adapting to the lifestyle.

   D He was challenged by the hard physical exercise required.

17 According to Peter, how can recent school leavers do well in the navy?

   A by accepting that their social life is of secondary importance

   B by recognizing that the navy can offer a long-term career

   C by learning to take responsibility for themselves

   D by delaying entry into the navy until they are older

18 For Peter, what is the most rewarding part of a trip back to his hometown?

   A Receiving respect from people he went to school with.

   B Experiencing a sense of pride in his achievements.

   C Relating his experiences to younger members of the community.

   D Hearing that other people have followed his example.

19 According to Peter, what do the public not understand about the navy?

   A The range of roles that the navy undertakes.

   B The length of time that navy personnel spend at sea.

   C The dangers that navy personnel have to face.

   D How much money is required to run the organization properly.

20 According to Peter, what advantage does a previous naval career give job seekers?

   A A sense of confidence in their own ability.

   B The discipline for later academic study.

   C The determination to succeed in their work.

   D Experience which can be transferred to other fields.

Part 4

You will hear five short extracts in which various people are talking about embarrassing situations.

TASK ONE

For questions **21–25**, choose from the list **A–H** the person who is speaking.

A   interpreter

B   student | 21 |

C   party organizer | 22 |

D   chef | 23 |

E   manager | 24 |

F   office worker | 25 |

G   photographer

H   old school friend

TASK TWO

For questions **26–30**, choose from the list **A–H** the situation the speaker finds embarrassing.

A   being unaware of social etiquette

B   losing customers | 26 |

C   making introductions | 27 |

D   meeting childhood rivals | 28 |

E   getting lost abroad | 29 |

F   being in unnatural social situations | 30 |

G   feeling inferior

H   impressing possible employers

In the exam you will have 5 minutes at the end of the test to copy your answers on to a separate answer sheet.

Before you check your answers, go to page 41.

WHAT'S TESTED

Part 4 of the Listening Paper is a multiple-matching exercise. This involves two tasks. In the first task, you may be required, for example, to identify the speakers (eg a salesman/a school teacher) or interpret their attitudes or opinions (eg anger/irritation), and in the second task, for example, to recognize the function of their monologue (eg complaining/apologizing), or recognize the context (eg traffic problems/rudeness).

TIPS

- Remember – you will hear the recording twice. You need to do both tasks while the recording is played.

- Read both Task 1 and Task 2 before the recording begins so you can anticipate the kind of vocabulary or functional language you are going to hear. For example, if one of the options is 'expressing disappointment', you might expect to hear 'What a pity' or 'It wasn't as good as I'd hoped for'.

- When you read Tasks 1 and 2, do not automatically assume that an option in Task 1 matches an option in Task 2. For example, 'an airline pilot' in Task 1 may not be talking about 'long flights' in Task 2.

A DETAILED STUDY

Listen to the recording again and fill in the gaps below. Answer the questions that follow each extract.

Speaker 1

1 … when I'm supposed to be showing .... around, I can never ....

2 … it doesn't exactly come across as .... for someone in my ....

3 I'd find myself saying things like '...'

4 My .... actually suggested I rehearse the whole thing.

What does the information in 1–4 tell you about the speaker and what he finds embarrassing?

Speaker 2

5 They come along and I'm setting up the ....

6 I just hide behind the ....

7 They feel .... and they're .... to have their kid's .... taken.

8 It's not exactly good for .... or personal ....

What does the information in 5–8 tell you about the speaker and what she finds embarrassing?

Speaker 3

9 I don't have much ....-...........…......... in general.

10 I'm the new girl in the ....

11 I'm fed up with them all .... me.

12 It makes me feel really .... at times.

What does the information in 9–12 tell you about the speaker and what she finds embarrassing?

Speaker 4

13 I didn't spend a lot of time there, a couple of .... I think.

14 Nobody had .... to anybody and the few conversations we had were utterly
....

15 What do you expect after a ....-odd years?

16 … everybody remembered hating the ....

What does the information in 13–16 tell you about the speaker and what he finds embarrassing?

Speaker 5

17 I'm going out there again in a month's time and .... to a couple of ....

18 At least my .... skills are alright.

19 There won't be many people prepared to .... unless I have some idea of the
language.

What does the information in 17–19 tell you about the speaker and what he finds embarrassing?

Now check your answers to Part 4 of the test.

PAPER 5 SPEAKING about 15 minutes

Part 1 (3 minutes)

Candidates may be asked:

- Where are you from?
- What do you do?
- How long have you been studying English?
- What do you enjoy most about learning English?

Candidates are then asked one or more questions from a selection of categories, for example:

Leisure time

- What do you enjoy doing in your free time?
- If you could take up a new sport or activity, what would it be?
- What kind of television programmes do you watch?
- How much time do you spend on leisure compared to work or study?

Future plans

- What are you most looking forward to in the next few months?
- How do you think you might use your English in the future?
- What do you hope to be doing this time next year?
- How far ahead in the future do you usually plan?

Travel and holidays

- What sort of holiday do you tend to prefer?
- Where in the world would you most like to visit?
- Do you prefer travelling alone or with others? Why?
- What do you find unpleasant about travelling?

Work and study

- What skills do you need for the job that you do or plan to do?
- What would make a job appeal to you?
- How do you help yourself to concentrate on your work or study?
- How have your ambitions changed over the last five years?

Experience

- How might learning English lead to new experiences?
- Who has had a significant influence on you?
- How has your life changed in the last few years?
- Are you the kind of person who likes to take risks and chances in life?

For further help, see page 46.

Part 2 (4 minutes)

1   Ambition

For both candidates: Look at the three pictures on page 141. They show people who have an ambition.

Candidate A: Compare two of these pictures and say what different ambitions these people might have and what they might be doing to achieve their ambitions. (*1 minute*)

Candidate B: Which of these people do you think has to work the hardest to achieve their ambition? (*approximately 30 seconds*)

2   Holiday destinations

For both candidates: Look at the three pictures on page 142. They show holiday destinations in different countries.

Candidate B: Compare two of these pictures and say what kind of people would choose a holiday destination like this, and what the reasons for their choice might be. (*1 minute*)

Candidate A: Which of these destinations do you think would have the least relaxing effect on people? (*approximately 30 seconds*)

For Further Practice and Guidance, see page 47.

Part 3 (4 minutes)

For both candidates: Look at the pictures on page 143. They show examples of different texts that people read.

First talk to each other about what each of these texts might tell us about life today. Then decide which three texts you would choose to put in a museum for future generations to see.

Part 4 (4 minutes)

For both candidates:

- Is there any other text you would choose to put in the museum?
- How do you think reading compares to watching films as a form of entertainment?
- What role do you think newspapers play in today's society?
- How important is it to encourage young people to read?
- How do you think written language might change in the future?

For further help, see page 47.

WHAT'S TESTED

In the Speaking Paper, candidates speak together in pairs or occasionally in a group of three if there is an odd number of candidates taking the test. There will be two examiners: the Interlocutor (the Examiner who asks the questions and gives you your tasks) and the Assessor who will listen, take notes and award marks. The test takes approximately 15 minutes and is divided into four parts.

Timing	Task Type	What the interlocutor asks	Focus
Part 1 about 3 minutes	Conversation between the interlocutor and each candidate	The interlocutor asks each candidate some general questions, eg about where they are from/their occupation/their experience of learning English, and some questions chosen from a range of general categories eg leisure/future plans/travel etc.	general interactional and social language
Part 2 about 4 minutes	Individual 'long turn' for each candidate	The interlocutor asks each candidate to compare and talk about two pictures from a different set of three. The other candidate is then asked to make a brief comment or give their response.	comparing, describing, expressing opinions, speculating
Part 3 about 4 minutes	Two-way conversation between candidates	The interlocutor gives the candidates a decision-making task – based on pictures and spoken instructions.	exchanging ideas, expressing and justifying opinion, (dis)agreeing, suggesting, speculating, evaluating, negotiating
Part 4 about 4 minutes	Discussion on topics related to the task	The interlocutor asks the candidates questions which develop and extend the theme of Part 3.	expressing and justifying opinion, (dis)agreeing.

ASSESSMENT CRITERIA

Your performance in the Speaking Paper is judged according to the following criteria.

Grammatical resource

Your ability to use a range of simple and complex grammatical structures accurately and appropriately.

Vocabulary resource

Your ability to use a range of vocabulary that will allow you to fulfil task requirements and express and exchange views on a variety of topics.

Discourse management

Your ability to link utterances together to form coherent speech without too much hesitation. The utterances should be relevant to the tasks and should be arranged logically to develop the themes or arguments required by the tasks.

Pronunciation

Your ability to produce individual sounds correctly, to use stress and intonation in a way that aids communication, and to link words together so that your spoken English sounds natural. You are not expected to have a perfect native-speaker accent, but your own accent should not interfere with communication, or require effort from the listener in order to understand you.

Interactive communication

Your ability to interact with the interlocutor and the other candidate(s) by initiating conversation (stating your opinion and ideas or asking your partner questions), allowing your partner time to respond without interruption, and responding to your partner's opinions, ideas or questions.

Global achievement

Your overall effectiveness in dealing with the tasks in the four separate parts of the speaking test. The global mark is an independent impression mark which reflects the assessment of your performance from the interlocutor's perspective.

Part 1: General and Social

1   In this part of the test, you are required to demonstrate your ability to use general interactional and social language and you will be mainly talking about yourself, your life and your experience. It is not a good idea to prepare a fixed speech; it may not be a suitable response to the exact questions the interlocutor has asked you, and your intonation will sound unnatural. However, you could make sure you are confident in using some accurate and appropriate grammatical forms. Read the following examples and add two more sentences which are true for you.

Your usual lifestyle/situation: *Present Simple*

I'm from Switzerland. I live in Ticino, which as you might know, is in the Italian-speaking part of Switzerland, and I work in a bank, in the personal loans department. I don't have much free time, but at weekends, I try to get out and do some sport, either tennis or golf.

....

....

Your temporary lifestyle/situation: *Present Continuous*

At the moment, I'm living in Oxford with a host family while I'm doing my English course. I'm working during the day so I'm studying English part-time in the evenings.

....

....

Talking about a situation or activity which started in the past and is still true: *Present Perfect*

I've been learning English since I was 13. It was a compulsory subject in school, but in the last few years, I've been having private lessons.

....

....

Talking about experiences where the exact time isn't important or mentioned: *Present Perfect*

Since I've been in London, I've visited loads of museums and galleries. Most of them were quite interesting and the best thing is that they're free. But I've also spent a lot of money on eating out and going to clubs. I haven't travelled outside of London yet – but I hope to.

....

....

Talking about the past: *Past Continuous, Past Simple, Past Perfect, used to*

Before I came here, I was working as an assistant in a nursery school. I used to help the young children with their reading, but after four years, I got a bit fed up with it. So, I decided to quit and to learn English to get a better job. My friend Carina had already studied English in Dublin and she recommended that I went to the same school. That's why I'm here.

....

....

Talking about future plans: *going to/Present Continuous/will*

After this course finishes, I'm going to hire a car and travel around Australia. [for plans/intentions]

I'm starting work as soon as the course finishes. [arrangements]

I'm not sure what I'll do … I think I'll probably look for a new job. [uncertainty/spontaneous decisions]

....

....

Comparing:

I think English is easier than French because French grammar is much more complicated.

In Barcelona, the bars and the cafés are open later than in the UK so I think the nightlife is better there.

....

....

2   The interlocutor is likely to ask questions similar to those on page 43. With a partner, take turns to be the interlocutor and the student. Ask each other the questions and use your sentences above to help you. Try to respond from memory and don't just read your answers.

Part 2: Talking about pictures

In this part of the test, you are given three pictures and you choose two of them to talk about. The interlocutor asks you to compare your chosen pictures and respond to two questions. You are able to see these questions above the pictures.

In order to respond to Part 2 tasks, you need grammatical structures and vocabulary that enable you to compare, express your opinions, describe and speculate.

Comparing

DO NOT SAY, for example, *'Here you can see a business man who looks anxious. This picture shows a boy who looks calm'.* (See the task on p.44 Ambition.)

DO SAY *'Compared to/Unlike the man in the first picture, the boy looks slightly/a lot/much calmer.'*

'The man here seems to be rather anxious, whereas/but the boy looks quite calm in comparison.'

'They're both in competitive situations but the difference is that the boy looks calm and the man seems much more anxious.'

Expressing your opinion

DO NOT SAY *'Let me think about that …'* and hesitate for too long.

YOU CAN SAY *'Let me think about that'* but then quickly add *'Well, in my opinion…'*, *'I'd guess that …'*, *'I imagine that …'*

Describing and speculating

DO NOT SAY *'They take part in a business meeting.'* *'He gives some kind of speech.'*

DO SAY *'They **are** tak**ing** part in a business meeting.'* *'He **is** giv**ing** some kind of speech.'*

DO NOT SAY *'… in the top left hand corner …'* *'… in the top picture of this page …'*

DO SAY *'… this man seems/appears to be giving orders to junior staff members …'*

'He looks quite confident … as if he knows he's in control.'

*'He looks quietly confident … I think he might/could/must have just realiz**ed** how to win the game.'*

DO NOT SAY if you can clearly see something, eg a chess board *'This might be a game of chess.'*

DO SAY *'There are other chess players behind the boy so it must be some kind of chess championship … perhaps it's somewhere in Russia because I know this game is quite popular there.'*

DO NOT SAY *'That's all'*, *'I've finished'*

DO remember that there are no right or wrong answers to the questions, so continue to speculate about the pictures until the examiner stops you. In this way, you can demonstrate a greater range of vocabulary and structure.

*****Using the highlighted language forms above, practise Part 2 'Ambition' and 'Holiday Destinations' on page 44. Take turns to be the interlocutor and the student.*****

CAE TEST TWO

PAPER 1 READING 1 hour 15 minutes

Part 1

You are going to read three extracts which are all concerned in some way with health. For questions **1–6**, choose the answer (**A, B, C** or **D**) which you think fits best according to the text.

HELP WITH MEDICAL EXPENSES

High Use Health Cards allow for cheaper consultation fees and prescription fees. To obtain one you must have consulted a doctor at least 12 times in the previous 12 months for chronic (long-term) conditions, not including treatment covered by the Accident Compensation Commission (ACC) or visits to specialists. If you think you qualify, please discuss this with your doctor. *Community Service Cards* also allow cheaper medical and prescription fees; applicants for this are assessed according to their income. If you are entitled to a *Community Services Card* then you may also qualify for a 'Disability Allowance', which is actually related to chronic conditions rather than disabilities as such. This allows a claim for costs relating to conditions that are expected to go on longer than six months.

In the case of serious accidents or severe injuries, whether they occur in the workplace or elsewhere, there is a widespread misconception that the ACC pays for all of a doctor's consultation fees. In fact they pay an ever-diminishing share and patients are responsible for the balance of the charge in these situations. To allow us to process your claims for compensation as swiftly as possible, please advise the receptionist on arrival at the surgery so that a claim form may be filled out before seeing the doctor.

1 A person may be able to get a Community Services Card depending on

    A the seriousness of their illness in their doctor's opinion.

    B the amount of money that they earn from work.

    C the cost of treatments they require refunded.

    D the effect of their disability on their day-to-day living.

2 In the second paragraph the reader is informed that

    A the compensation scheme does not include minor accidents.

    B ACC may decide to discontinue payments for injuries that happen outside of work.

    C patients are expected to pay some of the doctor's fees.

    D a compensation claim must be approved by ACC before seeing the doctor.

EXTRACT FROM A NEWSPAPER ARTICLE

Why does the term 'stress' spring to mind every time you are animated, nervous, hurried, tense, angry, worried or scared? It may interest you to know that scientific research has not identified any condition called 'stress'. However, this same word is used by the general public, the media, and also many psychologists, to refer to more than 650 quite different things, including most human emotions. Anxiety, annoyance and frustration may not be pleasant, but they are perfectly normal. Rushing about trying to survive is a natural phenomenon too – even tiny woodland shrews do it. So why do we think, when we are in a hurry or our emotions are aroused, that this is harmful, or that we have a condition called 'stress'? Well, it's because we are constantly being told by the purveyors of 'calm-down' products that if we are not calm, there is something wrong with us.

Since I first began studying stress management, I've been warning of its dangers. I have had my critics. One reviewer wrote that I was widely regarded as heartless, but I am the opposite of that. I have seen enough evidence to convince me that the stress-management industry is detrimental to people's health.

The principles of stress management make people wary of stress arousal. Yet if your problems don't get you up and running about and you don't face up to them but instead try to escape from unpleasant reality, then there really is something wrong with you. Such behaviour causes the brain to release natural opiates to numb the pain but it also shuts off the immune system. When stress researchers refer to 'long-term stress', they are really talking about helplessness, failure to address threats and inevitable biological decline.

3   Which of the following best summarizes the writer's argument in the first paragraph?

    A   Stress can only truly be associated with a few emotions.

    B   Stress is experienced in both positive and negative states.

    C   Stress has benefited both animals and humans during evolution.

    D   Stress is a term that is frequently used incorrectly.

4   What point is the writer making in the second paragraph?

    A   It is inadvisable to ignore problems that arise in life.

    B   These days people are unable to cope with the amount of stress.

    C   Too much stress can make you stop trying to succeed.

    D   It is best for a person to be calm when facing serious problems.

EXTRACT FROM A NON-FICTION BOOK

Not only do we spend money on things we don't need, we also use money to try and acquire things that either can't be bought with money at all, or certainly can't only be bought. Happiness. Health. Fitness. Slimness. Freedom from stress and anxiety. Peace of mind. Longevity. Goodness, we seem to be thinking to ourselves, if we can buy a smooth forehead by paying the cosmetic surgeon $500 for Botox injections, surely we can also buy something soothing for inside the head. If we can buy a lifestyle, can't we buy a life? A billion-dollar group of industries will tell you 'yes'. But the simple, commonsense rules that can make good skin, a good figure and physical and mental health available to almost everyone who doesn't have a serious disorder, get rather less coverage than products and regimens and services that cost money.

Walk around gardens and parks in the early morning and the greenery teems with people toiling away at their jogging and sprinting. Sometimes they are in groups, and are being lectured and bullied by an instructor who has them doing knee-jumps and sit-ups and squats. Whenever I walk past them, their eyes seem to roll agonizedly towards me, like those of cattle being herded with an electric prod. These are men and women who, 90 minutes later, will be decked out in high-priced suits and sitting in massive offices dealing in grave matters to do with money. They could achieve similar results for their health, mind and body by going for a gentle walk, but a walk takes longer, maybe three or four times as long, and they don't have that kind of time. Instead they must go for the painful, sweaty, joint-crunching, bosom-stretching, knee-crushing supervised jogging, exercising and running because they have been told it's the fast way, the best way to stay fit. Hang the expense!

5   What is the writer's main point in the first paragraph?

    A   People are becoming increasingly insecure about their looks.

    B   It is unrealistic to think that money can achieve a better quality of life.

    C   Wealthy people have different spending habits from poorer people.

    D   It is impossible to prolong life simply through cosmetic procedures.

6   In this piece, the writer is generally

    A   skeptical about people's ability to maintain long-term fitness.

    B   admiring of the way that some people can achieve a work–life balance.

    C   disapproving of the fact that people can be easily manipulated.

    D   amused by the tendency of over-ambitious people to compete with one another.

Part 2

You are going to read an extract from a magazine article. Six paragraphs have been removed from the extract. Choose from the paragraphs **A–G** the one which best fits each gap (**7–12**). There is one extra paragraph that you do not need to use.

The story of the lamb-plant

According to a recent survey, 70 per cent of ten-year-olds living in Scotland's big cities think that cotton comes from sheep. It's easy enough to mistake the soft white stuff sold in fluffy balls in plastic bags at the local chemist's shop or supermarket with the curly stuff on a sheep's back, especially when the only sheep you've seen are in books or on the TV.

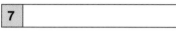
7

Rumours had first begun to circulate way back in the Middle Ages. The borametz, also known as the 'lamb-plant', was said to exist in Tartary, a far-away land stretching across Eastern Europe and Asia. None of those who told the various tales had actually seen it, but they'd always met men who had.

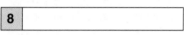
8

The man responsible for spreading the story in Britain was John Mandeville, a knight of England who left home in 1322, and for the next 34 years travelled about the world to many diverse countries. His account of what he saw was the medieval equivalent of a bestseller, and was translated into every European language. He wrote that he too had seen a type of fruit that when opened, proved to contain a small white creature that looked in every way to be a lamb.

9

This was apparently proof enough for Mandeville and those who passed on the story. With each telling, the story gained new details and greater credibility. But in the 16th and 17th centuries, people learned more about the world and its inhabitants. As doubts crept in, more sceptical travellers set out in search of the mysterious lamb of Tartary.

10

And so it went on. As soon as anyone voiced doubts, someone else popped up with new 'evidence' of the lamb's existence. In 1605, Frenchman Claude Duret devoted a whole chapter of a book on plants to the borametz. But then, 80 years later, the great traveller Engelbrecht Kaempfer went east looking for it. He found nothing but ordinary sheep. The number of believers was dwindling, and in London the renowned scientific academy, the Royal Society, decided it was time to 'kill off' the borametz for good.

11

This, the Society reckoned, was what had started the ancient rumours. They proclaimed it to be a 'specimen' of a borametz, in fact. Hans Sloane, founder of the British Museum, described the specimen in a contemporary publication: it was made from the root of a tree fern, had four legs and a head and seemed to be shaped by nature to imitate a lamb. The four-footed fake also had 'wool' of a dark golden yellow. Despite this discrepancy in the colour of its fleece, the Royal Society considered the case closed.

12

The answer was there all along in the writings of ancient travellers. While researching his book *Sea Monsters Unmasked*, the observant Henry Lee kept coming across detailed descriptions of plants that sounded far more like the prototype borametz. The Royal Society, Lee decided, had failed to spot the obvious connection and had settled for something so unlikely it had to be wrong. What so many had imagined to be a mythical animal in fact turned out to be ordinary cotton.

A And so it was, more or less, for 180 years. Then a little known naturalist pointed out that their so-called 'original' lamb-plant was a false clue. There was, however, a plant that had almost certainly given rise to the notion of the borametz.

B There's certainly doubt as to whether this was based on first-hand experience, but the contemporary guidebooks were certainly available. A few years earlier, a monk who came from a monastery near Padua, wrote that 'there grow fruits, which when they are ripe and open, display a little beast much like a young lamb'. He claimed he had heard this from reliable sources.

C The best way, it felt, was by showing people how the idea had begun. It was then lucky enough to suddenly receive a curious object from China, a sort of toy animal made from a plant with a few extra bits stuck on to give it a proper number of limbs.

D In some versions the 'vegetable lambs' were the fruits of a tree that grew from a round seed. When the fruits ripened, they burst open to reveal tiny lambs with soft white fleeces that the natives used to make their cloth. In others, the seed gave rise to a white lamb that grew on a stalk rooted in the ground, and lived by grazing on any plants it could reach.

Before you check your answers, go to page 52.

E There's less excuse for the generations of explorers, scholars and philosophers who were perhaps even more naïve. They were all happy to accept the story that the soft fibres from which eastern people wove fine white cloth came, in fact, from a creature that was half-plant, half-animal.

F Distorted descriptions of the cotton plants seen in India preceded the actual plants by many years. In the meantime, traders brought samples of cotton 'wool' along trade routes that passed through Tartar lands. To those who had never seen raw cotton, this fine 'Tartar wool' looked like something that might come from the fleece of a lamb.

G Still it eluded them, yet most came home convinced that it existed. One of these was a powerful baron who represented the Holy Roman Empire at the Russian court. The baron had dismissed the sheep-on-a-stalk as fable until he heard the creature described by a 'person in high authority' whose father had once been an envoy to the King of Tartary. The story was enough to convince the baron.

WHAT'S TESTED

Part 2 of the Reading Paper tests your ability to recognize the way a text is structured. You are required to read a gapped text on one page and then choose which extracts on the second page fit each gap. There is only one possible answer for each gap.

TIPS

* Read the gapped text first to understand the general idea of the content, meaning and structure.

* If the text is a narrative, look for tenses, words or phrases that indicate time (eg *shortly after this, from my previous experience, it was the first time I had ...*) and linkers that show cause and effect (eg *and it was for that reason, in order not to repeat that mistake, it was largely due to that advice that ...*).

* If the text presents an argument or discussion, you can look for cause and effect, phrases or linkers that show agreement or contrast (eg *Many people would go along with that/However, scientists discovered that this was not the case/Nevertheless, researchers continued to maintain ...*).

* It is also useful to look for repeated names, dates and pronouns (eg *At last one of **the archaeologists** found what seemed to be a **clue**. It was **this** [clue] that gave **them** [the archaeologists] hope*).

* Don't just read the first and last line of each extract. Often the clues or connecting ideas are in the middle of the extract.

A DETAILED STUDY

The questions below will help you to make sure that you have chosen the correct options for questions 7–12.

7 The text above 7 says that it is easy for children to confuse the product sold in supermarkets and chemists (manufactured cotton wool) with real wool from sheep. Which option A–G suggests that other people should have been able to recognize whether they were looking at real wool or not?

8 The text under 8 says he wrote that '*he too had seen a type of fruit that when opened, proved to contain ... a lamb*'. The '*too*' suggests that the option must contain a similar description. Which option seems similar? In the text above 8, notice the words '*various tales*', and under 8, '*the story*'. In the option you choose, which words refer to '*tales and stories*'?

9 In the text below 9, notice the words, '*This was ... proof enough for Mandeville*'. Which option gives an example of something that John Mandeville would believe he could trust?

10 The text above 10 finishes with '*more ... travellers set out in search of the...lamb*'. Which option starts with a reference to '*travellers*' (plural) and '*lamb*' (singular)? What word in the first line of that option means 'to avoid being found'? The text under 10 starts with '*And so it went on*'. What does '*it*' refer to in the option and in the following sentence?

11 In the text under 11, the text starts with '*This ... was what ... had started the ... rumours.*' It was a '*specimen*'. Which option contains a 'singular' reference?

12 The text above 12 finishes with '*the case* [this particular situation was] *closed*'. Which option begins with a reference to '*the case*'? The text under 12 also mentions '*Henry Lee*'. How has he been introduced in the option?

Now check your answers to Part 2 of the test.

Part 3

You are going to read a magazine article. For questions **13–19**, choose the answer (**A, B, C** or **D**) which you think fits best according to the text.

Virtuous Nature

Can animals really have a sense of right and wrong? Marc Bekoff thinks they do.

If you think that we are the only creatures on Earth with a moral sense, then you're in good company. Most experts in behaviour believe that morality is a uniquely human trait, without which our complex social life would never have emerged – yet I'm convinced that many animals can distinguish right from wrong. Decades spent watching wild and captive animals have persuaded me that species living in groups often have a sense of fair play built on moral codes of conduct that help cement their social relationships. The notion of Nature being naturally ruthlessly and selfishly competitive doesn't hold true for those of us who have observed and analysed animal relationships.

That's not all. I suspect that herein lies the origin of our own virtue. Biologists have had real problems trying to explain why people are frequently inexplicably nice to each other. It just doesn't make sense in evolutionary terms, unless there are ulterior motives behind our seemingly altruistic actions. Perhaps we expect a payback somewhere down the line, or maybe our good deeds are directed only towards kin, with whom we share a biological heritage. Nobody has really considered the possibility that being considerate to your neighbours might sometimes be the best way to survive. But I'm starting to find evidence that a well-developed sense of fair play helps non-human animals live longer, more successful lives.

I'm particularly interested in social play amongst youngsters because it has its own special rules of engagement, allowing participants to reinterpret acts that might otherwise seem aggressive. My studies of infant dogs, wolves and coyotes reveal that they use a special signal to prevent misinterpretation of playful actions. They perform a 'bow' – which entails crouching on the forelimbs while keeping the rear upright – when initiating play, or in association with aggressive actions such as biting, to modify their meaning. And role reversal is common, so that during play a dominant animal will often allow a subordinate to have the upper hand. Such behaviours reduce inequalities in size, strength and dominance between playmates, fostering the co-operation and reciprocity that are essential for play to occur. Indeed, on the rare occasions when an animal says 'Let's play' and then beats up an unsuspecting animal, the culprit usually finds itself ostracized by its former playmates.

My belief is that a sense of fairness is common to many animals, because there could be no social play without it, and without social play individual animals and indeed, entire groups would be at a disadvantage. If I'm right, morality evolved because it is adaptive. It helps many animals, including humans, to survive and flourish in their particular social environment. This may sound like a radical idea, particularly if you view morality as uniquely human and a sort of mystical quality that sets us apart from other animals. But if you accept my argument that play and fairness are inextricably linked, you're halfway there.

The challenge then is to demonstrate that individual animals benefit from fair behaviour and social play, but the more we learn about how play affects the brain, the more apparent it becomes that the activity is far from idle time-wasting. On the contrary, it is essential food for the brain. In fact what this does is sharpen an individual's cognitive skills,   *(line 59)* including logical reasoning and behavioural adaptability.

I am not putting the case forward for a specific gene for fair or moral behaviour. As with any behavioural trait, the underlying genetics is bound to be complex, and environmental influences may be large. No matter. Provided there is variation in levels of morality among individuals, and provided virtue is rewarded by a greater number of offspring, then any genes associated with good behaviour are bound to accumulate in subsequent generations. And the observation that play is rarely unfair or unco-operative is surely an indication that natural selection acts to weed out those who don't play by the rules.

What does this tell us about human morality? First, we didn't invent virtue – its origins are much more ancient than our own. Secondly, we should stop seeing ourselves as morally superior to other animals. True, our big brains endow us with a highly sophisticated sense of what's right and wrong, but they also give us much greater scope for manipulating others – to deceive and try to benefit from immoral behaviour. In that sense, animal morality might be 'purer' than our own. We should accept our moral responsibility towards other animals, and that means developing and enforcing more restrictive regulations governing animal use. While animal minds may vary from one species to another, they are not so different from our own, and only when we accept this can we truly be moral in our relations with nature as a whole.

13 In the first paragraph, what does the writer state about morality?

   A Humans are the only creatures that demonstrate true emotional behaviour.

   B A well-developed moral code does not lead to civilization.

   C Humans and animals share the same selfish instincts for survival.

   D There is a common misconception that animals are not moral.

14 What point does the writer make in the second paragraph?

   A People who are generous to others are not always sure why they behave this way.

   B People who do not possess good social skills achieve less in life.

   C People who behave considerately to others have selfish reasons for doing so.

   D People who treat acquaintances better than relatives are unusual.

15 What has the writer deduced about social play from his observation of animals?

   A It provides an opportunity for physically weaker animals to develop their survival skills.

   B It allows animals to prove who is dominant in the group without using real aggression.

   C It requires animals to abide by the rules or they will be excluded from the rest of the group.

   D It demonstrates that certain animals possess a large range of emotions.

16 Which of the following best summarizes the writer's argument in the fourth paragraph?

   A There are different degrees of morality between various cultures.

   B Groups benefit from social play more than individuals do.

   C Spirituality and morality are inseparable.

   D Humans adopted moral behaviour as a means of survival.

17 The pronoun 'this' (line 59) refers to

   A the challenge facing the writer.

   B the concept of fair behaviour.

   C the activity of play.

   D the development of the brain.

18 What does the writer state about the evolution of morality in the sixth paragraph?

   A There may be a particular gene responsible for morality.

   B Moral development depends on physical hardships.

   C There is little point seeking the origin of moral behaviour.

   D Animals that behave fairly are more likely to breed.

19 In the final paragraph, the writer concludes that people

   A must treat animals on equal terms with humans.

   B should be less arrogant in their view of themselves.

   C are more advanced as they use immorality to their advantage.

   D should discriminate between which animals display morality and those that don't.

Part 4

You are going to read an extract from a magazine which has been divided into eight sections. For questions **20–34**, choose from the sections (**A–H**). The sections may be chosen more than once.

In which section of the article are the following mentioned?

evidence that an increasing number of people wish to learn traditional dance   **20**

the influence of another art form on the growing interest in traditional dance   **21**

the idea that it is a human instinct to dance   **22**

a negative reaction to a particular form of traditional dance   **23**

the belief that modern dancing reduces communication between people   **24**

travel allowing certain people to become more exposed to foreign dance   **25**

dance allowing interaction between people who would otherwise be unlikely to meet   **26**

a reference to certain young people's contempt for traditional forms of dance   **27**

the fact that ability and enthusiasm are the most valued qualities   **28**

reasons why people who usually dislike dancing sometimes do it anyway   **29**

certain physical benefits that dance can bring to the body   **30**

examples of ways in which dancing can offer psychological advantages   **31**

the fact that the British have never been acclaimed as good dancers   **32**

a particular individual being responsible for traditional dancing's decreasing popularity   **33**

the idea that dance can be spontaneous as well as something that requires practice   **34**

Before you check your answers, go to page 57.

Let's Dance

We do it when we feel good and we feel good when we do it.

A   Who really doesn't like dancing? Can even the most bad-tempered dance-floor-avoider last an entire lifetime without a shameless display at a wedding, or a particularly good goal – or refrain from a secret shuffle around the privacy of their living room? Dance can take many forms: whether it comes as an impulsive release of energy and emotion, or within a skilful display of choreography after much rehearsal; to dance is as fundamental to humans as breathing. The great dancer Martha Graham wasn't overstating it when she said, 'Dance is the hidden language of the soul, of the body.' The first human art form, dancing is an innate celebration of physical existence, something automatic to us, a language that can be spoken by anyone and understood by everyone. Beyond speech, learnt behaviour, or even conscious thought, we do it when we feel good, and we feel good when we do it.

B   It's a little sad, then, for Britons, that as a nation, our reputation as dancers has historically earned us no points and no recognition. Always ever so slightly embarrassed by fun, Britain has failed to give dancing the status and support it deserves. But times, and dance-floors, are changing. More and more of us are returning home from foreign adventures with glowing memories of cultures in which dance, including traditional forms, are a vital part of life, and musical cross-pollination has accustomed our ears to exotic dance rhythms from all over the world.

C   Cinema too has had an effect. *Evita, The Tango Lesson* and *Strictly Ballroom* all celebrated traditional dance artistry, and we can expect the profile of the incredible Argentine style to skyrocket after several new releases. Yet for many years, the modern pop music played in British night clubs was the only kind the young generation would dance to, and formal ballroom dancing, and Latin styles were perceived as embarrassingly old-fashioned and bizarre. These kinds of traditional dance were dismissed as something to be practised by old people in shiny, spangly outfits.

D   Lyndon Wainwright, of the British Dance Council, lays the decline of traditional dancing squarely at the fast feet of the actor John Travolta, who as disco dancer 'Tony Manero' in *Saturday Night Fever* struck an iconic, swaggering solitary figure up on stage. But now dancing in all its different styles has made a revival. Behind its rebirth lies a confluence of factors: the global village, delight in the accessories – the glittery hair and the extravagant costumes, and boredom with the loud unfriendliness of modern dance clubs.

E   On an average week in London, the entertainment guide *Time Out* usually lists around 50 Latin dance nights, many of them offering tuition. Meanwhile, traditional dance schools too have started to report significant attendance rises. 'In just traditional ballroom and Latin styles, we know that 240,000 amateur tests were taken last year,' Wainwright says. 'The schools tell me business is booming, with salsa and Argentine tango especially on the rise.' For those unconvinced, he points to the following: 'An evening's dancing is as good for you as a three-hour hike. It pumps blood up your legs, so it's good for your heart, and it helps posture and breathing, too. And you don't get that kind of fun on an exercise bike.'

F   Dance is also good therapy too, busting stress, promoting relaxation and, with the mastery of a new skill, brings self-confidence and a sense of achievement. 'There is nothing more notable about the Greek philosopher Socrates than that he found time, when he was an old man, to learn music and dancing, and thought it well spent,' the French philosopher Michel de Montaigne once mused. Professor Cary Cooper, of UMIST, says that dancing allows people to have physical contact in a safe, sanctioned environment, that it literally puts people in touch. All humans need tactile contact. The touch of another person affirms that we are real, that we are alive.

G   Whether you're in it purely for the social contact or the romance, there's no denying that traditional dancing offers unparalleled opportunities to interact with a range of partners we would not normally encounter, in a forum where your partner's skill, aptitude and passion for dancing count for far more than their age, gender and class. 'We live extremely insecure, isolated lives,' Cooper says. 'More and more of us in Britain leave our native communities, work long hours, sacrifice our relationships, neglect our social lives. Today, clubbing, with its deafening music, solo dancing and heavy competitiveness, provides less and less social contact, and becomes an avoidance activity. Now people are embracing the old forms again. Traditional dancing allows people to reconnect with others.'

H   However, one step forward, another back; not all are ready to welcome recent developments. One venue in Suffolk has banned line-dancing at its USA-style Country and Western nights,despite the fact that it has been practised in the USA ever since European migrants introduced it in the 1800s. The DJ Vic Stamp, 77, fumed: 'I'm not against line-dancing but I resent them gate-crashing and taking up all the dance floor. There is nothing worse than dancing round the floor and bumping into people doing a line dance. It stops your rhythm.' Oh dear. Perhaps he should follow the advice offered by the Indian sage, Krishnamurti: 'You must understand the whole of life, not just one little part of it. That is why you must … sing, and dance … for all that is life.'

WHAT'S TESTED?

Part 4 tests your ability to find specific information in a single long text or set of short texts which are connected by theme. There will be a set of questions which you will need to match to the relevant information in the text. Some examples of matching tasks are:

- matching a list of attitudes to a set of people

- matching a list of opinions to a set of book or film reviews

- matching a list of statements to different sections of a text.

TIPS

- For multiple matching, read the questions first and highlight any key words. The questions are written in a very precise way, which means that wrong answers will not match them. By reading the questions first, you will also have an idea of what to look for while you are reading. If you start by reading the text first, you may waste time trying to understand part of the text or some vocabulary that is not being tested.

- Beware of choosing an answer just because you notice a word in the question that is a synonym for a word in the text.

A DETAILED STUDY

Look at the *italicized words* in a selection of questions 20–34 below and answer the Part 4 checking question which follows. Use a dictionary if necessary.

(20) *evidence* that an increasing number of people wish to learn traditional dance

    1 Are you looking for:

    a people's opinions   **b** a set of suggestions   **c** something which proves a fact?

(21) the influence of another *art form* on the growing interest in traditional dance

    2 What are some of the different kinds of art form?

(22) the idea that it is a human *instinct* to dance

    3 If we behave in an instinctive way, is this:

    a something we do naturally   or   **b** something we must learn to do?

(23) a negative *reaction* to a particular form of traditional dance

    4 Are you looking for:

    a a result   **b** a person's attitude   **c** the reason why traditional dance has become popular?

(24) the belief that modern dancing *reduces* communication between people

    5 How could you paraphrase this sentence?

(25) travel allowing people to become more *exposed* to foreign dance

    6 'Exposed to' can be replaced with:

    a able to see and experience   **b** skilled in   **c** scared of trying

(26) dance *allowing* interaction between people who would otherwise be unlikely to meet

7 In this context, does 'allowing' mean:

a giving permission for   or   **b** providing an opportunity for?

(27) a reference to young people's *contempt* for traditional styles of dance

8 If you feel contempt for something, do you:

a show great interest in it   **b** find it difficult   **c** believe that it is inferior in some way?

(28) the fact that ability and enthusiasm are the most *valued* qualities

9 What is the best explanation for 'valued'?

a typical   **b** admired   **c** leading to success

(31) examples of ways in which dancing can offer *psychological* advantages

10 What is the difference between 'physical' and 'psychological'?

(32) the fact that the British have never been *acclaimed* as good dancers

11 'Acclaimed as' could be replaced with:

a interested in becoming   **b** known to be   **c** proud of being

(34) the idea that dance can be *spontaneous* as well as something that requires practice

12 If you do something spontaneously, do you:

a plan it in advance   **b** do it immediately without thinking about it
c practise it many times?

Now check your answers to Part 4 of the test.

PAPER 2 WRITING 1 hour 30 minutes

Part 1

You **must** answer this question. Write your answer in **180–220** words in an appropriate style.

1   The principal of the college where you study has asked you to write an article for international students to help them when they first arrive.

Read an extract from the principal's note below and some comments from current international students. Then, **using the information appropriately**, write an article, describing some aspects of local culture students might find unusual and suggesting how they can adapt.

We think students would do better in their studies if they got over their culture shock more quickly. Some of them only seem to mix with people from their own country, and I think this just isolates them even more. Any advice would be great.

Behaviour of men and women – different here.

Academic lectures fine, but informal conversation - confusing!

Making friends with local people - how?

Will watching TV help me understand the culture here?

Write your **article**. You should use your own words as far as possible.

Before you write your answer, go to page 60.

A DETAILED STUDY

Content

Read question 1 again. What four general topics do you need to include in your answer?

Read the sample article below. Underline parts of the text where the writer deals with the four topics.

NEW ZEALAND: WHAT YOU NEED TO KNOW!

You've arrived in New Zealand, made it to your college accommodation, unpacked your bags and now you're ready to have a look around. You ask directions to the local supermarket and you're surprised when the man addresses you as 'mate'. Then the supermarket check-out girl says 'How's your day going?' Should you give a one-word answer or have a ten-minute conversation? Don't worry – you'll soon get used to life in our country.

Most students comment that they find New Zealanders very friendly on the street but they don't know how to meet them socially. One thing you will do is join a college sports team; netball for woman and rugby or football for men. You'll soon get to make friends – and get fit at the same time. Alternatively, New Zealanders love foreign food so why not to invite some of your fellow students around for dinner? What happens if you're having a chat and they start using colloquial language you don't understand? Don't be afraid asking for an explanation. Even North Americans and British people don't always know we mean. You could also try some of the soap operas on TV; this will help you pick up some common expressions. Watch the evening news will help you find out what's happening in the country – which is always useful when you starting conversations.

One thing that might surprise you is that men and women are both very direct and opinionated. Many people have strong views about politics, sport and social issues. You don't have to agree with them; New Zealanders would rather you just speak your mind.

Good luck with your studies and enjoy your time here.

Effect on target reader

An article needs to be engaging and lively. Where in the text does the writer:

a   use questions to get the reader's attention?

b   use some common scenarios to capture the reader's imagination?

Range and Accuracy

The text contains various structures for giving advice or making suggestions to a friend, but there are five of these structures which contain errors. Find and correct the structures.

Part 2

Write an answer to **one** of the questions 2–5 in this part. Write your answers in **220–260** words in an appropriate style.

---

2   You have been asked to provide a reference for a friend who has applied for a job as a guide with a tour company. The company is looking for a person who could deal with a range of people from different countries and who has an interest in local history.

You should include information about your friend's personal qualities and skills, previous work experience that might be relevant, and explain why they would be a suitable person for the job.

Write your **reference**.

Before you write your reference, go to page 62.

3   An international research group is gathering information on the dietary habits of young people around the world. You have been asked by the group to write a report about your country.

You should include information on the ways that diet has changed in recent times, giving reasons for the changes, and suggesting what impact the changes may be having on young people's health and lifestyle.

Write your **report**.

4   Recently there has been an increasing problem with safety and security at the college you attend. You have been asked to prepare an information sheet which will help students avoid these kind of problems. Your information sheet should:

   • describe typical safety and security problems that can occur

   • suggest what students can do to avoid these problems

   • explain what students should do if they ever experience these problems.

Write your **information sheet**.

5   Answer **one** of the following two questions based on **one** of the [set books] below.

   a   A popular literary magazine has invited its readers to send in a review of a book. You decide to write a review of [the set book], giving a brief outline of the plot, explaining the relevance of the title, and saying whether or not you would recommend it to other readers and why.

Write your **review**.

   b   Your teacher has asked you to write an essay saying which character in [the set book] you think is most interesting. You should describe the character and explain why you think he or she is the most interesting character in the story.

Write your **essay**.

Before you write your review, go to page 64.

A DETAILED STUDY – Reference

Content and Effect on target reader

1   Look back at the instructions for question 2 on page 61. You are told to write about three general areas such as qualities and skills, relevant work experience, suitability. What two specific things need to be included in these areas that will help the target reader (the manager at the tour company) make a decision about hiring your friend?

2   To inform your target reader fully, you need to extend your points and ideas beyond a single sentence. Read the sample answer below and decide where extracts **A–E** best fit.

To whom it may concern

Karen Adams

I have known Karen since July 2002 when we were employed as tour guides by City Escapes. We worked closely together during the summer and I was immediately impressed by her attitude towards her work. Although City Escapes provided us with information about the sites on our itinerary, Karen spent a great deal of time doing further research and background reading. **(1)** ....
....

Karen was also a valuable member of our team due to her fluency in both Spanish and German. The visitors who spoke these languages very much appreciated the friendly conversations they had with Karen. **(2)** ....
.... Karen also communicated very well with English-speaking tourists from other countries.
(3) ....
....

Karen's attitude towards teamwork was another attribute that I admired. When we worked together again in the summers of 2003/2004, she spent considerable time helping the newer employees. **(4)** ....
....

She was also the person that less experienced guides turned to for advice and guidance when problems arose.

Karen's experience and aptitude for the role of tour guide would make her an asset to any tour company she worked for. **(5)** ....
....

I wish her well in her application.

A This was especially the case with the elderly tourists who required more care and attention, and the younger children who spoke no English.

B For these reasons I have no hesitation in recommending Karen for the position you are advertising.

C An example of this is when she helped them prepare for each day by providing useful notes and assisting them with bookings for museums and galleries.

D This enabled her to give very informative talks to the people in our tour groups and really bring local history alive for them.

E She always took time to respond to their questions and make sure they were enjoying their trip.

Further practice

Write a suitable preposition in each gap below. Read back through the sample reference to find your answers.

Useful phrases for references and job applications

1   I was employed .... a primary school teacher in Basel for three years.

2   She had a positive attitude .... professional development.

3   The course I attended provided me .... a better understanding of customer relations.

4   Having lived in Italy for five years, I have developed a reasonable degree of fluency .... the language.

5   He demonstrated an ability to communicate effectively .... both clients and colleagues.

6   The way that Yulia responds .... problems shows that she is practical and level-headed.

7   Grace assisted me .... the day-to-day running of the business.

8   I feel that my proven leadership skills show that I have the right aptitude .... the position.

9   I have no hesitation .... supporting Abdullah's application to your company.

A DETAILED STUDY – Review

Describing the plot

1   What tense is mainly used to describe the facts and stages of the plot?

2   Which tense is used to give background information?

3   Which tense is used to show previous events/past actions?

Springtime in Paris is a romantic novel set in 1920s France. The heroine is Adrienne, who is a lonely young girl living with her widowed father. He is still grieving for his wife twelve years after she has passed away, and pays little attention to his daughter's emotional needs. Over the years since her mother's death, Adrienne has kept a secret from her father. She has an imaginary friend called Oliver, with whom she shares all her dreams. Even at the age of eighteen, she still can't quite stop talking to him and begins to wonder if she is going a little insane. Then one day a stranger moves in to the house across the street and he looks just the way that Adrienne has always pictured Oliver. The story unfolds as Adrienne seeks different ways to meet him and find out if he really is her dream come true. This all becomes more urgent when her father announces that they will soon be emigrating to America.

Describing characters, expressing your opinion, making recommendations

Choose a word from the box to complete sentence (**b**), so that it has the opposite meaning to sentence (**a**).

predictable	likeable	straightforward	impressive	dull	close	weak

1a The characterization is very convincing in regards to the minor characters.

 b The characterization is .... when it comes to the minor characters.

2a What makes Eric such a detestable man is the way he …

 b One of the reasons that Eric is such a .... character is that …

3a Emily's ex-husband comes across as a very intriguing character.

 b Emily's ex-husband is portrayed as a .... man.

4a Jack and Anna become increasingly distant after this conversation.

 b The conversation leads to Jack and Anna feeling .... to one another.

5a At times the story becomes rather complicated which makes it hard to follow.

 b The story is generally .... so it requires little concentration.

6a The ending comes as a complete surprise when …

 b The ending is rather .... when …

7a I personally found the book disappointing as it does not give a true picture of Japan.

 b I would highly recommend this .... book to anyone interested in Japan.

PAPER 3 USE OF ENGLISH 1 hour

Part 1

For questions **1–12**, read the text below and decide which answer (**A, B, C** or **D**) best fits each gap. There is an example at the beginning (**0**).

Example:

0   **A** paying   **B attracting**   **C** causing   **D** devoting

---

Smart Dog!

Animal behaviourists used to think that a dog's bark was simply a way of **(0)** ....

attention. Now a new study suggests that dogs have **(1)** .... barks, and that they vary

the pitch and pace of these to **(2)** .... different messages. The scientists who carried out

the research are now **(3)** .... that dogs usually use high-pitched single barks when they

are **(4)** .... from their owners and a lower, harsher superbark when strangers

(5) .... towards them or the doorbell rings.

During their research, the scientists also wondered what other abilities dogs possessed; for example,

were they able to recognize quantity? To test this, the dogs were first **(6)** .... treats

before a screen was lowered so that the treats were out of **(7)** .... Then the treats were

either left as they were, added to or reduced. If a treat was added or taken away, the dogs looked at

them for longer, presumably because the numbers did not meet their **(8)** .... The scientists

concluded that dogs know they are receiving fewer treats because they have a basic mathematical

ability that **(9)** .... them to tell when one pile of objects is bigger than another. This

ability may be present because dogs are **(10)** .... from wolves, which not only have a

large neo-cortex – the brain's centre of reasoning – but live in large social groups. This mathematical

ability could have been used to work out how many enemies and allies they had in a pack. However,

in order to truly 'count', an animal has to recognize that each object in a set **(11)** .... to

a single number and that the last number in a **(12)** .... represents the total number of objects.

1 A specific   B exact   C detailed   D specialized

2 A transfer   B convey   C bear   D suggest

3 A converted   B persuaded   C determined   D convinced

4 A split   B detached   C separated   D divided

5 A approach   B appear   C draw   D move

6 A tempted   B demonstrated   C shown   D presented

7 A view   B notice   C perception   D sight

8 A estimates   B calculations   C suspicions   D expectations

9 A assists   B facilitates   C enables   D informs

10 A descended   B related   C connected   D evolved

11 A corresponds   B ties   C fits   D complements

12 A system   B sequence   C progression   D succession

Before you check your answers, go to page 67.

WHAT'S TESTED

Part 1 of the Use of English Paper is primarily a test of vocabulary. Questions typically focus on fixed phrases, collocations, linkers, idioms, and phrasal verbs.

TIPS

- Read the whole text through carefully before choosing the correct option for each space.
- Look at the choice of four words and choose the one that best fits both in terms of meaning and grammar.

A DETAILED STUDY

In the exercise below, use the words in the box to complete the sentences. Use each word once only.

0

a   By *attracting* attention to themselves, they were rescued from the island.

b   He laughed in a very strange way, *causing* everyone to turn round and look.

c   She won the award for *devoting* her whole life to looking after the poor.

d   By *paying* attention to the directions, she arrived quicker than anyone else.

> paying
> attracting
> causing
> devoting

1

a   'Does someone have the .... time, please?'

b   You need to be highly trained and have .... skills to work in engineering.

c   She wrote a .... account of the time she spent travelling across Africa.

d   I gave him .... instructions about what to say during the meeting.

> specific
> exact
> detailed
> specialized

2

a   If you're bored, I .... you go to the cinema.

b   The colour red can often .... a sense of energy and strength to people.

c   I wouldn't like to be senior manager. You have to .... a lot of responsibility.

d   When he retires, he'll .... his power to his son.

> transfer
> convey
> bear
> suggest

3

a   Sue is .... that she can sing, but everyone else thinks she's terrible!

b   The government say they are .... to improve the education system.

c   I used to eat anything from the supermarket but recently I .... to organic foods.

d   Jim .... his mother to lend him the car for the weekend.

> converted
> persuaded
> determined
> convinced

4

a   There were ten of us for dinner, so the food was .... up carefully.

b   The log of wood was .... into two halves.

c   Simon became more and more .... from reality as his illness progressed.

d   The child cried when he became .... from his mother in the crowd.

> split
> detached
> separated
> divided

5

a   Jane tends to .... on my doorstep whenever I'm about to go out.

b   We watched his train .... into the station.

c   There was a long queue for the sales, but eventually we began to .... towards the shop entrance.

d   The trainer told us to .... the horse slowly and quietly.

> approach
> appear
> draw
> move

6

a   Jane was .... with a beautiful crystal vase when she left her department.

b   I was .... to book the holiday immediately, but I thought I should check with my wife.

c   The surgeon .... how the operation should be performed.

d   We were .... our rooms by the owner of the hotel.

> tempted
> demonstrated
> shown
> presented

7

a   If we build that hotel there, the ocean will be hidden from ....

b   The kite rose into the sky until it was out of ....

c   Don't take any .... of Chris – he's always rude to everyone.

d   He showed great .... of the situation – he could see exactly what was really happening.

> view
> notice
> perception
> sight

8

a   Unfortunately, the holiday did not meet our ....

b   The man's strange behaviour aroused the .... of the police officer.

c   According to my .... , we should have enough money for the rest of the month.

d   We were given three very different .... for the cost of repairs to our car.

> estimates
> calculations
> suspicions
> expectations

9

a   Richard is great. He .... people whenever he can.

b   Your assistant .... me that the delivery will be here today.

c   The money I inherited .... me to do a lot more things.

d   The new system .... a faster service.

> assists
> facilitates
> enables
> informs

10

a   We share the same surname but we're not .... to one another.

b   I don't think the problem with this software is .... to a virus.

c   He said he was .... from a French king!

d   The idea .... from a brainstorming session with the team.

> descended
> related
> connected
> evolved

11

a   Are you sure that a British plug .... a continental socket?

b   This strange weather .... in with global warming.

c   I don't think this remote control .... to this particular model of TV.

d   People who know about wines will choose one that .... their meal.

> corresponds
> ties
> fits
> complements

12

a   We had a .... of temporary teachers before the school hired a permanent one.

b   To open a bank safe, you need to remember the exact .... of numbers.

c   How does the .... work if I want to order some new stationery?

d   There are many opportunities for career .... if you work for that company.

> system
> sequence
> progression
> succession

Now check your answers to Part 1 of the test.

Part 2

For questions **13–27**, read the text below and think of the word which best fits each gap. Use only **one** word in each gap. There is an example at the beginning (**0**).

Example: 0 WOULD

Born liars?

Little babies are not so innocent after all, it (**0**) .... seem. A recent study claims that infants

as young as six months are capable of lying to their parents, which they do (**13**) .... crying

when they are not truly (**14**) .... pain or distress. They do it simply to draw attention to

themselves, but once they start receiving the loving hugs they (**15**) .... badly desire, the

babies then do (**16**) .... best to prolong this reward with fake smiles. This and similar

research has led to suggestions that only humans beings lie but this is actually (**17**) .... from

the truth.

A young chimpanzee in captivity, for example, is just as capable of 'lying', most commonly when

human handlers go away for a while. (**18**) .... human babies, the chimpanzees really hate

(**19**) .... left alone, and for this reason, their handlers, (**20**) .... have become their

'family', should ideally never be out of sight. Even (**21**) .... the handlers always do their

best to avoid going away for too long, some absence is unavoidable. In (**22**) .... a situation,

and as soon as the young chimp knows it is going to be left alone, it will start making the most vocal

protests, which can be heard as the handler leaves the building. The screaming stops after the door is

slammed (**23**) .... at this point the chimpanzee knows that the handler can

(**24**) .... longer hear him. It has total control (**25**) .... its crying and can switch it

on and off whenever it likes.

The crying is actually a deliberate signal, rather (**26**) .... an uncontrollable outburst. But

(**27**) .... this is a case of 'real' lying rather depends on how you look at it.

Part 3

For questions **28–37**, read the text below. Use the word given in capitals at the end of some of the lines to form a word that fits in the gap **in the same line**. There is an example at the beginning **(0)**.

Example: 0 HORRIFIES

There can be little that **(0)** .... a homeowner more than discovering   **HORROR**

they have been burgled. Even if the thief has only taken a box containing

something he **(28)** .... believed to be valuable but which in   **MISTAKE**

fact only contains some family photographs, the effect on the owner can be

devastating. They may be **(29)** .... to the thief, but these   **WORTH**

these items are considered **(30)** .... by the owner.   **REPLACE**

Moreover, the owner's sense of loss is often **(31)** .... by a feeling of   **COMPANY**

being unsafe in their own home as they know that, in all **(32)** ...., the   **LIKELY**

items will not be found and the thieves not caught.

So what can we do to **(33)** .... the chance of our valuables being   **LESS**

taken? First of all, burglars prefer homes which are easily **(34)** ....   **ACCESS**

to them, so it's a good idea to take some simple **(35)** .... such as   **CAUTIOUS**

locking all your windows and doors. Also, do not **(36)** .... the   **ABLE**

burglar to break into your house unnoticed by erecting high fences around your

property. Burglars are also deterred by the **(37)** .... of dogs on a   **PRESENT**

property, so if you are not a pet owner, record the loud barking of a friend's and

play the recording while you're out.

Part 4

For questions **38–42**, think of **one** word only which can be used appropriately in all three sentences. Here is an example **(0)**.

Example:

0   Explain to me the .... of having another meeting.

    It was at that .... that most of the audience got up and left.

    We lost a .... because one person in our team started the race too early.

Example: POINT

---

38   My mother .... down an old photograph album for us to see.

    The pollution from the factory has .... local people many problems.

    The concert was watched by millions of viewers and .... people together from all

    around the world.

39   When Laura checked the shirt label, she saw that it .... 'Hand wash only'.

    Unfortunately I .... the map wrongly and we ended up too far south.

    The sergeant .... out the names of the officers who would work on the case.

40   I think it's .... to say that our team was the most successful.

    The council seems to have a .... idea of what the people really want.

    Kate has a .... complexion, unlike the others in her family.

41   The .... between our two companies should be profitable for both of us.

    In my opinion, the principal didn't .... with the students in the right way.

    A great .... of time and money was invested in the new project.

42   The two teams .... each other in the final match this weekend.

    The photographer asked the bride and groom to .... each other for the final shot.

    We need to .... the fact that the problem has got out of control.

Before you check your answers, go to page 72.

WHAT'S TESTED?

Part 4 of the Use of English paper tests your knowledge of items of vocabulary with a range of meanings. There are five questions, and for each question, you need to choose **one** word that can be used in three sentences.

TIPS

- When you are learning and recording a new word in English, do not just write down the translation. You need to write down words that are commonly associated with it. The two examples below show the new words in bold and common collocations.

	a friendship		heavy	
to **establish**	a business	to receive a	light	**sentence**
	the reason for something		long	

- When you are answering the questions in Part 4, read all three sentences in each question before you decide on the missing word. Each sentence can be completed by more than one missing word, so it is easy to choose the wrong one if you only read the first and second sentences.

A DETAILED STUDY

The words in bold in the sentences below provide the biggest clues for the missing word.

- Read the meaning of the missing word and word in bold combination which follows each sentence.

- Guess what the missing word is, and check your dictionary to see if you are correct.

38 My mother ………….. **down** an old photograph album for us to see.

(This phrase means to move something somewhere, from a higher place to a lower one)

The pollution from the factory has ……………. local people many **problems**.

(In this context, the meaning is *to be the cause of a situation*)

The concert was watched by millions of viewers and ………. people **together** from all around the world.

(This phrasal verb means to create a situation in which people meet and do something together, especially when they would not usually do this)

39 When Laura checked the shirt **label**, she saw that it ……………. 'Hand wash only'.

(This verb can be used to say that a short written text contains those particular words)

Unfortunately I ……………. the **map** wrongly and we ended up too far south.

(In this context, the verb means that you can understand the information presented in a map)

The sergeant ……………. **out** the names of the officers who would work on the case.

(This phrasal verb means to say aloud the words in a text so that other people can hear them)

40 I think it's ……………….. to say that our team was the most successful.

(This adjective forms part of an expression which is used to suggest that a particular statement is likely to be true)

The council seems to have a ……………….. **idea** of what the people really want.

(The adjective can be used with *idea* or *guess* to say that something is likely to be correct)

Kate has a ……………….. **complexion**, unlike the others in her family.

(The adjective is a synonym for *pale* ie *to have pale skin*)

41 The ……………….. **between** our two companies should be profitable for both of us.

(This noun means a formal agreement, mainly in business or politics)

In my opinion, the principal didn't ……………….. **with** the students in the right way.

(This phrasal verb means to take the action that is required when you are involved with a particular person)

A **great** ……………….. **of** time and money was invested in the new project.

(This phrase means a large amount or quantity of something)

42 The two **teams** ……………….. **each other** in the final match this weekend.

(This verb means to have to compete against a team or another person)

The photographer asked the bride and groom to ……………….. **each other** for the final shot.

(In this context, the verb means to stand opposite another person/group of people, so that you are looking at them)

We need to ……………….. **the fact** that the problem has got out of control.

(In this context, the verb means to accept that a bad situation exists and try to find a solution)

Part 5

For questions **43–50**, complete the second sentence so that it has a similar meaning to the first sentence, using the word given. **Do not change the word given**. You must use between **three** and **six** words, including the word given. Here is an example (**0**).

Example:

0   As he continued to listen to the speech, Richard became increasingly sleepy.

SLEEPIER

The more Richard listened to the speech, ... became.

Example: **0**   THE SLEEPIER HE

---

43   It was very easy for someone to steal the car because Dad forgot to lock it.

STOLEN

Dad forgot to lock the car which explains .... easily.

44   Anne told me that she doesn't intend to stop working.

INTENTION

Anne told me that she .... up her job.

45   I don't usually learn anything useful from the television, but last night I did.

CHANGE

It .... useful from the television last night.

46   Despite usually feeling comfortable when he spoke in public, John felt quite nervous this time.

USED

Even .... in public, John felt quite nervous this time.

47   Jill wished she had tried to have a better relationship with her father.

GET

Jill regretted .... better with her father.

48   We protested when Jim offered to pay but he wouldn't accept our refusal.

TAKE

We protested when Jim offered to pay but he refused .... for an answer.

49   The team are determined to finish the race however tough it is.

MATTER

The team are determined to finish the race .... be.

50   Jack did not feel like going to the party.

MOOD

Jack .... to go to the party.

Before you check your answers, go to page 75.

WHAT'S TESTED?

Part 5 of the Use of English paper has eight questions. There are three parts to each question: a lead-in sentence which is complete, a key word, and a second sentence which is incomplete. You have to complete the second sentence so that it has a similar meaning to the first, using three to six words, including the key word. The key word must not be changed in any way. Contractions count as two words.

A DETAILED STUDY

Look at the lead-in sentence in question 43 below. It can be separated into three parts, A and C which contain the main information, and B, showing the connection between them.

Decide: a   what question word comes after 'explains'.
          b   what pronoun can replace 'the car'.
          c   how 'stolen' can form part of a passive construction.
          d   what adverb should go in front of 'easily'.

43   It was very easy for someone to steal the car   because   Dad forgot to lock it.
                      A   B   C

STOLEN

Dad forgot to lock the car   which explains ……… ………………………………. easily.
         C   B   A

Now do the same for questions 44–50.

44   Anne told me that she   doesn't intend to   stop working.
       A   B   C

INTENTION

Anne told me that she   ……………………………………   …………… up her job.
    A   B   C

Decide: a   what verb is needed to complement the noun 'intention'.
          b   what tense this verb must be in.
          c   what negative word must go in front of 'intention'.
          d   what preposition is used after 'intention'.
          e   what phrasal verb (with 'up') means 'to stop doing something that you do regularly'.
          f   what effect the preposition in (d) has on the phrasal verb.

45   I don't usually   learn   anything useful from the television,   but last night I did.
      A   B   C   A

CHANGE

It …………… ………………………………… ……………. useful from the television last night.
   A   B   C

Decide: a   what verb is needed to complement the noun 'change'.
          b   what article needs to go in front of the noun.
          c   what structure comes next ie, 'learn', 'to learn', 'learning'.
          d   how 'anything' must be changed to a positive form

46   Despite   usually feeling comfortable when he spoke   in public, John felt quite nervous this time.
      A   B   C

USED

Even ………… ………………………………. in public, John felt quite nervous this time.

     A   B   C

Decide: **a**   what adverb needs to follow 'even', so that these words together mean the same as 'despite'.
           b   what pronoun comes next.
           c   what form of the auxiliary verb goes in front of the adjective used.
           d   what preposition comes after 'used'.
           e   what effect the preposition has on the verb 'speak'.

47 Jill wished   she had tried   to have a better relationship with her father.
           A   **B**   **C**

    GET

    Jill regretted   .... better with her father.
        A   **B**   **C**

Decide: **a**   what form of 'try' comes after the verb 'regret'.
           b   how to make this form negative.
           c   what phrasal verb is formed with 'get' that means 'to have a good relationship with someone'.

48 We protested when Jim offered to pay but   he wouldn't accept   our refusal.
                A   **B**   **C**

    TAKE

    We protested when Jim offered to pay but   he refused   .... for an answer.
                A   **B**   **C**

Decide: **a**   which verb is a synonym for 'accept' in this context
           b   the form of this verb after 'refused'.
           c   what preposition fits between 'no' and 'an answer'.

49 The team are determined to finish the race,   however   tough it is.
                A   **B**   **C**

    MATTER

    The team are determined to finish the race   .... be.
            A   **B**   **C**

Decide: **a**   what three-word phrase, beginning with a negative and including 'matter', can replace 'however'.
           b   which words from part **C** can be kept the same.
           c   what modal verb often follows the three-word phrase, and must go in front of 'be'.

50 Jack   did not feel like   going to the party.
    A   **B**   **C**

    MOOD

    Jack   ....   to go to the party.
    A   **B**   **C**

Decide: **a**   which auxiliary verb goes with the noun 'mood'.
           b   what preposition precedes 'mood'.
           c   what article goes directly in front of 'mood'.
           d   how to make the sentence negative.

PAPER 4 LISTENING approximately 40 minutes

Part 1

You will hear three different extracts. For questions **1–6**, choose the answer (**A, B** or **C**) which fits best according to what you hear. There are two questions for each extract.

Extract One

You hear two people on a radio programme discussing the effect of price on consumers.

1   If the woman had known the real cost of her hotel room, she says she would have

    A   chosen another hotel.

    B   appreciated her stay more.

    C   hidden the price from her husband.

2   What do the two speakers agree about?

    A   Expensive wine is worth the money for the effect it creates.

    B   People tend to trust scientific researchers too easily.

    C   It is usually luxury items that people are happy to pay high prices for.

Extract Two

You hear part of an interview with a woman called Petra Davies who is training for a marathon.

3   Petra was reluctant to do much running in her training because she

    A   found it had not been an effective strategy before.

    B   was still suffering from an injury.

    C   did not want to put in the effort it required.

4   According to Petra, what is Sean Deacon's attitude to preparing for a marathon?

    A   He rejects the idea of there being one correct way to train successfully.

    B   He is insistent that athletes do long runs soon after training has started.

    C   He believes in the importance of strength training over long-distance running.

Extract Three

You hear two people on a radio programme talking about the idea of educating children at home.

5   What is the woman's opinion of traditional school education?

    A   It is essential as it demonstrates school leavers' academic ability.

    B   It is not a suitable form of education for all children.

    C   It does not encourage a children's imagination to develop.

6   What does the man conclude about 'unschooling'?

    A   It is unproven whether 'unschooling' is better than schooling.

    B   'Unschooling' will become an increasingly popular form of education.

    C   Being educated at home may cause children to lack social skills.

Part 2

You will hear a radio presenter called Lewis Reed talking about an extreme-sports event that takes place in Britain. For questions **7–14**, complete the sentences.

The National Adventure Sports Show

Lewis says that fans of the show are mainly interested in the performers' [**7**].

[**8**] will be on sale to fans on the day of the show.

Lewis recommends seeing the [**9**] as well as the competitions.

According to Lewis, many fans describe the competitors as [**10**].

He agrees with the fans that there is a [**11**] atmosphere at the sports show.

Lewis describes a new sport that requires a [**12**] to be attached to a pair of skates.

He suggests that people think about [**13**] before trying a new sport.

He says that the increase in [**14**] shows how popular extreme sports are becoming.

Before you check your answers, go to page 79.

WHAT'S TESTED?

For Part 2 of the Listening Paper, you will hear a monologue for about three minutes. This monologue may be an extract from a radio broadcast, a speech, presentation or talk. You will have to write a word or short phrase to complete eight sentences.

TIPS

• Use the pause before the recording to read each sentence carefully and guess the kind of information that would make sense in the gap.

• Write down the exact word or short phrase that you hear. The words will be nouns, proper names, a single adjective, or an adjective plus noun.

• Make sure you write the correct form of a noun, ie singular or plural. If you didn't manage to hear it during the recording, read the sentence carefully to help you decide.

• Write your answers in CAPITAL letters on the answer sheet.

• Spell the words correctly, either using British or American English.

A DETAILED STUDY

You can prepare for Part 2 by predicting what the missing information might be. Even if the words you think of are not exactly the same as the words used in the recording, the process of prediction will give you an idea of the kind of information to listen for.

Question 7: Does the gap require an adjective or a noun? Extreme sports are fast, require a lot of skill and can be quite dangerous, so what kind of thing would fans want to see an extreme sports show?

Question 8: What might you be able to buy at a sports show?

Question 9: What kind of structures or phrases should you listen for when someone is recommending something? Is the missing word likely to be the name of a sport or not? How do you know?

Question 10: 'Describe as' can be followed by a noun or an adjective. If the answer is a noun, will it be plural or singular? If the answer is an adjective, will it be something positive or negative?

Question 11: What kind of structures or phrases should you listen for when someone is agreeing with something? The missing word must be an adjective. Will it be positive or negative? What adjectives might describe the atmosphere at a sports show?

Question 12: If you were taking part in an extreme sports competition, what would you attach to a pair of skates in order to go faster?

Question 13: Like question 9, what kind of structures or phrases should you listen for when someone is suggesting something? What kind of suggestions might Lewis make to people before they try a new sport at the competition?

Question 14: What would show or prove that extreme sports are becoming more popular by increasing?

Part 3

You will hear part of a radio interview in which a graphic designer called Sandra Cammell is talking about her work as a children's book illustrator. For questions **15–20**, choose the answer (**A, B, C** or **D**) which fits best according to what you hear.

15 What does Sandra find difficult about working as a freelance illustrator?

    A   being expected to be available all the time

    B   having to work to a tight schedule

    C   not knowing when she will next be working

    D   lacking the opportunity to develop her style

16 How did Sandra feel about working at the advertising agency?

    A   She appreciated the opportunities it gave her.

    B   She found the work she was given very dull.

    C   She resented not being able to devote herself to her college work.

    D   She felt challenged by the style she was asked to use.

17 What is the advantage for Sandra of working with editors she knows well?

    A   She can illustrate books for the age group she prefers.

    B   She can disagree with the editor's decisions

    C   She has freedom in how she chooses to illustrate books.

    D   She is allowed to work on illustrations before receiving the story.

18 For Sandra, what aspect of drawing people requires most effort?

    A   persuading other people to model for her drawings

    B   keeping the figures realistic rather than cartoonish

    C   making the postures of children seem convincing

    D   forming a mental picture of a book's main character

19 According to Sandra, what effect did her work have on her children?

    A   They had to learn to play by themselves.

    B   They thought that all mothers worked at home.

    C   They developed their own interest in art.

    D   They became good readers at an early age.

20 What advice does Sandra give to young people hoping to be illustrators?

    A   send samples of your work to publishers

    B   be prepared to spend time on self-promotion

    C   show that you specialize in particular subjects

    D   avoid being distracted by other kinds of work

Before you check your answers, go to page 81.

WHAT'S TESTED?

For Part 3 of the Listening Paper, you will hear a conversation for about four minutes. This conversation will be an extract from a broadcast interview or a discussion between two or three speakers. There are six four-option multiple-choice questions, which mainly test your ability to understand the attitude and opinion of the speakers. There may also be questions which require you to understand the gist of the conversation or particular detail. Questions follow the order of the recording.

TIPS

- Use the pause before each recording is heard to read the questions. It is more important that you focus on the questions during preparation time, rather than the options A–D, so you can listen for a suitable answer.
- After you hear a suitable answer, then match it to the most similar option.
- Remember that the options are paraphrases of what is said during the conversation, so it is important that you know the meaning of a range of reporting verbs, (eg denies/admits/regrets) and adjectives for attitude, feeling and opinion (eg irritated/disappointed/resentful).
- It is also important that you understand how stress and intonation affect meaning, for example:

I *was* going to become an artist. = That was my original intention but I changed my mind.

I suppose you *could* try sending in your CV. = It's an idea but I don't really think it's a good one.

A DETAILED STUDY

- Do task 1 for all the questions 15–20 first.
- Then play the recording and do task 2 for questions 15–20.

Task 1: Match parts of the text 1–4 with options A–D that they are most similar to.

Task 2: Listen to the recording and match parts of the text 1–4 with the additional information i–iv.

15 What does Sandra find difficult about working as a freelance illustrator?

TASK 1	
1 meeting the deadline 2 you can work any time of the night or day 3 you resort to a similar style 4 you have periods of time when you haven't got any work coming in	**A** being expected to be available all the time **B** having to work to a tight schedule **C** not knowing when she will next be working **D** lacking the opportunity to develop her style
TASK 2	
i if you like a variety ii is the hardest part iii it's ideal iv you have to accept that	

16 How did Sandra feel about working at the advertising agency?

TASK 1	
1 while I was at college, I also worked for an advertising agency **2** way of networking with people and making contacts **3** I lost count of how many buns and loaves I had to draw **4** the company wanted very realistic pictures	**A** She appreciated the opportunities it gave her. **B** She found the work she was given very dull. **C** She resented not being able to devote herself to her college work. **D** She felt challenged by the style she was asked to use.

TASK 2
i   from that perspective it was great   ii   gives me immense satisfaction   iii you try and work in the situation you're heading for while you're training   iv   I didn't mind

17 What is the advantage for Sandra of working with editors she knows well?

TASK 1	
1 then you receive …the actual story **2** that brief [instructions] can be quite flexible when I receive it **3** that's little children who are learning to read **4** You can't have a drawing of someone on one page wearing a certain sort of clothing and then change it on the next	**A** She can illustrate books for the age group she prefers. **B** She can disagree with the editor's decisions. **C** She has freedom in how she chooses to illustrate books. **D** She is allowed to work on illustrations before receiving the story.

TASK 2
i   then they will give you a brief , which is a page-by-page idea of what they want to see   ii   they understand that I've been doing this long enough   iii that just wouldn't work   iv   they need a very strong picture–word relationship

18 For Sandra, what aspect of drawing people requires most effort?

TASK 1	
1 then you receive…the actual story **2** if it's not an animal or cartoon idea **3** take a lot of photos of that person **4** the poor child has had to pose doing all sorts of things	**A** persuading other people to model for her drawings **B** keeping the figures realistic rather than cartoonish **C** making the postures of children seem convincing **D** forming a mental picture of a book's main character

TASK 2
i   children are quite tricky to draw   ii   I immediately see it in my mind   iii I try to think of someone I know and I base the character on that person   iv   if they agree, to sort of help me get some idea about facial expression

19 According to Sandra, what effect did her work have on her children?

TASK 1		
1 me illustrating at home **2** it's all about the contact you have with your child **3** they used to look at the pictures a lot **4** I have a deep belief in reading to children right from the word go	**A** They had to learn to play by themselves. **B** They thought that all mothers worked at home. **C** They developed their own interest in art. **D** They became good readers at an early age.	

TASK 2
i   they had a reading ability way beyond some of their friends ii   they've always been part of their lives iii children are missing out on that more and more, perhaps with everybody being busy iv   has always been part of what they know

20 What advice does Sandra give to young people hoping to be illustrators?

TASK 1	
1 market yourself really well **2** trained teachers **3** I suppose you could send in your CV first **4** a range of ethnic backgrounds	**A** send samples of your work to publishers **B** be prepared to spend time on self-promotion **C** show that you specialize in particular subjects **D** avoid being distracted by other kinds of work

TASK 2
i   versatility is the key ii   but I tended to ring and make an appointment and go and see them iii you need to generate your own work iv   it's always handy to have something else up your sleeve

Now check your answers to Part 3 of the test.

Part 4

You will hear five short extracts in which people are talking about other people who have had an effect on them.

TASK ONE

For questions **21–25**, choose from the list **A–H** the person who the speaker is describing.

A   a writer

B   a pop star

C   a policeman | 21 |

D   a TV star | 22 |

E   a parent | 23 |

F   a coach | 24 |

G   a teacher | 25 |

H   a childhood friend

TASK TWO

For questions **26–30**, choose from the list **A–H** the effect that the speaker describes.

A   I was encouraged to develop a talent

B   I got into trouble for behaving like him

C   I felt able to cope with my life | 26 |

D   I tried to develop the same qualities | 27 |

E   I became less interested in academic study | 28 |

F   I became interested in experiencing new things | 29 |

G   I realized I could change my career | 30 |

H   I was unable to trust people again

In the exam you will have 5 minutes at the end of the test to copy your answers on to a separate answer sheet.

PAPER 5 SPEAKING approximately 15 minutes

Part 2 (4 minutes)

1   Different Professions

For both candidates: Look at the three pictures on page 144. They show people in different kinds of profession.

Candidate A: Compare two of these pictures, and say what skills these people require in their work and why they might have chosen these professions. (*1 minute*)

Candidate B: Which profession do you think requires more natural talent than learnt skills? (*30 seconds*)

2   In the forest

For both candidates: Look at the three pictures on page 145. They show people in the forest.

Candidate B: Compare two of these pictures, and say why the people might be in the forest and what the atmosphere might be like in each situation. (*1 minute*)

Candidate A: Which of these people do you think is taking part in the most useful activity? (*30 seconds*)

Part 3 (4 minutes)

College Magazine

For both candidates: Imagine that your college wants a new cover for the brochure it gives to prospective students. On pages 146 and147 you can see some of the images for the cover that have been suggested.

First talk to each other about what aspects of student life these images show. Then decide which two images should be chosen for the front and back covers of the brochure.

Part 4 (4 minutes)

For both candidates:

- How far do you agree that further education is necessary to be successful in life?

- What kind of difficulties do students face in your country?

- Some people believe that education should be free for everyone. What's your opinion?

- What might be the advantages and disadvantages of entering further education many years after leaving school?

- A lot of students are nowadays choosing to take degrees in business and technology, rather than science and the arts. Why do you think this is?

For Further Practice and Guidance, see page 86.

WHAT'S TESTED?

Problem-solving activity

In Part 3 of the Speaking Paper, you are asked to discuss a problem-solving task with your partner(s) based on a set of visual and written prompts. The task may require you to discuss, justify, evaluate, select or speculate about a number of ideas and choices. There is no right or wrong answer to these problem-solving tasks, and it is better to speak about all or most of the pictures before you start to reach a conclusion, so that you can demonstrate your range of grammatical forms and vocabulary.

This part of the Speaking Paper tests your ability to interact with your partner. This means you need to ask questions as well as respond to them and carry out the task in a way that reflects a normal conversation. It is possible to use natural conversation fillers such as 'Well, let me think...' or 'That's a good point. I hadn't thought about that,' etc.

It is important that candidates allow each other equal participation in the discussion and both make the effort to keep the conversation going.

Using the phrases below, practise Part 3 on page 85 with your partner.

Conversation fillers

- *Well, let me think…*

- *Let me see…*

- *That's a good/interesting/difficult question…*

- *Well, I haven't really thought about this before but…*

Stating your opinion

- *Personally, …*

- *In my opinion, …*

- *If you ask me, …*

- *The way I see it, …*

- *I think/feel/reckon/guess/believe/would say that…*

Asking your partner

- *In your opinion, what would you say is…?*

- *What do you think/reckon/feel about…?*

- *Do you think that…?*

- *Would you agree?*

Responding to your partner

- *On the whole, I agree with you but…*

- *I see what you mean but…*

- *That's true but…*

- *I'm not sure I agree with you on that.*

- *Yes, I think you're right about that and...*

- *Good point/True and what about...?*

Reaching a conclusion

- *So, what have we decided? Do you agree that we should choose this one?*

- *So, we're going for/choosing this one, are we?*

- *I think we've agreed on this one and maybe this one?*

- *I think we both agree on this one but we have different opinions about our second choice.*

Further Discussion

In Part 4, the interlocutor will ask the students a series of questions which relate to the topic(s) in Part 3. These questions tend to become more general and more abstract as the discussion develops. You will only hear and not see these questions. If necessary, you can ask the examiner to repeat the question.

This part is testing your ability to express your opinion further by using a range of structures and vocabulary. Don't worry about having different ideas to the examiners – they are only interested in listening to your English. For this reason, try to develop the conversation as much as possible. If you only give short answers, you are not demonstrating your ability.

CAE TEST THREE

PAPER 1 READING 1 hour 15 minutes

Part 1

You are going to read three extracts which are all concerned in some way with memories. For questions **1–6**, choose the answer (**A, B, C** or **D**) which you think fits best according to the text.

EXTRACT FROM A REVIEW

Last night Channel 8 brought us the first episode of the much-publicized series on space exploration *Dark Voyages*. In it there were glimpses of defining moments in extraterrestrial travel including the launch of the Sputnik satellite and the 1969 moon landings, as well as the background to each event. Cleverly, the programme makers have chosen to simplify the technological details of these missions and instead draw the audience in by keeping the excitement and mystery of the subject in focus, mainly through the striking use of original film footage.

Where the programme is less successful is in its interviews with those who have travelled in space and to the moon. Given the potential for bringing to life memories of highly unique and potentially fascinating experiences, the program makers opt to include fragments of interviews interrupted by generally redundant narration that prevents the viewer from gaining a real sense of the memories that are being recalled. So, although several of the interviewees briefly reflect on the overwhelming emptiness of space and the surreal beauty of the Earth below, we are denied a chance to hear what they may have said in a more meditative fashion.

1 In the television programme *Dark Voyages* there is an emphasis on

    A presenting new images.

    B appealing to the viewers' emotions.

    C contrasting two particular events.

    D introducing certain aspects of technology.

2 What does the writer find particularly disappointing about the documentary?

    A the way the interviews are edited

    B the choice of interviewees

    C the lack of purpose in the interviews

    D the subject matter the interviewees discuss

GOING BACK IN TIME

As part of a nationwide survey shoppers in Stoke-on-Trent were recently asked to exchange memories from 40 or more years ago, the aim being to piece together a picture of what constitutes the perfect first few years of life. The older shoppers were in no doubt about one thing: material possessions do not make children happy. Many had low-cost recollections of long bike rides and making up games out in the street. In fact, it wasn't until around the start of the 1980s that people's memories started to be about things,

such as particular brand-name dolls like Barbie or the popular Scalextric racing cars, popular with boys and girls alike.

I admit that nostalgia often colours our view of the past, but things do seem to be tougher for today's young generation. In my day, despite the cold houses, tough schooling and sometimes severe illnesses, what made it all bearable was the sense of everyone living through it together, whereas now, so many of the things that children do are isolating. There has been a retreat from the outdoors into individual rooms and if children have a computer up there the irony is that they're not safer at all. What they see on their screens is a world that was unknown to those elderly shoppers in their childhood. And most of these pensioners would be grateful that it was.

3   The writer refers to 'Barbie' and 'Scalextric' in order to emphasize

   A   the division of toys according to gender.

   B   the effect of consumerism on play time.

   C   the lack of creativity in modern cildren.

   D   the idea that children need constant stimulation.

4   What is the writer doing in the second paragraph?

   A   explaining why it is difficult to be a child in the modern world

   B   suggesting why it is that people tend to forget bad experiences

   C   illustrating the change in society's attitude to parental responsibility

   D   showing how the general standard of living has improved for children

EXTRACT FROM A SCIENCE MAGAZINE

It's seven years since AJ first wrote to neuro-psychologist James McGaugh, asking for help. She was locked in a cycle of remembering that she described as 'a running movie that never stops.' Her constant recall was a 'burden' of which she was both warden and victim. Intrigued, McGaugh set about investigating her memory. In initial tests he found that she could identify the day of the week for any date since 1980. Convinced her condition was new to science, he dubbed it 'hyperthymestic syndrome' – from the Greek 'thymesis' for remembering. Whereas normally the human mind weeds out irrelevant or out-of-date material and discards it, clearly AJ's memory does not work in quite the same way.

Crucially, though, while AJ's memory is impressive, it is not indiscriminate and could not be described as photographic. McGaugh's team discovered this several hours into a testing session by asking AJ to close her eyes and describe what the researchers were wearing. She had no idea. Similarly, she could not recall which dates the team had quizzed her about a month earlier. 'Her autobiographical memory, while incredible, is still selective and even ordinary in some respects,' McGaugh says. This was evident in AJ's poor performance on tests in which she was asked to memorize word lists or recognize faces. Not only that, AJ had been an average student, unable to apply her prodigious memory to her studies.

5   What does the writer suggest about AJ's memory?

   A   It made AJ forget things which might have been useful.

   B   It could be advantageous to AJ in some ways.

   C   She had once been able to control it through certain strategies.

   D   It retained the kind of non-essential information most people forget.

6   What point is exemplified by the reference to the researchers' clothes?

   A   AJ's visual recall is the weakest area of her memory.

   B   AJ's long-term memories are stronger than recent ones.

   C   AJ's memory does not retain everything that she sees.

   D   AJ's concentration is frequently disturbed by her constant recall.

Part 2

You are going to read an extract from a magazine article. Six paragraphs have been removed from the extract. Choose from the paragraphs **A–G** the one which fits each gap (**7–12**). There is one extra paragraph which you do not need to use.

Mountain Challenge

When the Army asked him to go on a climbing mission, Alex Wade said 'Yes, sir!'

I was managing the mountain climb fairly well until we got to the crevasse – a two-metre wide crack in the ice. 'What do I do with my ice axe?' I yelled. 'Don't worry about it,' the leader of the expedition, Mark Smyth, shouted back at me. 'Just jump.' I obeyed but with the knowledge that a tumble on the other, lower, side would result in an express ride to the perilous glacier below. I just about made it. For an average climber like myself, this seemed more like a military operation!

| **7** | |

I had met Mark a year previously on a climb in Russia. He had dropped me a line: 'I'm climbing Mont Blanc in June. Interested?' I'd had a rough time there on a previous attempt, failing to reach the summit because of altitude sickness. Here was a chance to try again with a serious mountaineer. But still, this was a full military expedition, so, technically, I wouldn't be his responsibility. If I climbed with them, would I be OK? 'Put it this way, I'm not going to let you fall off,' he said.

| **8** | |

As Mark put it, 'Climbing Mont Blanc from this approach is not technically difficult but is never to be underestimated. The weather can change in minutes, and freezing temperatures and 120kph winds are common. At over 5000 metres, these extreme conditions test the endurance limit of all but the hardiest of mountaineers.'

| **9** | |

Looks can be deceptive. After a few days' walking to acclimatize to the altitude I was exhausted. Come the climb itself, we camped on the Col du Midi (3542 metres), having hiked down the exposed ridge from the cable car station. Everyone was coping fine with the altitude, and the warm sunlight made Mont Blanc seem harmless. Around 3am the next morning we began the long slog up Tacul. From the shoulder of Tacul we had a perfect view of the route across the Col du Mont Maudit. It was on the Col that I had turned back two years ago.

| **10** | |

Even digging snow pits for the tents was a real struggle. Teams of two or three dug holes, got their tents up and got warm. On my own, I was the first to start digging and the last to finish. No one said much, too exhausted to waste energy on speech.

| **11** | |

I couldn't have been more wrong. The descent made everything that had gone before seem easy. After eventually negotiating the crevasses, we staggered down to just above the glacier – all that lay between us and safety. The ice on the glacier would be unstable, but there was a chance we would make it. Then a lump of ice the size of a house crashed to pieces right on our prospective path.

| **12** | |

Sure enough, as I forced my legs to go down the agonizingly steep slope, I slipped. Though I managed to slam my axe into the ice, I committed the worst crime of failing to secure my feet before I stood up. I slid further down, ice axe stuck in the snow above me, into the next man on the rope. Fortunately neither of us slid any further. It was several more hours before we made it back down but as Mark said 'The aim of the expedition was achieved. Now you know what it's like to be on a mountain.'

A   This time it seemed I was having better luck and the climb went well save for the near-vertical ice wall which stood before our next brief stop on the Col de la Brenva. We laboured up the wall and I could scarcely stand by the time we came to camp. By this stage, though, everyone was suffering and slowing down.

B   It looked like the decision had been made for us. There was no choice but to trudge back up the mountain and spend the night at the Grands Mulets refuge. Next morning we headed off to re-attempt our glacier crossing. But it only takes a moment to make a mistake, and they usually happen when you're tired.

C   I wasn't the only one! Our destination seemed no nearer although we'd been on the move for hours, and so far, we'd all managed to maintain a reasonable pace. But at this point, we could hardly turn around and head back. And more than this, I didn't want to let Mark down.

D   Despite that welcome reassurance, I wondered whether I could keep up with the other, very fit expedition members. I didn't feel too optimistic when I learned of the route – 'The Grand Traverse' – which takes in two other mountains, Mont Blanc du Tacul and Mont Maudit, and is often done in a day starting from the Aiguille de Midi cable car station. We would be carrying full rucksacks with food and equipment for three days.

Before you check your answers, go to page 91.

E   After another early start in temperatures of around –20, we finally made it to the summit. The wind was now roaring and I could barely see the peaks of the mountains around us. It was a long way to come for such a poor view but at least the worst was over.

F   To add to my apprehension, it was this same route that had beaten me the last time around. But after two months of frantic aerobic training since Mark's invitation, there I was, with the army in Chamonix. They seemed a decent bunch, and didn't appear too fit.

G   But that, however, was exactly what it was. I was the 13th man on an army expedition to climb Mont Blanc. As Mark said, 'The aim is to put the soldiers into a challenging environment in order to develop the qualities of team spirit and self-confidence.' A good aim, yes, but the difference between them and me is that I was the sole civilian.

A DETAILED STUDY

Below you can see extracts from the paragraphs **A–G**. Read the extracts and answer the questions.

A 1 'This time it seemed I was having better luck and the climb went well…'

This part of the sentence suggests the writer has already mentioned:

a   a bad experience.

b   a reasonable experience.

c   a good experience.

2 'We laboured up the wall… I could scarcely stand by the time we came to camp.'

This part of the sentence suggests the writer:

a   improved his climbing technique.

b   needed to stop and have a rest.

c   wanted to continue the climb.

3 'By this stage, though, everyone was suffering and slowing down.'

What would you expect to follow this sentence?

a   An example of how well some of the soldiers were doing.

b   An example of what the soldiers managed to do with difficulty.

c   An example of how the writer was coping better than the soldiers.

B 4 'It looked like the decision had been made for us. There was no choice but to trudge back…'

This means that:

a   everyone decided to return.

b   Mark [the leader] wanted everyone to return.

c   something else forced everyone to return.

5 '…we headed off to re-attempt our glacier crossing.'

This suggests that:

a   they had already tried to cross the glacier.

b   it was the first time they tried to cross the glacier.

c   they had tried to cross a different glacier before.

6 'But it only takes a moment to make a mistake.'

What is the purpose of this sentence?

a   To warn the reader about the dangers of mountain climbing.

b   To introduce an example of a mistake.

c   To suggest that everyone on the team did very well.

C 7 'Our destination seemed no nearer although we'd been on the move for hours.'

What does this sentence mean?

a   We were close to our destination and we had only been travelling a short time.

b   We were far away from our destination because we had only been travelling for a short time.

c   We were far away from our destination and we had been travelling for a long time.

8 '…we'd all managed to maintain a reasonable pace.'

This means that:

a   the team had made a lot of progress on the climb.

b   the team had done fairly well on the climb.

c   the team had moved quite slowly on the climb.

9 '…we could hardly turn around and head back.'

What is the writer suggesting?

a   He thinks they should return to the starting point.

b   He thinks it will be a challenge to find the same route home.

c   He thinks that they must continue in the same direction.

D   10 'Despite that welcome reassurance…'

This suggests that someone has said something to the writer to make him feel more:

a   nervous.

b   confident.

c   enthusiastic.

E   11 '…we finally made it to the summit.'

What does this tell you about the team's progress?

a   They reached the lower slopes.

b   They reached a flat area.

c   They reached the highest point.

12 '…but at least the worst was over.'

The writer believes:

a   the climb will get easier.

b   he is experiencing the most difficult part of the climb.

c   the worst part of the climb is coming next.

F   13 'To add to my apprehension…'

This suggests that the writer has just heard something that:

a   worries him.

b   makes him feel safe.

c   interests him.

14 'They [the soldiers] … didn't appear too fit.'

The writer believes the physical condition of the soldiers is:

a   excellent.

b   quite good.

c   not as good as it should be.

G   15 'But that, however, was exactly what it was.'

This sentence means that the writer has:

a   correctly identified something.

b   incorrectly identified something.

Now check your answers to Part 2 of the test.

Part 3

You are going to read a magazine article. For questions **13–19**, choose the answer (**A, B, C** or **D**) which you think fits best according to the text.

A career in comedy? It's no laughing matter!

At one time the notion of a career on stage may have been frowned upon by certain sections of society, but nowadays parents would be well advised to actually push their offspring into the safe and lucrative world of comedy. If the number of awards, the profusion of clubs and the amount of lucrative broadcasting work available are anything to go by, comedy is the new accountancy. Where once a stand-up comedian would have to endure years on the circuit of small-time venues and get paid in free drinks and curled-up sandwiches, comedians can now work in several media and even be paid a regular salary for writing jokes for TV and media. The live comedy circuit has mushroomed and the general public seem to have an insatiable appetite for comedic talent both in front of and behind the camera.

'The advent of multi-channel TV is behind this comedy revolution', says William Burdett-Coutts, artistic director of one of the top venues for comedy during the famous Edinburgh Festival Fringe. 'I put it down to when television programmers at Channel 4 created a new interest in comedy. That's what sparked it off, and now with so many channels there are hours of airtime to be filled. There is a fairly constant demand for new talent.' The festival sees the culmination of five comedy awards that are regarded in the industry as one long audition for lucrative TV work. 'The eventual winners will possibly get guaranteed runs at the prestigious Montreal and Melbourne comedy festivals but the ultimate lure for many, though, is the thought of being snapped up by a top agent', he says.

Edinburgh is only one of the many comedy festivals in Britain where comedians can ply their trade. Several other British cities have festivals but Burdett-Coutts cautions that it's not all milk and honey for those seeking fame and fortune. 'Manchester struggles to keep its venues going, Newcastle has closed them all, and London is a hard one to crack as there is so much going on there all the time. There are many, many comedians who have been around for years without a breakthrough.' Nevertheless, he still maintains that there's room for another comedy festival in a seemingly overcrowded market and points out that October sees the opening of the Brighton Comedy Festival.

Despite the risk of obscurity, the openings for talented funny people are many and varied – and it's not necessarily performers that TV wants to lure. As Lisa Thomas, director of an agency which handles several top comics, says, 'Not so long ago, TV producers would want to see someone up there performing live, and audience reaction was the bottom line. What you have these days is a concern with the comic's creative potential. They may think someone doesn't quite have it on stage, but has a talent that could be put to better use coming up with ideas for sketches in established TV shows or even for editing scripts.'

While Thomas welcomes the extra money and audience interest that awards attract, she believes they are hardly an automatic guarantee of well-paid comedy life, but rather they act as an industry 'shop window'. 'They are definitely the foot in the door', she says. 'The awards do secure work for newcomers and a lot of them feel they have to pay their dues and do live performance for a couple of years before they can call themselves a comedian. It certainly helps in terms of knowing whether a joke is "sayable" or if the timing's right when they go into writing or production.'

One comedian who made the deviation from delivering the jokes himself to writing for others is Phil Whelans. Although he does the occasional live performance and voiceover work for commercials, he now considers himself a writer and made the career change in the late 1990s after his comedy act with a partner broke up. 'I couldn't face starting over, doing try-out sessions', says Whelans. 'The scene is so diluted now – there are hundreds of competent, blandish, slightly uninteresting stand-ups who I would be up against and my heart sank at the thought.' And the money? 'The rates vary wildly', says Whelans, who is currently devising an improvised sitcom for TV. 'I've seen writers turn ashen with jealousy when they hear what others can earn, but believe me, it's a very decent living for most.'

13 What does the writer state about a career in comedy in the past?

   A Comedians used to expect a reasonable salary.

   B There was a range of awards comedians could aim for.

   C It offered a longer career than most comedians achieve today.

   D It was not always regarded as a respectable profession.

14 According to William Burdett-Coutts, comedians often take part in the Edinburgh Festival

   A to challenge current notions of comedy.

   B to secure more work in the future.

   C to appear to as diverse an audience as possible.

   D to compete with each other for money.

15 What does Burdett-Coutts state about the current opportunities for comedians?

   A A career in comedy may not always be rewarding.

   B Comedians should avoid venues in large cities.

   C There are many inadequate comedians seeking work.

   D The launch of another festival is fairly pointless.

16 According to Lisa Thomas, TV producers are looking for comedians who

   A are capable of producing material for others.

   B come across as confident in live performance.

   C enjoy a good rapport with their audiences.

   D are realistic about their chances of success.

17 What does Lisa Thomas say about comedy awards?

   A They ensure comedians gain experience before entering comedy festivals.

   B They usually mean that comedians will enjoy a successful career.

   C They lead to opportunities where comedians can experiment with material.

   D They help comedians decide which branch of comedy they are suited to.

18 Why did Phil Whelans choose to become a comedy writer?

   A He felt he was no longer at competition standard.

   B He believed he would earn a regular salary as a writer.

   C He had found it difficult to work as part of a team.

   D He did not have the enthusiasm to develop a new act.

19 The writer's overall purpose in writing this text is to

   A dissuade people from taking up a career in comedy.

   B explain the steps necessary to gain success as a comedian.

   C highlight the positive and negative aspects of being a comedian.

   D illustrate the kind of comedy which will have most public appeal.

Part 4

You are going to read a magazine article containing interviews with five men who have outdoor jobs. For questions **20–34**, choose from the list of men (**A–E**). Each man may be chosen more than once.

Note: When more than one answer is required, these may be given in any order.

For which man are the following sentences true?

He appreciates the fact that his work has received professional recognition. | 20

His job requires a constant high level of concentration. | 21

He does not consider himself to be a full-time professional. | 22

He has more of a managerial role than he used to. | 23

His current career is the result of a desire to work from a permanent location. | 24

He admits that he does not perform one of his duties particularly well. | 25

He appreciates the ability of the people he is responsible for. | 26

He gets a sense of satisfaction from knowing people rely on him. | 27 | 28

He appreciates the comments that other people have made about his skills. | 29

He resents the bureaucracy that is part of his job. | 30

His training did not require any academic component. | 31 | 32

He accepts the fact that there is a negative aspect to his work. | 33 | 34

Take a step outside!

*Do you ever feel 'stuck in the office'? We spoke to five men with outdoor jobs
and asked them about the reality of working outside.*

A John Hughes: Academic Leader for Adventure Recreation

I've been working in the outdoor sports and activities industry since I was 22, but whereas I used to go climbing myself, I've got more of an academic position now I'm at the polytechnic. I work with students and focus my skills on demonstrating how mountaineering groups should be run and organized. The best aspect of the work is the quality of the students. I've always got a lot out of my job but a day that jumps to mind was when we had to climb down into the crater of Mt Erebus in Antarctica. The volcano started throwing bits and pieces at us, so it was pretty amazing being inside while it was partly erupting. That kind of thing appeals to me. I can't think of anything that is particularly frustrating about working outdoors but I am bothered by the endless meetings and things to do within the polytechnic system, which don't always seem relevant to how you might actually improve the programme for students.

B Mick Beasley: Mountain Guide

For 25 years I was going back and forth between the USA and New Zealand teaching skiing. Eventually, I just wanted to settle down and find a base. That meant I needed a summer job so I started learning about summer mountain guiding. I prefer trips which aren't technical, but difficult, and where without a guide it would be beyond most people's ability, and it's rewarding to know they appreciate that fact. I only deal with groups of four to five people as it's hard to find wilderness when you travel in large numbers. I'm at an age when I resent doing things that I don't enjoy so I offer places to the clients that I want to go to anyway. Working with people is not difficult in the mountains; they are so far out of their element that they tend to have faith in you implicitly and are easy to get along with. To do a job like mine I think it's essential that you attend the best courses. To go through such training and have other people look at your work and get their input is invaluable.

C Johnny Kitts: Jet-boat driver

I've been driving commercially for 18 years on various rivers and every day is different. What isn't so pleasant is picking hikers up on dangerous parts of the river – sometimes it's just not safe enough to attempt. There's probably not a dull part with any jet-boat job, especially on commercial trips. You've got to be aware of what is happening all the time, you can't switch off at any point on the trip. That's when the boat ends up stuck in the shallows. I am now more involved in scheduling other drivers, so I don't spend as much time on the river as I did, which is a bit of a downpoint at times. For commercial driving it's learning as you go – time on the river with checks done by the local harbour master. There's no course. You get a good idea of a driver's ability after about 25 hours. It's experience of the river and conditions that counts and that continues for as long as you drive your boat.

D Chris Macrae: Snow sports photographer

All my training for this career has been completely hands-on, rather than through study. I've been skiing since I was a kid and was lucky enough to get sponsorship which allowed me to get up to serious competition level. But I'd also been into photography since I was twelve and my camera always went with me to the slopes. This year I was invited to take part in the biggest ski photography competition in the world. It was overwhelming just to be asked along to the competition and then I was over the moon to actually win something! I've been skiing in Alaska for seven years now and every time it's unique. Basically my whole life is just waiting for that period to come around. In the meantime, waiting on payment from people you work with is a frustration you have to put up with. It's difficult because sometimes you might spend $400 or $500 on film and then there's the travel costs, and you might not get paid for months while you wait for magazines to run the shots. And filing photos is not my strong point. It's the most tedious and most important part of the job.

E Jarrod Scott: Black-water rafting guide

The caves we raft through really are astonishing – a totally different world. One of the best things is meeting people from different backgrounds and you get to see them at their highs and lows. Occasionally some people get scared stiff and I get a lot out of helping someone overcome that. I've also had a few incidents where clients have completely ignored me because I'm still quite young. I used to get really offended, but now I'm resigned to it. When I started out I had no caving experience so I was 'tagged' for 10 trips. That means you join in like a normal client on a guided trip. During that time the other guides assess you: the idea is that they train you in the technical skills but you won't make a guide if you don't have what it takes regarding personality. Once you're accepted, it's full on into training, like water safety and risk management. Having said all this, and although I love caving, I wouldn't class myself as a caver. In my spare time I prefer above-ground activities like training in different martial arts.

PAPER 2 WRITING 1 hour 30 minutes

Part 1

You **must** answer this question. Write your answer in **180–220** words in an appropriate style.

---

1 You work part-time in the sports centre of an international college. The manager has asked you to write a report on the centre in order to help her increase customer satisfaction and membership.

Read the summary of feedback from a questionnaire that was given to sports centre members below, and the notes you have made on it. Then, **using the information appropriately**, write your report for the manager, providing details of the feedback you received and making suggestions for improvements.

Summary of members' feedback	
Area	**Quality Rating**
Facilities: changing rooms + gym equipment	Poor ★ – *explain why members unhappy/suggest what improvements necessary*
Staff	Good ★★★ – *much better than last year! Say why*
Cafeteria	Poor ★ – *prices OK – but other problems*
Other problems:	

- Opening times – *don't forget members are college students and staff!*
- Fees mentioned as high – *say what we could do about this.*

Write your **report**. You should use your own words as far as possible.

Before you write your report, go to page 98.

A DETAILED STUDY

Content

Read the question again. What are the five content points that should be included? How would you expand on each main point? (In other words, what else would you say to develop each point and to inform the target reader fully?)

Effect on target reader

Who are you writing this report for? What register should you use?

Now read the sample answer and compare your ideas for content and register.

Report on customer satisfaction with the health club

This report is based on a total of 125 questionnaires that health club members returned to us.

I would like to start by saying that members are happy with staff and the service they provide. It would seem, therefore, that the training courses (1) **staff were sent on** have been effective. However, there is significant dissatisfaction with a number of other areas.

Firstly, the condition of the changing rooms (2) **was felt to be** poor. I realize that the showers (3) **have been renovated** only three years ago but I would strongly recommend that we have them done again. Perhaps the changing rooms (4) **could decorated** with lighter colours to create a brighter atmosphere? Secondly, some of the cycling machines are regularly breaking down and the floor mats are generally worn. I would suggest that (5) **these are replaced** as soon as possible.

Regarding the cafeteria, the feedback indicated that there were few healthy options available on the menu. It might be an idea to introduce some salad-based meals instead.

Two other areas of concern are opening times and fees. I would recommend that we consider extending our opening hours to fit in with the college timetable and that a reduced rate (6) **will be offered** to students who attend the health club on weekday afternoons. We could do this for a trial period, of, say, two months, and see what effect on membership it has.

I appreciate that all the suggestions above would involve considerable expenditure but I feel that the cost would be worth it in the long term.

Organization

How has the writer organized the report? How does he make the report clear to read?

Range

The passive is often used in formal reports. Which structures in bold are correct forms of the passive? Which ones are incorrect?

Further practice

A question regarding 'suggestions, advice and recommendations' may require you to be diplomatic and polite when you are writing to a senior person, or someone you need to make a good impression on. As always, the effect on the target reader is vital and for this type of question you will have to choose your language very carefully to achieve the right effect. It is very easy to sound tactless and rude instead of tactful and reassuring if the wrong words and expressions are used.

Look at the pairs of sentences below and choose the sentence which sounds the most polite.

1a **How about** hold**ing** the conference elsewhere?

b I **wonder if** the conference **might be held** elsewhere.

2a I **was hoping** that the office **could be** redecorated.

b I **hope** we **can** redecorate the office.

3a **Can** we go to a different venue?

b **Would it be possible** to go to a different venue?

4a **Perhaps** we **could** encourage younger people to join our group.

b **Maybe** we **can** encourage younger people to join our group.

5a I suggest **you should reduce** the prices if possible.

b I suggest **that** the prices **should be reduced** if possible.

6a I **feel** that our employees' morale **would** improve if we **gave** them a bonus.

b I **think** that our employees' morale **will** improve if we give them a bonus.

7a If we **offer** our visitors a range, I feel certain that there **will** be far fewer complaints.

b If we **offered** our visitors a range, I feel certain that there **would** be far fewer complaints.

Part 2

Write an answer to **one** of the questions **2–5** in this part. Write your answers in **220–260** words in an appropriate style.

2   An English-speaking friend of yours will soon attend their first job interview. Your friend is feeling nervous about the interview and has written to you asking for your advice.

Write to your friend, describing a job interview that you attended and suggesting what your friend should do at their interview.

Write your **letter**.

Before you write your letter, go to page 101.

3   You see the following announcement in your college magazine.

In next month's issue we will be looking at how the Internet can help you improve your English. We invite students to send in reviews of two English-language teaching websites they have visited, describing the features of each site, suggesting which one might be the most useful, and giving reasons for your choice.

Write your **review**.

4   An international current affairs magazine called *GLOBAL ISSUES* has announced that it plans to feature a series of articles on the impact of tourism around the world. You have decided to write a contribution to the series. Your contribution should:

•   give details of the kind of tourist activities that are popular in your country

•   explain what impact tourism has had on your country so far

•   suggest how tourism may develop in your country in the future.

Write your **contribution** to the series.

5   Answer **one** of the following two questions based on **one** of the [set books] below.

a   Your teacher has asked you to write an essay giving your opinion on the following statement:

The most likeable characters are those who make mistakes and show signs of human weakness.

In your essay, you should explain your opinion with reference to one or more characters in [the set book].

Write your **essay**.

b   A literary magazine has invited readers to send in articles on books they have read on the theme of motivation. In your article, briefly describe the personality and any known background details of one of the major characters in [the set book], say what you think he or she hopes to achieve, and explain what you think it is that motivates them.

Write your **article**.

A DETAILED STUDY – Informal letter

Effect on target reader

Read question 2 again. How do you want the reader (your friend going to the interview) to feel after they have read your letter? How can you achieve this?

Content

What two things do you need to include in your answer?

Read the sample letter below. In which paragraphs are these two things contained?

> Hi Martin,
>
> .... I'm surprised, though, that you've got time for extra work **on top of** your studies. But if you can get some practical work experience in a law firm before you graduate, I'm sure **it'll stand you in good stead** for the future.
>
> I've only had one serious interview myself when I applied to the *South Post* newspaper. It wasn't as awful as I expected. I was interviewed by a panel of three editors but they were all really friendly and one of them actually **started off** the interview by talking about the history of the paper and the direction they wanted to go in. Of course they wanted to see the material I'd written for the college magazine, but they also wanted to find out what kind of a person I was. I think a lot of the questions they asked me were designed to **figure out** whether I'd be able to meet deadlines and fit into their team.
>
> **In your case**, I'd definitely do some background reading on the firm you're applying to. It'll help you prepare something useful to say when they ask 'Why do you want to work for us?' I'm sure **this goes without saying** – but look the interviewer in the eye when you're answering questions, and rather than **just come out with** things like 'I'm a quick learner' – you need to **back it up** with an example. Finally – remember your potential employers will partly be making their decision based on whether they like you or not ...so smile!
>
> .... , Tom

Starting and finishing your informal letter

Choose the best phrase below to start and finish your letter:

START:

    a   You will soon attend an interview and you are nervous.

    b   I am writing in response to your recent request for help.

    c   It was good to hear from you

FINISH:

    a   Hope it all goes well!

    b   See you soon!

    c   Thanks for all your help!

Range

What do the phrases and phrasal verbs in bold mean? Try to work them out by using the surrounding context. Then check in your dictionary.

PAPER 3 USE OF ENGLISH 1 hour

Part 1

For questions **1–12**, read the text below and decide which answer (**A, B, C** or **D**) best fits each gap. There is an example at the beginning (**0**).

Example:

0   **A** getting   **B** sending   **C putting**   **D** setting

---

Burglars beware! Don't touch the food

It seems that a burglar's inability to say no to his stomach could go a long way towards

(0) .... him behind bars. Indeed, **(1)** .... a crime actually seems to work

up an appetite. According to a 1973 article in the *British Dental Journal*, 'Criminals appear to be unable

to **(2)** .... food, chocolate or fruit that they find on **(3)** .... into which they

enter illegally. There's also a **(4)** .... to leave, at the site, the unconsumed portions.' For

years, forensic experts have examined these food traces in the **(5)** .... of finding bite-

mark evidence, but with DNA identification now **(6)** .... , investigators try to uncover

molecular fingerprints as well. A handful of criminals have been **(7)** .... this way in the

past ten years.

Californian researchers recently wanted to test the **(8)** .... of recovering DNA from

foods. They organized a dinner party in which guests were asked to **(9)** .... themselves

to a few bites of whatever they fancied and leave the **(10)** .... behind. Cheese, carrots,

apples and pizza returned the most complete DNA profiles while chocolate was **(11)** ....

useless. The researchers think the chocolate failure was more to do with the fact that the pieces were

small, **(12)** .... that less saliva was left behind.

1 A enacting   B realizing   C committing   D performing

2 A resist   B decline   C deny   D refuse

3 A houses   B locations   C grounds   D premises

4 A habit   B tendency   C behaviour   D likelihood

5 A reason   B chance   C hope   D view

6 A commonplace   B regular   C typical   D average

7 A confirmed   B accused   C shown   D convicted

8 A dependency   B reliability   C suitability   D methodology

9 A control   B limit   C restrain   D ration

10 A extra   B spare   C excess   D remains

11 A hardly   B extremely   C virtually   D barely

12 A meaning   B showing   C requiring   D causing

Part 2

For questions **13–27**, read the text below and think of the word which best fits each space. Use only **one** word in each gap. There is an example at the beginning (**0**).

Example: 0 WOULD

Too late to learn?

After I had fallen over for the eighth time in 25 minutes, I realized I **(0)** .... not be able

to teach myself to ski. I had fallen forwards, backwards and to both sides. I had landed on my wrists,

arms, knees, thighs and shoulders and it seemed **(13)** .... were no new ways left to fall,

(14) .... I got in the way of other learners and **(15)** .... knocked down

by someone else. I asked a friend **(16)** .... I could do to improve my technique. 'Stop

crashing into things,' she said, at **(17)** .... point I gave up. I tucked my skis under one

arm, dropped them, tucked them under the **(18)** .... and stomped home through the

snow in my very uncomfortable snow boots. **(19)** .... my anger, I booked a lesson with

an instructor called Jane who was surprised that a 37-year-old could live life **(20)** ....

no co-ordination. It was **(21)** .... disability that meant my first lesson was wildly

unsuccessful. The difference **(22)** .... skiing and sliding out of control down a steep hill

is **(23)** .... ability to 'snowplough', meaning that you have to position the skis in an open

V-shape with the apex parallel to your nose. If you **(24)** .... make a snowplough, you

simply aren't going to stop. I found **(25)** .... impossible to turn my feet to the correct

angle, and when I finally **(26)** .... make a V-shape, it was **(27)** .... wide I

could not move out of it! Jane was unimpressed.

Part 3

For questions **28–37**, read the text below. Use the word given in capitals at the end of some of the lines to form a word that fits in the gap **in the same line**. There is an example at the beginning (**0**).

Example: 0 EXTENSIVE

Bilingual Graduates Required for Sunworld Travel

Sunworld Travel has a widespread and **(0)** .... network of travel agencies   **EXTEND**

across the country, and due to recent **(28)** .... , we have a number of   **GROW**

(29) .... for graduates who are interested in pursuing a career in tourism.   **VACANT**

Suitable candidates will be hardworking, ambitious and **(30)** .... They   **RELY**

will have the **(31)** .... ability to work successfully within a team, for   **PROVE**

for example in a work-experience or college situation, but should also be able to work

(32) ....   **DEPEND**

They should have good interpersonal skills skills, and because much of our

business is conducted with overseas operators, **(33)** .... in a second language   **FLUENT**

is also required, **(34)** .... in Spanish or French. If achieving customer   **PREFER**

(35) .... appeals to you, and you meet the above criteria, come along   **SATISFY**

to our **(36)** .... day on 16th March, at the Queen's Hotel, South Malden.   **RECRUIT**

Our regional managers will be giving presentations and arranging interviews with

(37) ....   **APPLY**

Part 4

For questions **38–42**, think of **one** word only which can be used appropriately in all three sentences. Here is an example (0).

Example:

0   Please explain to me the .... of having another meeting.

It was at that .... that most of the audience got up and left.

We lost a .... because one person in our team started the race too early.

Example: POINT

---

38   Australia is a .... of diverse nationalities and cultural traditions.

We saw the bird .... briefly on a nearby fence before it flew off.

Even the strongest swimmer couldn't swim to .... in such rough water.

39   The man shouted at us to .... out as he ran down the street towards us.

I wouldn't .... him staying if he agreed to do some of the housework.

Can you .... the children for half an hour while I go to the dentist's?

40   We hope to .... more people from the disease by making the treatment freely available.

Please do not attempt to .... a seat in the library by leaving your bag there.

The government has said that low-income families should .... more, but this is unrealistic.

41   A member of the rescue team suffered a .... cut to his hand.

The .... roaring sound of the ocean was never far away.

Laura was .... in thought and didn't hear the teacher call her name.

42   The new exams will .... students under even more pressure.

The police advise homeowners not to .... spare keys under the door mat.

In our culture, we .... our children's education before everything else.

Part 5

For questions **43–50**, complete the second sentence so that it has a similar meaning to the first sentence, using the word given. **Do not change the word given**. You must use between **three** and **six** words, including the word given. Here is an example (0).

Example:

0   As he continued to listen to the speech, Richard became increasingly sleepy.

SLEEPIER

The more Richard listened to the speech, ... became.

Example: 0 THE SLEEPIER HE

---

43   Although we booked a table, it wasn't necessary because the restaurant was empty.

NEED

There was .... made a reservation because the restaurant was empty.

44   John resigned because he wants to travel, not because he wants a new job.

DO

John's resignation is .... desire to travel than wanting a new job.

45   Albert's wife said he had to start being interested in their children's lives.

TIME

Albert's wife said .... an interest in their children's lives.

46   I almost didn't recognize Takeshi because he had lost so much weight.

DUE

I hardly .... the amount of weight he'd lost.

47   I wish Jack had bought tickets for Venice but we went to Paris instead.

RATHER

Jack bought us tickets to Paris but I .... to Venice.

48   From the time Elena and Alex finished their relationship, they've both been sad.

SEEING

Ever .... other, Alex and Elena have both been sad.

49   It was wrong of you not to tell me that information.

KEPT

You should .... me.

50   The council officer promised to get someone to remove the rubbish.

HAVE

The council officer promised he .... away.

PAPER 4 LISTENING approximately 40 minutes

Part 1

You will hear three different extracts. For questions **1–6**, choose the answer (**A, B** or **C**) which fits best according to what you hear. There are two questions for each extract.

Extract One

You hear part of an interview with an author called Marian Bly.

1   Marian mentions the woman in Brighton in order to show how people

   A   seem to find tragedy in fiction very appealing.

   B   tend to forget that they are reading fiction, not fact.

   C   want something in common with the writer they read.

2   What does Marian say about the increasing public interest in stories about suffering?

   A   It is probably a temporary trend.

   B   It shows that people are generally unhappy.

   C   Publishing companies are responsible for it.

Extract Two

You hear two people on a radio programme talking about consumerism.

3   What does the man imply when he describes his shopping trip?

   A   Children expect to receive more material things nowadays.

   B   Parents are buying gifts instead of spending time with children.

   C   Packaging has become far more sophisticated than it used to be.

4   The woman says that people do not return goods to stores because they

   A   forget to keep their receipts.

   B   doubt they will get their money back.

   C   did not pay much for them.

Extract Three

You hear part of an interview with Kesaia Tavola, the organizer of an exhibition of tapa, a kind of decorated cloth.

5   According to Kesaia, what led to the decline of tapa-making in Hawaii?

   A   the availability of other material

   B   the migration of Hawaiian communities

   C   the preference amongst native Hawaiians for European fashion

6   What does Kesaia say is behind the resumed interest in tapa-making?

   A   a sense of cultural pride

   B   the need for financial security

   C   increased demand from tourists

Part 2

You will hear a radio presenter called Andrew Young talking about food trends in Britain.
For questions **7–14**, complete the sentences.

FOOD TRENDS IN BRITAIN

Andrew says that [_____ **7**] were not involved in the study carried out by the

Restaurant Association.

The study showed that [_____ **8**] food had become the nation's favourite

restaurant meal.

It also showed that Italian restaurants were more popular than [_____ **9**]

restaurants.

According to the study, 40% of restaurants are part of corporate-owned [_____ **10**] .

The fact that 30% of restaurants are now making a [_____ **11**] does not surprise

Andrew.

Sushi became a popular lunchtime meal with businessmen when restaurants offered a

[_____ **12**] .

Andrew is unimpressed with the sushi that [_____ **13**] sell.

Not everyone agrees about the amount of [_____ **14**] that sushi

contains.

Part 3

You will hear part of a radio interview in which television presenter and volcanologist Callum Gray is talking about his work with volcanoes. For questions **15–20**, choose the answer (**A, B, C** or **D**) which fits bests according to what you hear.

15 How do many people react after hearing Callum is a volcanologist?

    A They expect him to be boring in some way.

    B They are keen to learn more about his work.

    C They want to hear about dangerous incidents.

    D They are unwilling to show how little they know about volcanoes.

16 What does Callum say about his decision to become a volcanologist?

    A It occurred spontaneously.

    B It was prompted by his father.

    C It had originated in his childhood.

    D It has caused him some slight regret.

17 How did Callum feel during the flight over the erupting Hawaiian volcano?

    A fascinated by the force of the eruption

    B frightened that he was not going to survive

    C guilty because he had put the pilot in danger

    D annoyed there was no warning of bad weather

18 Which aspect of his job does Callum find most difficult?

    A having to handle the media during an eruption

    B being constantly aware of danger while on an active volcano

    C assessing the risk to life that an eruption might cause

    D dealing with people who could be affected by an eruption

19 According to Callum, what surprises students about being a volcanologist?

    A the time that is allocated to different aspects of the job

    B the need to have good communication skills

    C the difficulty in finding regular employment

    D the possibility of seeing an entire eruption take place

20 Why does Callum prefer working at volcanoes to being a TV presenter?

    A It gives him a sense of freedom.

    B It is possible to see unusual places.

    C He finds the work more challenging.

    D He enjoys the unpredictability of events.

Part 4

You will hear five short extracts in which people are talking about an aspect of tourism.

TASK ONE

For questions **21–25**, choose from the list **A–H** the person who is speaking.

A   pilot

B   restaurant owner

C   tour guide | 21 |

D   coach driver | 22 |

E   flight attendant | 23 |

F   tourist | 24 |

G   hotel receptionist | 25 |

H   travel agent

TASK TWO

For questions **26–30**, choose from the list **A–H** the word that best describes the person's attitude.

A   irritated

B   unenthusiastic

C   worried | 26 |

D   keen | 27 |

E   accepting | 28 |

F   afraid | 29 |

G   disappointed | 30 |

H   angry

In the exam you will have 5 minutes at the end of the test to copy your answers on to a separate answer sheet.

Before you check your answers, go to page 112.

A DETAILED STUDY

Listen again to Part 4 of the test on page 111 and answer the following questions by either writing T (true) or F (false) in the box provided. You may wish to change your answers to this part of the test after you have done this.

Speaker 1 says:

1 he has a job she always wanted. ☐

2 he stays in hotels. ☐

3 he enjoys a good social life. ☐

4 he travels long distances by plane. ☐

5 his work is repetitive. ☐

6 he has to deal with complaints. ☐

7 the job is what he expected it to be. ☐

Speaker 2 says:

8 she works at an airport. ☐

9 she is affected by plane delays. ☐

10 she has to wait for tourists to arrive. ☐

11 she doesn't mind working overtime. ☐

12 she is often told she has to stay at work at short notice. ☐

Speaker 3 says:

13 he helps customers find what they're looking for. ☐

14 some customers take a long time to make decisions. ☐

15 his customers have to pay a lot of money. ☐

16 he finds his customers' behaviour irritating. ☐

Speaker 4 says:

17 she has enjoyed holidays in St Lucia and Antigua. ☐

18 she knows a lot about Greek history. ☐

19 she is interested in learning about Greek customs. ☐

20 she is anxious about making mistakes. ☐

Speaker 5 says:

21 he was willing to go to an art gallery. ☐

22 he is responsible for a group of people. ☐

23 he would prefer to relax than go sightseeing. ☐

24 he believes that every statue he sees is unique. ☐

Now check your answers to Part 4 of the test.

PAPER 5 SPEAKING approximately 15 minutes

Part 2 (4 minutes)

1 Risk at work

For both candidates: Look at the three pictures on page 148. They show people who take risks as part of their job.

Candidate A: Compare two of these pictures and say in what ways these people benefit society and what risks they might face in their work. (*1 minute*)

Candidate B: Which of these people do you think should be paid the most for the risks they take? (*approximately 30 seconds*)

2 Emotions

For both candidates: Look at the three pictures on page 149. They show people experiencing different emotions.

Candidate B: Compare two of these pictures, and say how the people might be feeling towards one another, and what might have happened to make them feel this way. (*1 minute*)

Candidate A: Which of these people are most likely to have a lasting memory of their feelings at this moment? (*approximately 30 seconds*)

Part 3 (4 minutes)

A sense of fulfilment

For both candidates: Look at the pictures on pages 150 and 151. They show some different aspects of people's lives.

First talk to each other about how these different aspects of life might contribute to people's sense of fulfilment. Then decide which three things you think would lead to the most satisfaction in the long run.

Part 4 (4 minutes)

For both candidates:

- What other aspects of life may provide a sense of fulfilment?
- Are the things that make people happy today different to what made people happy in the past?
- How far do you agree with the statement 'Money can't buy happiness'?
- Is it desirable to reach a point in life where you are completely satisfied? Why/Why not?

CAE TEST 4

PAPER 1 READING 1 hour 15 minutes

Part 1

You are going to read three extracts which are all concerned in some way with travel. For questions **1–6**, choose the answer (**A, B, C** or **D**) which you think fits best according to the text.

EXTRACT FROM A LEAFLET

Notice to Customers – Devonport-City Ferry Service

We apologize to customers who are still awaiting the return of the Devonport-City ferry, Dolphin I. As regular passengers will know, Dolphin I was temporarily withdrawn from service in early July when it was scheduled to undergo its annual inspection and maintenance checks. While we are pleased to announce that it met all test requirements, it was highly unfortunate that on the due date for its return to public service, it was involved in a collision with an unmanned smaller vessel that had broken free of its moorings during the recent storms. As a result of this incident, the outer hull sustained slight damage which will require at least two weeks to repair.

During this time, Dolphin II will continue to stand in for its sister ship but its smaller passenger capacity means that customers may not be able to travel at their usual time. Commuters who are unable to board their regular service will be entitled to a 20% refund on day return or weekly tickets which can be immediately claimed at the destination ticket office, provided they are able to produce proof of ticket purchase. For customers with a currently valid monthly pass, a 10% discount will be granted when they are next renewed.

1 The regular ferry is not running because

   A it was damaged in bad weather.

   B it requires a yearly service.

   C it was hit by another boat.

   D it has taken longer to repair than expected.

2 Passengers can get some money off the cost of travel

   A only if they take their trip at their regular time.

   B when they apply to buy their tickets.

   C once they return from their destination.

   D when they purchase a new monthly pass.

EXTRACT FROM A MAGAZINE

As policy director for a well-known multinational, Andrew Sims spends his days thinking globally. But when he travels on holiday, it's always closer to home; several years ago he made the decision to never again to take a vacation by air. 'It was partly driven by a concern for the environment,' says Sims, 'but also by a desire not to overlook what's on your doorstep, and to travel in a more leisurely way.' Now Sims and his family would rather board a sleeper train from London to Scotland's west coast. They spend unstructured days amid the islands, hiking, cooking or just dreaming. The journey itself is a key part of the trip. No matter that it takes three times longer than flying; for Sims and his family, enjoying breakfast in bed while chugging past some of the world's most beautiful scenery is the end, not the means to get there.

More and more people are living for their next vacation, and like Sims, are opting to travel in the slow lane. They are bargaining with their employers for more time to savour their travels.

For them there seems to be an easy transition from the drudgery of work and responsibilities of bringing up children to the pleasures of time off – and back again. And today's trips are more like narratives in which the next page is yet to be written, and the traveller is the storyteller. The whole idea of 'If it's Tuesday, it must be Belize' is completely over. So is the desire to come back with an object, or even a picture. They want to come back with a story.

Article from *Newsweek* 14/5/07 www.newsweek.com

3   According to the writer, Andrew Sims chose not to travel abroad because he

   A   has too many work-related responsibilities.

   B   wishes to spend more time with his family.

   C   wants to appreciate what local holidays could offer.

   D   had never enjoyed overseas trips as much as ones at home.

4   What are we told about many travellers in the third paragraph?

   A   They are keen to bring back souvenirs of their experience.

   B   They are likely to cause difficulties for the companies they work for.

   C   They believe their children will benefit from travelling with them.

   D   They do not follow a fixed schedule during their holiday.

EXTRACT FROM A NOVEL

He found he had been allocated a window seat, and that was fine, because Robbie knew he would need some intense distraction on the long flight home. As always, it was only a matter of moments before he found his limbs longing to break free of the designated area. The resentful compromise of space and the enforced human cohabitation for the next seven hours would test his powers of endurance to the limit, and yet he would suffer in silence. It was every man for himself in this place, save for the rare conspiratorial glances shared between those like himself, who were child-free, and bore only hand luggage, as those others herded their untamed offspring down the aisle, seeking out their seats and adjacent victims. The smaller the child, the more potential for extreme disturbance, and this was hardly the same as distraction.

Robbie was spared this time, and to his relief, had the row to himself. Once the plane was airborne, he began to reflect on the purpose of the flight; his father's funeral. Indeed, it was actually a fitting place to think about the old man; the confinement of his seat could well describe their interaction; there was his father's relentless attempt to shape him and Robbie's equally obstinate refusal to stay contained. He thought of his sisters; Emily who had willingly given in and whose role as nurse was predestined, Helen the oldest, sitting in mouldy, stone-faced judgement over all the others, Janice whose disappearance for years had generally gone unobserved. They would stand by the grave as a family unit with all lines of communication severed.

5   What did Robbie find particularly irritating about flying?

   A   the inability to move freely

   B   the risk of losing luggage

   C   the time it took certain people to board

   D   the minimal conversation people shared

6   In the second paragraph, the writer makes a comparison between the seat and Robbie's

   A   sense of direction in life.

   B   relationship with his father.

   C   sisters' attitude towards one another.

   D   sense of separation from his family.

Part 2

You are going to read an extract from a newspaper article. Six paragraphs have been removed from the extract. Choose from the paragraphs **A–G** the one which fits each gap (**7–12**). There is one extra paragraph which you do not need to use.

Baby Talk

As much as you may want to believe it, there is no basis to the feeling that your infant is smiling at you, and smiling because he knows you're his mother. He might look as wise as the ages when he gazes into your eyes – but face up to the facts. There's nothing in there, unless we count the blank slate. And don't read too much into his babbling either. He's just learning how to use his face muscles. That's what my doctor told me when I took my baby for his check-ups. I doubted this, but I knew science was on her side so I kept my opinion to myself.

7

This is not just hopeful theorizing. Thanks to new technology that allows scientists to study living brains, the bank of evidence is growing fast. Another great advance was made last week with the publication of research by neuroscientist Laura Ann Petitto of Dartmouth College. The aim of the study was to challenge the traditional understanding of early language development, which holds that babies must develop motor skills before they can begin to connect sounds to meanings.

8

They looked at the way babies moved their mouths when babbling (making sounds with a consonant-vowel repetition) and contrasted this with the movements when they smiled or made non-babbling noises. They studied five English infants, five French infants and five Spanish to be sure they weren't studying mouth movements specific to one language.

9

'The mouth is being carved out depending on the function of what's coming out,' Petitto explains. 'And this function could only occur if different parts of the brain are participating in the control of different functions.' Her researchers deduced that 'the right side of the face – used for smiling – is controlled by the left hemisphere of the brain, where the emotional control centres are located.'

But babbling 'is a left-side mouth function and controlled by the right side of the brain – the centre for speech.'

10

And that is not all it can do. According to other researchers in the field, babies can 'distinguish human faces and voices from other sights and sounds and prefer them'. Although they are born short-sighted, they can see people and items clearly at a distance of about 30cms. Their preference for stripes and other patterns shows they are imposing order on their perceptions in early infancy. Long before they can crawl, they can tell the difference between happy features and sad features.

11

They can grasp simple arithmetic by using the same capacity, according to Petitto. 'It is well established that infants look longer at things that are unexpected or surprising to them. In a recent study, the researchers built up the expectation that a puppet would jump, say two times.' When the infants lost interest, they continued to show one group of infants what they had already been watching. Another group was shown a puppet that jumped three times. Petitto explains, 'The infants looked longer at the puppet when it jumped three times, showing they had detected the change in number.

12

But this is not the end of the story, as the nature side of the nature/nurture divide has claimed for so long. Despite this standard capacity, babies depend on their vast reserves of innate knowledge in the way you and I depend on the programs we put into our computers. What matters most is what we do with these programs, and it's the same with babies. They're born with powerful learning tools that allow them to explore and learn about the world around them. And what they learn goes on to determine the way their brains are wired, and how they think.

A 'What this tells us', says Petitto, 'is that language processing starts far earlier than we ever thought and without much language experience. As young as five months, the brain is already discriminating between a purely physical response and an oral one.'

B But they depend on more than innate knowledge and learning abilities. People instinctively want to help babies learn. A lot of this tuition is, they claim, unconscious and unwilled. The typical example would be the stern businessman who, if left holding the baby, lapses into baby talk.

C The results showed uniformity in all cases. When the babies smiled, they opened the left sides of their mouths, using more muscles on the left side of the face. When they were making 'non-babbling' noises they used the middle of the mouth, and when they babbled they pulled down on the right side of the mouth, using more right-side muscles.

D Now at last it is science that is having second thoughts. It turns out that babies know a lot more than our best minds previously suspected. If they smile, it may well be because they recognize your voice. When they babble, they are probably not speaking nonsense but practising speech.

E This is borne out by the fact that they can imitate these same expressions, and by the time they're old enough to pick up a phone they can mimic what they've seen others doing with it. This means they can learn how to use things just by watching people.

F So much for the blank slate then. Much of this research would seem to disprove many of our oldest and fondest assumptions, not just about speech but about how people are like us and how we are like other people. It appears that our brains all start out with the same approach to learning and development.

G Petitto and her team take a different view. 'When a child babbles, it's not just trying to get control over its facial muscles,' she says. Babies are 'literally trying to say the sounds' they hear, and trying to make sense of 'the patterns of sounds in the world around them.'

Part 3

You are going to read a magazine article. For questions **13–19**, choose the answer (**A, B, C** or **D**) which you think fits best according to the text.

Writing and Wishing

Felicity Price loves to write, but even with her fifth novel just out, she has yet to make a living from literature.

By the time I finished the 180 000-word draft of my first novel, I imagined myself travelling the globe to meet adoring fans, being the toast of international book festivals, and juggling offers for the film rights. But then I tried to find a publisher and the bubble burst. One after another, publishers rejected it. When it was eventually accepted, that wasn't the end of the battle. I had to cut 85 000 dearly beloved, hard-earned words, followed by endless revisions by my editor. And just as I was preparing to chill the champagne for the launch party, another wave of anxiety arose over the title, the cover, the promotion and a publicity blurb that would somehow describe it in 20 words or fewer.

Finally, with the book in front of me to touch and hold, the bubble burst all over again. I'd anticipated an ecstatic feeling. But as soon as I opened the cover and started to read it, what leapt out at me but a typing error and I was ready to give it all up for good. Then the reviews came out and almost all of them were upbeat, praising the book, and I decided against indulging in self-pity. But one sarcastic reviewer picked it to pieces and I was back to throwing down my pen forever.

A bookseller asked me to do a book signing and I was on a high again. The store manager showed me to a little table where people would queue to meet me, the author of the book they were clutching. I sat down and waited. I thumbed through the book and smiled at passersby – because yes, they did pass me by. At last, someone came up to the table. My heart skipped a beat. 'Where is the new Jamie Oliver cook book, please?' 'Sorry, I don't work here. But would you like to buy my book?' I held it up hopefully. They feigned polite interest, then headed purposefully in the direction of the cooking section. Final tally: five books sold and autographed, including one to a friend. But at least the bookshops where you go for signings have your books prominently displayed. I admit that I went around other bookstores looking for any sign of my novel and pushed it towards the front of the display but I stood no chance against celebrity memoirs.

Getting published is an emotional rollercoaster. So why do it? Hardly for the fame and certainly not the fortune. The best part of writing a novel is being tucked away in a room with a good CD on the stereo and a laptop recording every word you write – and rewrite. It's much more fun than journalism because you don't have to worry about facts getting in the way of a good story. You can improve on real people, or merge several into one malevolent anti-hero; you can embellish a true story and the characters you create can take over and almost tell the story themselves. Sure, sometimes you have to force yourself to do it. I've been known to go to the dentist just to put off the hour when I have to start a new chapter. But once I get going, I don't want to stop.

There is one other compelling reason to sit in front of the computer for endless hours until your back aches and your brain hurts – and that's your readers. There is nothing more gratifying than being stopped in the street by someone wanting to tell you how much they enjoyed your book and asking you about one of the characters in such detail they seem to think it was real. But you rarely get to experience such joy for very long. 'I loved it so much I lent it to my friend,' they go on to say. 'And she lent it to…' You grind your teeth, counting lost sales as it gets passed from one reader to the next because that's the next thing to worry about – will it sell?

Even if booksellers agree to stock your novel, writing fiction may not pay well unless you hit the big time, but writing on commission – that is being asked to write a book on a specific subject – certainly helps makes ends meet. I've written several books on commission, including a pictorial history of Lake Tekapo and a company history. Providing you are dealing with a subject which is interesting, writing on commission can be both professionally and financially rewarding, paying you a more realistic rate for your labours, not hard when your fiction earns you less than a dollar an hour. But you need to write more than one commissioned book a year to make the equivalent of a full time wage, and then you won't have any time left to write a novel.

In the end, it's not about the money or public recognition. Let's face it, few authors are asked to sell their wedding photos to a women's magazine. Writing novels isn't a ticket to a celebrity circuit, which is hardly surprising when you have to spend all your productive time tucked away in your study, writing in anonymous isolation, but it does bring its own rewards. The joy of writing is in the creating of something that has a life of its own and that can give pleasure to others. But just the same, it would be nice to make the top spot on the best-seller list just this once.

13 How did the writer feel about the process of getting her first novel published?

    A She resented having to abandon the book and begin another.

    B She felt she had been misled about the book's potential success.

    C She had last-minute doubts about the marketing of the book.

    D She was dismayed that her writing was not as good as she had believed.

14 Which phrase in paragraph two is echoed by 'throwing down my pen forever'?

    A the bubble burst all over again

    B what leapt out at me

    C to give it all up for good

    D decided against indulging in self-pity

15 What are we told about the writer's experience during the book signing event?

    A She felt reluctant to attend this promotional event in person.

    B She was surprised by the amount of interest shown in her book.

    C She was resentful that her book was not clearly on display.

    D She tried to remain optimistic despite being ignored.

16 The writer compares fiction writing to journalism in order to emphasize

    A the greater amount of public admiration that fiction writers receive.

    B the point that fiction allows writers more creative freedom.

    C the limitations journalists face when they want to criticize people.

    D the effort it requires to make certain news stories appealing to readers.

17 What point does the writer make about some of her readers in paragraph five?

    A They frustrate her when they allow their friends to borrow her books.

    B They are harder to please because they are familiar with her previous work.

    C They often bother her at inappropriate moments.

    D They do not appreciate the effort that is required in writing a novel.

18 What is the writer doing in the penultimate paragraph?

    A discouraging people from taking up novel writing

    B explaining the pros and cons of writing commissioned books

    C specifying which kinds of commissioned books are worth writing

    D criticizing the publishing industry for the way it treats writers

19 In the last paragraph, the writer draws a comparison between 'the celebrity circuit' and

    A public recognition.

    B productive time.

    C anonymous isolation.

    D the top spot.

Part 4

You are going to read a magazine article in which four successful career women talk about emigrating to New Zealand. For questions **20–34**, choose from the list of women (**A–D**). The women may be chosen more than once.

Which woman ...

mentions the way in which she was disadvantaged in the country she left? | 20 |

mentions a negative point about a job she has had? | 21 |

explains an advantage of choosing to pursue her career in New Zealand? | 22 |

mentions an aspect of living in New Zealand that she can find difficult? | 23 |

appreciates the approach to achieving goals in New Zealand? | 24 |

expresses a sense of regret about leaving her country? | 25 |

appreciates the honesty she feels exists in New Zealand? | 26 |

denies conforming to a certain stereotype? | 27 |

appreciates New Zealand for its sense of calm and normality? | 28 |

explains how a potential hazard in New Zealand requires special consideration
in her work? | 29 |

explains that she had not planned to stay in New Zealand permanently? | 30 |

states that her original nationality puts her in an advantageous position in New Zealand? | 31 |

recognizes the fact that conflicting opinions can lead to improvements? | 32 |

recommends that New Zealanders take more pride in their country? | 33 |

appreciates working in a friendly environment? | 34 |

The Brain Gain

With New Zealand becoming renowned as a great place to live, it was the first-choice destination for a new generation of talented migrants looking for a better life. Sharon Stephenson talks to four of them.

A Nicky Meiring, Architect

Listen to Nicky Meiring talk about South Africa and it soon becomes evident that she's mourning for a country she once called home. 'The current economic situation has made South Africa quite a hard place to live in,' she says, 'but I do miss it.' Nicky first arrived in Auckland in 1994 and got a job in an architectural practice in Auckland where she soon settled in. She says 'New Zealand often feels like utopia. I just love the tranquillity and the fact you can lead a safe and ordinary life.' She lives and works from a renovated factory where her mantelpiece is littered with awards for the design of her summer house on Great Barrier Island. 'Although the design of buildings is fairly universal, houses here are generally constructed of timber as opposed to brick and when it comes to the engineering of buildings, I have to take great heed of earthquakes which isn't an issue in South Africa,' she says. 'But the very fact that my training and experience are different means I have something to offer. And I'm so glad I have the opportunity to leave my stamp on my new country.'

B Jenny Orr, Art Director

American Jenny Orr's southern accent seems more at home in the movies than in New Zealand's capital, Wellington. 'I'm from Alabama, but no, we didn't run around barefoot and my father didn't play the banjo!' she jokes, in anticipation of my preconceptions. Having worked in corporate design for ten years in the USA, she was after a change and thought of relocating to New Zealand. It didn't take long for her to land a job with an Auckland design firm, where she was able to gain experience in an unfamiliar but challenging area of design – packaging – and before long, she was headhunted by a direct marketing agency which recently transferred her to Wellington. While she admits she could have the same salary and level of responsibility at home, 'it would probably have been harder to break into this kind of field. I'm not saying I couldn't have done it, but it may have taken longer in the US because of the sheer number of people ahead of me.' Ask Jenny how she's contributing to this country's 'brain gain' and she laughs. 'I don't see myself as being more talented or intelligent but opposing views are what make strategies, concepts and designs better and I hope that's what I bring.'

C Sarah Hodgett, Creative Planner

What happens when all your dreams come true? Just ask Sarah Hodgett. Sarah says that she had always dreamed of a career in advertising. 'But I was from the wrong class and went to the wrong university. In the UK, if you're working class you grow up not expecting greatness in your life. You resign yourself to working at the local factory and knowing your place.' New Zealand, on the other hand, allowed her to break free of those shackles. 'It's a land of opportunity. I quickly learned that if you want to do something here, you just go for it, which is an attitude I admire beyond belief.' Within a month of arriving, she'd landed a job in customer servicing with an advertising agency. Then, when an opening in research came up, she jumped at the chance. 'My job is to conduct research with New Zealanders,' she explains. 'So I get to meet people from across the social spectrum which is incredibly rewarding.' Being a foreigner certainly works in her favour, says Sarah. 'Because a lot of my research is quite personal, respondents tend to see me as impartial and open-minded and are therefore more willing to share their lives with me.' She certainly sees New Zealand in a good light. 'I wish New Zealanders could see their country as I do. They don't think they're good enough on the global stage – and they definitely are – whether it's to do with sports, politics, the academic world, whatever!'

D Lucy Kramer, School Director

Born in Sydney, Australia, Lucy Kramer left for London when she was 23 to further her career as a stockbroker. 'London certainly lived up to my expectations and I had a very exciting lifestyle,' Lucy explains. But after four years she felt burnt out and was disillusioned with her job. 'People at work were far too competitive for my liking,' she says. It was at this time she made a life-changing decision. 'I signed up for a teacher-training course and shortly after that met my partner, Graeme. He asked me to come back to New Zealand with him and I agreed, on the condition we'd eventually go back to London.' It wasn't long before she found work in a large Auckland school and, since then, she has rapidly worked her way up to a management position. 'It's fair to say I'm not earning what I used to but my New Zealand colleagues are much more easy-going. A good atmosphere more than makes up for the drop in salary. Another thing that impresses me is that you can leave your stuff on a seat in a café and it'll still be there half an hour later. People are pretty trustworthy here. Sometimes it bothers me that we're so remote – you can feel a bit cut off from what's going on in the rest of the world, but on the whole, I'd say it's one of the best moves I ever made. This is home, now.'

PAPER 2 WRITING 1 hour 30 minutes

Part 1

You **must** answer this question. Write your answer in **180–220** words in an appropriate style.

1   You are a student at an international college. You have been asked by the college social club to write a proposal recommending a suitable place for the end-of-year party.

Read some students' comments below, and the advertisements for two places which have been suggested. Then, using the information appropriately, write your proposal for the social club, describing the two possibilities, recommending one of them and providing reasons for your choice.

Students' comments:

1 Not too expensive.

2 Should offer food.

3 Entertainment a must!

4 Easy to get there?

5 Last year it ended too quickly.

River Boat Disco

Top-class DJ

$25 includes entry and

all-you-can-eat buffet

Boat departs 7.30pm

returns 10.30pm

Milford Comedy Club

Excellent night of comedy

Four great performers

Snacks available

Group bookings (30+)

$20 tickets

Doors open 8pm–2am

(on High Street, near Milford Underground Station)

take Exit 5 on motorway towards Crofton Harbour, 10 minute drive to boat on Pier 1.

Write your **proposal**.

Before you write your answer, go to page 123.

A DETAILED STUDY

Effect on target reader

Before you read the sample answer below, decide what it is that you need to make clear at the end of any proposal.

Content

Should you refer to the information from both advertisements or just one of them?

Now read the sample answer and find the answers to the questions above.

Proposal for a suitable venue for the college end-of-year party

Introduction

Two venues have been proposed for the party; a River Boat Disco and Milford Comedy Club. Both of these venues could potentially (**1**) **give us what we need**.

Entertainment and food

The boat option offers its own DJ so we would not have to hire one ourselves. However, the disco ends rather early at 10.30pm and I do not think students would (**2**) **like that**. A buffet is available which I think would be (**3**) **better than** a sit-down meal. Regarding the comedy club, the students would be able to see four comedians and moreover, the entertainment continues much later, until 2am. Unfortunately, it only sells snacks which might not (**4**) **make everyone happy**, but we could (**5**) **tell** students to eat before they came.

Price

The disco is (**6**) **not too expensive** at $25 and includes food. Tickets would be $5 cheaper at the comedy club, but this only pays for entry. Students would have to pay more for any snacks they wanted. I feel that there is very little difference between these venues (**7**) **to do with** cost .

Accessibility

Travelling to the disco would require students to drive to Crofton Marina or for the college to hire a bus. Getting to Milford Comedy Club, (**8**) **though**, would be much easier as there is an underground station nearby. It is also located on the high street so students would easily be able to find taxis.

Recommendation

Bearing all the above points in mind, I would propose that the college (**9**) **chooses** Milford Comedy Club. It would offer our students an excellent night out at a reasonable price.

Appropriacy of register

Replace the informal words and phrases in bold with more formal ones from below.

a in terms of   **b** suit everybody's needs   **c** opts for   **d** reasonably priced
e on the other hand   **f** preferable to   **g** advise   **h** meet our requirements   **i** appreciate

Part 2

Write an answer to **one** of the questions **2–5** in this part. Write your answers in **220–260** words in an appropriate style.

---

2   You read the following announcement in an international students' magazine.

> ## THE ATLAS CHANNEL: NEW DOCUMENTARY SERIES COMPETITION
>
> Our producers are looking for locations to include in a documentary about your country. If you can recommend an interesting place, please write to us. You should explain why the location should be included in the documentary, and suggest which local features and local people should appear, giving reasons for your choices.
>
> The winners will have the chance to appear in the documentary.

Write your **competition entry**.

3   The Principal of the college where you study has asked you to prepare an information sheet for recently arrived international students. The purpose of the information sheet is to provide them with practical advice about travelling in your area.

In your information sheet you should:
- describe the most useful form of public transport
- make suggestions about buying and driving cars.

Write your **information sheet**.

Before you write your answer, go to page 125.

4   You see the following job advertisement on your college notice board.

 AMERICAN SUMMER CAMPS

We are currently recruiting international staff to look after young American children between the ages of 9–13 on one of our many summer camps across the USA.

Successful candidates will be able to work well with children, help them develop either their sporting ability or creative talents, and have experience of working successfully within a team.

If you are interested, apply to us in writing, telling us what you can offer and why you are suitable.

Write your **letter of application**.

Before you write your answer, go to page 126.

5   Answer **one** of the following two questions based on **one** of the [set books] below.

a   A bookshop website has invited readers to send in articles entitled 'Making Choices' on books they have read. Write an article about some of the choices that the main character makes in [the set book], suggesting why he or she makes them, and describing the impact that these choices have on the outcome of the story.

Write your **article**.

b   A popular literary magazine has invited readers to submit reviews of books they have read, with a focus on relationships. In your review, briefly outline the plot of [the set book], explain what connection the major characters have with one another and how their relationships develop, and say whether or not you would recommend the book to other readers.

Write your **review**.

A DETAILED STUDY – Information sheet

Before you read the sample information sheet, decide whether the 'tips' below are true or false.

TIPS

- It is necessary to use subheadings.
- Bullet points should not be used.
- The register is always formal.
- The imperative is avoided.

Content

Before you read the sample information sheet, look back at question 3 and decide what information you would include about a) buses b) buying and driving cars.

Now read the sample answer. What information is mentioned concerning buses and cars? Are any of your ideas for information the same?

Guide to travelling around the city

It is **(1) rel**........................ easy to find your way around the city on foot, but if you do not enjoy walking, buses are **(2) fa**.......................... affordable and may be your best option for travelling to and from the college.

Buses

Getting round the inner city couldn't be easier as there is now a free CityLink bus available, and this will drop you off right outside college. It leaves from the main bus station opposite the Downtown Ferry Building and runs **(3) re**.............................. every ten minutes from 7am to 7pm, seven days a week. When you're waiting at a stop, wave to the driver to indicate that you want to be picked up.

Buying a car

Many students, whether local or international, **(4) co**........................... choose to buy a second-hand car. There are several ways to look if you're searching for one: The *Express* newspaper, local community newspapers and www. BuyIt.com are **(5) fr**...................... used to advertise cars for sale, at a range of prices. To be sure you are buying a safe and roadworthy vehicle, you can have it checked out by a **(6) rel**................... expert from the Automobile Association for a fee. They will look at all the main areas of the car and provide you with a **(7) th**.................... report.

Driving around town

First of all, be aware that the speed limit is 40kmph in the inner city and suburban areas and that it is a legal requirement to wear a seat belt. It is also **(8) vi**................... that you know about our unique rule that says that drivers turning left have to give way to oncoming traffic that wants to turn right.

Finally – don't forget that we drive on the left!

Range

Using adjectives and adverbs in writing will make your information sheets, articles, reviews etc more interesting and more informative for your reader. Complete the gaps 1–8 by using a suitable adjective or adverb.

A DETAILED STUDY – Letter of application

Content

Read question 4 again. What points do you need to respond to? Find them in the sample application below.

Dear Sir or Madam,

I have read your advertisement for camp counsellors this summer and I am (1) .... interested in applying for one of these positions.

I am in my second year at university, studying Foreign Languages, and I (2) .... to become an interpreter for the United Nations after my graduation in June 2010. My (3) .... language is Swedish but I am also quite fluent in English and Spanish so (4) .... with the children and other camp counsellors would not be a problem.

(5) .... I have never worked on a summer camp before, I think I have some suitable qualifications and skills that a counsellor might need. Firstly, I am able to (6) .... to different routines quickly and learn the (7) .... in a new situation. I am used to working with children since I have a (8) .... job teaching Swedish to 8–11 year olds who have recently emigrated here with their families. Part of the job requires me to co-operate with other volunteers in planning lessons; in this situation I am willing to listen to other people's ideas as well as (9) .... my own.

I would be happy to get (10) .... with the sports activities at the camp as I usually play volleyball or take (11) .... in tennis tournaments most weekends. I also have several certificates in life saving which I think might be quite useful.

Could you please send me a list of the (12) .... and dates of recruitment days in Northern Europe? I would be willing to travel to an interview if no recruitment fairs are planned for Sweden.

I look forward to hearing from you,

Yours faithfully,

Christina Rehn

Christina Rehn

Range

Now do the multiple-choice vocabulary task below.

1 a	so	b	very	c	too	d	much
2 a	hope	b	like	c	desire	d	dream
3 a	first	b	mother	c	country	d	original
4 a	understanding	b	contacting	c	communicating	d	responding
5 a	Despite	b	Even	c	Although	d	However
6 a	manage	b	deal	c	modify	d	adapt
7 a	strings	b	lines	c	words	d	ropes
8 a	part-time	b	half-time	c	sometime	d	overtime
9 a	participate	b	contribute	c	involve	d	donate
10 a	included	b	participated	c	involved	d	concerned
11 a	place	b	part	c	turn	d	time
12 a	situations	b	sites	c	localities	d	locations

Further practice

Choose the right word or phrase in the sentences below. All the sentences are fairly neutral and could be used in formal or polite letters.

1   I am used to **deal/dealing** with the public.

2   **I am/have been** at Peugeot for three years.

3   I am writing to apply **for/to** the position of interpreter, which was advertised in last Thursday's *Guardian*.

4   From 1989 to 1993, I **had worked/worked** for Crédit Suisse in Zurich in the Customer Relations Department.

5   I am familiar **to/with** all the major software systems.

6   I graduated **from/at** the Korean University in Seoul in 1991.

7   I have a pleasant telephone **behaviour/manner**.

8   I feel that my **experience/experiences** would be extremely relevant to the position.

9   My responsibilities **involve/consist** managing a team of five people, **discussing/liaising** with our offices abroad, and **making/setting** up meetings with clients.

Paper 2 General Impression Mark Scheme

BAND 5

For a Band 5 to be awarded, the candidate's writing has a very positive effect on the target reader. The content is relevant* and the topic is fully developed. Information and ideas are skilfully organized through a range of cohesive devices, which are used to good effect. A wide range of complex structures and vocabulary is used effectively. Errors are minimal, and inaccuracies which do occur have no impact on communication. Register and format are consistently appropriate to the purpose of the task and the audience.

BAND 4

For a Band 4 to be awarded, the candidate's writing has a positive effect on the target reader. The content is relevant* and the topic is developed. Information and ideas are clearly organized through the use of a variety of cohesive devices. A good range of complex structures and vocabulary is used. Some errors may occur with vocabulary and when complex language is attempted, but these do not cause difficulty for the reader. Register and format are usually appropriate to the purpose of the task and the audience.

BAND 3

For a Band 3 to be awarded, the candidate's writing has a satisfactory effect on the target reader. The content is relevant* with some development of the topic. Information and ideas are generally organized logically, though cohesive devices may not always be used appropriately. A satisfactory range of structures and vocabulary is used, though word choice may lack precision. Errors which do occur do not cause difficulty for the reader. Register and format are reasonably appropriate to the purpose of the task and the audience.

BAND 2

For a Band 2 to be awarded, the candidate's writing has a negative effect on the target reader. The content is not always relevant. Information and ideas are inadequately organized and sometimes incoherent, with inaccurate use of cohesive devices. The range of structures and vocabulary is limited and/or repetitive, and errors may be basic or cause difficulty for the reader. Register and format are sometimes inappropriate to the purpose of the task and the audience.

BAND 1

For a Band 1 to be awarded, the candidate's writing has a very negative effect on the target reader. The content is often irrelevant. Information and ideas are poorly organized, often incoherent, and there is minimal use of cohesive devices. The range of structures and vocabulary is severely limited, and errors frequently cause considerable difficulty for the reader. Register and format are inappropriate to the purpose of the task and the audience.

BAND 0

For a Band zero to be awarded, there is either too little language for assessment or the candidate's writing is totally irrelevant or illegible.

*Candidates who do not address all the content points will be penalized for dealing inadequately with the requirements of the task. Candidates who fully satisfy the Band 3 descriptor will demonstrate an adequate performance in writing at CAE level.

PAPER 3 ENGLISH IN USE 1 hour

Part 1

For questions **1–12**, read the text below and decide which answer (**A, B, C** or **D**) best fits each gap. There is an example at the beginning (**0**).

Example:

0   **A** searching   **B seeking**   **C** requesting   **D** enquiring

What does every top corporate boss need? Lego

The success of many leading companies depends on an effective management team and they are always (**0**) .... ways to encourage those managers to (**1**) .... along with each other. In previous years, those ways have (**2**) .... from weekends where managers went camping together to white-water rafting. Now the latest corporate team-building technique that is becoming increasingly popular in the management (**3**) .... is sitting for hours round a table making shapes out of Lego, the well-known building bricks that so many children have grown up with. But don't be (**4**) .... by those familiar green and yellow plastic blocks – this is Lego for adults, and among senior executives it is the hottest management (**5**) .... since the go-everywhere laptop. Companies are now (**6**) .... to send senior staff along to learn what Lego can do for their corporate ethos, and management consultants are even (**7**) .... themselves to running Lego sessions to (**8**) .... the demand. They claim that the multicoloured bricks can (**9**) .... free managers from a limited imagination. What does this mean in (**10**) .... ? For a start, staff (**11**) .... a session are encouraged to 'unlock their creative potential' while they build models to understand how their businesses work. By (**12**) .... their firms as three-dimensional structures, they can build models which are metaphors for the issues that often occur at work.

1 A go   B come   C get   D work

2 A covered   B included   C ranged   D consisted

3 A circle   B world   C level   D area

4 A attracted   B concerned   C directed   D fooled

5 A tool   B equipment   C instrument   D gadget

6 A enthusiastic   B agreeable   C eager   D excited

7 A specializing   B focusing   C concentrating   D dedicating

8 A fill   B recognize   C meet   D supply

9 A assist   B help   C aid   D support

10 A theory   B truth   C demonstration   D reality

11 A joining   B following   C participating   D entering

12 A symbolizing   B demonstrating   C illustrating   D representing

Part 2

For questions **13–27**, read the text below and think of the word which best fits each gap. Use only **one** word in each gap. There is an example at the beginning (0).

Example: 0 BY

The world's rubbish dump

In 1997 American oceanographer Charles Moore discovered **(0)** .... chance a vast floating

mass of plastic garbage in the Pacific Ocean. Since then, the 'plastic soup' has been growing at

(13) .... scientists believe to be an alarming rate and covers an area double

(14) .... size of the USA. The garbage is held **(15)** .... place by swirling

underwater currents and stretches across the northern Pacific. In fact the 'soup' consists of two linked

areas, on **(16)** .... side of the islands of Hawaii, known **(17)** .... the Western

and Eastern Pacific Garbage Patches. About one-fifth of the garbage, **(18)** .... everything

from footballs and kayaks to Lego blocks and carrier bags, gets thrown off ships or oil platforms, with

the rest of **(19)** .... coming from land. Historically, ocean rubbish has biodegraded but

modern plastics are **(20)** .... durable that objects half-a-century old **(21)** ....

sometimes found in the north Pacific dump. Plastic garbage causes the deaths of more than 100 000

marine mammals every year, **(22)** .... to mention over a million seabirds. Syringes, lighters

and toothbrushes end up inside the stomachs of these creatures, **(23)** .... mistake them

for food. There is a risk to human health, too, **(24)** .... hundreds of millions of tiny plastic

pellets, the raw materials for the plastic industry, become lost or get spilled every year, working

(25) .... way into the sea. These pollutants act as sponges attracting man-made chemicals

(26) .... as hydrocarbons and the pesticide DDT. It does not take **(27)** ....

before they enter the food chain: after being consumed by small fish they eventually end up on dinner

plates.

Part 3

For questions **28–37**, read the text below. Use the word given in capitals at the end of some of the lines to form a word that fits in the gap **in the same line**. There is an example at the beginning **(0)**.

Example: 0   OBESITY

New food labelling system

The government may soon force restaurants to introduce a 'traffic light' labelling

system on menus to help slow down rising levels of **(0)** .... A green circle   **OBESE**

would show food is safe and **(28)** .... to eat, while amber foods should be   **ADVICE**

eaten in moderation and red foods eaten occasionally. Supermarkets already

(29) .... follow a similar code, but ministers believe a radical   **VOLUNTEER**

(30) .... of the system to restaurant chains is necessary. They intend to   **EXTEND**

(31) .... government policies on public health as recent statistics show that   **HARD**

two thirds of adults are **(32)** .... or worse, obese. Abroad, New York city   **WEIGH**

has already forced restaurant chains to list calorie content on menus, believing

this will lead to a dramatic **(33)** .... in the number of people who are obese or   **REDUCE**

who suffer from diabetes. If the government here goes ahead with the 'traffic

light' system it will no doubt face considerable **(34)** .... from the food   **RESIST**

industry, which would be forced to spend money on **(35)** .... menus.   **DATE**

This new system would also be **(36)** .... for small restaurant chains   **CONTROVERSY**

because menus are **(37)** .... and constantly change, and many dishes do   **SEASON**

not contain standardized levels of ingredients.

Part 4

For questions **38–42**, think of **one** word only which can be used appropriately in all three sentences. Here is an example (**0**).

Example:

0   Please explain to me the .... of having another meeting.

It was at that .... that most of the audience got up and left.

We lost a .... because one person in our team started the race too early.

Example: POINT

---

38   We need to agree on what .... of punishment is appropriate in this case.

A strange .... suddenly appeared out of the fog and began to walk towards them.

Please hand in the completed .... to the receptionist before you see the doctor.

39   The company directors say they will .... out a way to prevent further job losses.

The vaccine did not .... as well as the researchers had hoped.

Taking regular exercise will help people .... up an appetite.

40   My sisters have had a .... relationship with one another since they were children.

A .... wind suddenly came out of nowhere and we turned the boat around.

Even after recent injuries, we have a .... team for the next game.

41   I had to .... the entire business when the manager became ill.

Two rivers .... down the mountain and feed the lake below.

We need to .... through the song one more time before we record it.

42   I'd like to .... this meeting by welcoming our guest speaker.

It is a generalization that women tend to be more .... to new ideas than men.

Private health care is not an option that is .... to many people.

Part 5

For questions **43–50**, complete the second sentence so that it has a similar meaning to the first sentence, using the word given. **Do not change the word given**. You must use between **three** and **six** words, including the word given. Here is an example (**0**).

Example:

0   As he continued to listen to the speech, Richard became increasingly sleepy.

SLEEPIER

The more Richard listened to the speech, ... became.

Example: 0 THE SLEEPIER HE

---

43   The damage to the painting is so minor that it won't be very noticeable to most people.

HARDLY

I'm sure that most people .... minor damage to the painting.

44   I hate it when people lie to me which is why I split up with Simon.

STAND

I .... to, which is why I split up with Simon.

45   Do you think you could help me take these boxes outside?

MIND

Would .... a hand taking these boxes outside?

46   Senator Jackson announced his intention to resign a short time ago.

KNOWN

Senator Jackson has just .... to resign.

47   Joe would only agree to continue the trip if he could drive instead of Paul.

TAKING

Joe insisted .... as the driver before he would agree to continue the trip.

48   Remember that there's a chance it will rain when you pack for the camping trip.

POSSIBILITY

Please bear .... mind when you pack for the camping trip.

49   John needs to arrive soon or we'll have to go without him.

BEHIND

We'll have to .... turns up soon.

50   We managed to escape just before the whole building caught on fire.

HAD

No .... the whole building caught on fire.

PAPER 4 LISTENING approximately 40 minutes

Part 1

You will hear three different extracts. For questions **1–6**, choose the answer (**A, B** or **C**) which fits best according to what you hear. There are two questions for each extract.

Extract One

You hear part of an interview with James Finn, a young musician.

1   James no longer owns a television because he

    A   dislikes the immoral content of some of the programmes.

    B   is irritated by the frequency of the advertisements.

    C   feels that he becomes too easily absorbed in watching it.

2   What is James' opinion about the future of television?

    A   It will be replaced by the Internet.

    B   It will become increasingly commercial.

    C   It will show more and more poor quality programmes.

Extract Two

You hear part of an interview with Martin Greenwood, an education specialist.

3   What does Martin blame for the lack of male teachers in secondary education?

    A   the low salary

    B   the lack of status

    C   the perception that it is a female job

4   Martin mentions the argument in the playground to illustrate

    A   the lack of control some female teachers have over male students.

    B   the different ways men and women handle conflict.

    C   the fact that boys need to be taught how to manage aggression.

Extract Three

You hear part of an interview with a woman called Shelley Sumner, who appeared on a TV reality show.

5   Shelley says she decided to take part in the reality show because she

    A   needed the prize money that was offered.

    B   was attracted by the idea of fame.

    C   felt pressured into it by her friends.

6   Why does Shelley compare herself to a new member of royalty?

    A   To show how she has lost her privacy.

    B   To show how relationships with former friends have changed.

    C   To show the advantages she has gained from celebrity.

Part 2

You will hear a historian called Sarah Potts talking about Easter Island. For questions **7–14**, complete the sentences.

EASTER ISLAND

Sarah says the stone heads on Easter Island probably show their makers'

[_____ **7**].

She disagrees with researchers who say [_____ **8**] led to Easter Island's

deforestation.

Palm trees on the island provided wood and [_____ **9**] for transporting the

stone heads.

The shells of palm seeds provide evidence that [_____ **10**] destroyed forests.

Sarah explains that [_____ **11**] were ruined by strong winds.

Many of Easter Island's [_____ **12**] became extinct.

Sarah thinks it is particularly sad that European sailors brought [_____ **13**]

to Easter Island.

According to Sarah, what happened on Easter Island is still [_____ **14**]

today.

Part 3

You will hear part of a radio interview in which a young man called Toby Burrow is talking about a year he spent doing voluntary work in Madagascar. For questions **15–20**, choose the answer (**A, B, C** or **D**) which fits best according to what you hear.

15 Why did Toby choose to work in Madagascar?

    A He thought it would offer interesting travel experiences.

    B He knew other students who had been there before him.

    C He believed it would offer challenging opportunities.

    D He had been influenced by a television programme.

16 How did Toby's mother respond when he announced he was going to Madagascar?

    A She tried to dissuade him from taking the job.

    B She told him about her experience of working abroad.

    C She insisted he take measures to protect his health.

    D She did some research on the country.

17 What aspect of life in the village did Toby originally find hard?

    A the constant noise

    B the lack of privacy

    C the basic facilities

    D the sense of isolation

18 How did Toby feel after the incident with his wallet?

    A He wanted to quit his job and go home.

    B He thought it was a shame that not all people were honest.

    C He no longer trusted the people he worked with.

    D He believed he was partly responsible for the situation.

19 What does Toby say about his return to the UK?

    A He was eager to discuss his adventures with friends.

    B He felt relieved to be back in familiar surroundings.

    C He was keen to return to Madagascar.

    D He felt critical of his own country.

20 What advice does Toby offer students who are about to graduate?

    A Have the right attitude towards people you are helping.

    B Give up your voluntary work if you are unhappy.

    C Avoid just going abroad for your own pleasure.

    D Travel with someone you already know well.

Part 4

You will hear five short extracts in which various people are talking about the problems of living in a city.

TASK ONE

For questions **21–25**, choose from the list **A–H** the problem being described.

A   being alone

B   longer working hours | | 21 |

C   heavy traffic | | 22 |

D   high prices | | 23 |

E   inconsiderate neighbours | | 24 |

F   crime | | 25 |

G   pollution

H   lack of open spaces

TASK TWO

For questions **26–30**, choose from the list **A–H** the reaction the speaker has had to the problem.

A   I'm thinking of changing my job.

B   I made a formal complaint.

C   I have become less healthy. | | 26 |

D   I decided to move. | | 27 |

E   I often get angry. | | 28 |

F   I feel depressed all the time. | | 29 |

G   I spend a lot of time complaining about it. | | 30 |

H   It doesn't bother me anymore.

In the exam you will have 5 minutes at the end of the test to copy your answers on to a separate answer sheet.

PAPER 5 SPEAKING approximately 15 minutes

Part 2 (4 minutes)

1 Spending money

For both candidates: Look at the three pictures on page 152. They show people who might be interested in buying something.

Candidate A: Compare two of these pictures and say what the people might want to buy and how they might be feeling. (*1 minute*)

Candidate B: Which of these people might get most enjoyment out of what they buy? (*approximately 30 seconds*)

2 Chimpanzees

For both candidates: Look at the three pictures on page 153 of people and chimpanzees.

Candidate B: Compare two of the pictures and say what kind of relationship the people and chimpanzees have with each other, and what different reasons these people might have for observing the chimpanzees. (*1 minute*)

Candidate A: In which of these situations do you think the chimpanzee is the happiest? (*30 seconds*)

Part 3 (4 minutes)

Science

For both candidates: Look at the pictures on page 154. They show different ways in which science affects our lives. First talk to each other about how these pictures show the role of science nowadays. Then decide which two pictures reflect the greatest impact that science will have on our lives in the future.

Part 4 (4 minutes)

For both candidates:

- What do you think attracts people to studying or working within science?
- What future scientific achievement do you think would be the most beneficial to mankind? Why?
- In your opinion, what is more likely to lead to scientific achievement – competition or teamwork?
- Some people believe that there should be more laws restricting some scientific experiments. What do you think?

Test 1 Part 2 Ambition

- What different ambitions might these people have?
- What might they be doing to achieve their ambitions?

Test 1 Part 2 Holiday destinations

- What kind of people would choose a holiday destination like this?
- What might the reasons for their choice be?

Test 1 Part 3 Discussion about texts

- What does each of these texts tell us about life today?
- Which three texts would you choose to put in a museum for future generations to see?

Newspapers

Children's fiction

Text messages

Personal websites

Women's magazines

College magazine

Test 2 Part 2 Different professions

- What skills do these people require in their work?
- Why might they have chosen their professions?

Test 2 Part 2 In the forest

- Why might the people be in the forest?
- What might the atmosphere be like in each situation?

Test 2 Part 3 College magazine

- What aspects of student life do these images show?
- Which two images should be chosen for the front and back covers of the brochure?

Test 3 Part 2 Risk at work

- In what ways do these people benefit society?
- What risks might they face in their work?

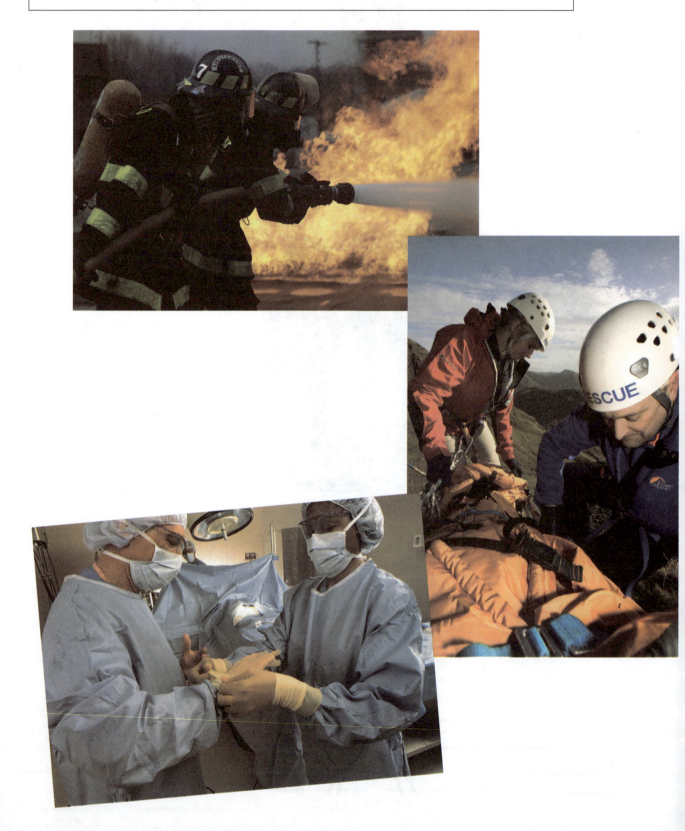

Test 3 Part 2 Emotions

- How might the people be feeling towards one another?
- What might have happened to make them feel this way?

Test 3 Part 3 A sense of fulfilment

- How might these different aspects of life contribute to people's sense of fulfilment?
- Which three things do you think would lead to the most satisfaction in the long run?

Maintaining friendships

Keeping fit and doing sport

Cooking and eating

Developing a career

Going on holiday

Spending time with family

Learning

Test 4 Part 2 Spending money

- What might the people want to buy?
- How might they be feeling?

Test 4 Part 2 Chimpanzees

- What kind of relationship might the people and chimpanzees have with each other?
- What different reasons might these people have for observing the chimpanzees?

Test 4 Part 3 Science

- How do these pictures show the role of science nowadays?
- Which two pictures reflect the greatest impact that science will have on our lives in the future?

PAPER 1 READING ANSWER SHEET

UNIVERSITY *of* **CAMBRIDGE**
ESOL Examinations

Do not write in this box

Candidate Name
If not already printed, write name in CAPITALS and complete the Candidate No. grid (in pencil).

Candidate Signature

Examination Title

Centre

Supervisor:
If the candidate is ABSENT or has WITHDRAWN shade here ⬜

SAMPLE

Centre No.

Candidate No.

Examination Details

Candidate Answer Sheet

Instructions

Use a PENCIL (B or HB).

Mark ONE letter for each question.

For example, if you think B is the right answer to the question, mark your answer sheet like this:

0 A B̶ C D E F G H

Rub out any answer you wish to change using an eraser.

1	A B C D E F G H		21	A B C D E F G H
2	A B C D E F G H		22	A B C D E F G H
3	A B C D E F G H		23	A B C D E F G H
4	A B C D E F G H		24	A B C D E F G H
5	A B C D E F G H		25	A B C D E F G H
6	A B C D E F G H		26	A B C D E F G H
7	A B C D E F G H		27	A B C D E F G H
8	A B C D E F G H		28	A B C D E F G H
9	A B C D E F G H		29	A B C D E F G H
10	A B C D E F G H		30	A B C D E F G H
11	A B C D E F G H		31	A B C D E F G H
12	A B C D E F G H		32	A B C D E F G H
13	A B C D E F G H		33	A B C D E F G H
14	A B C D E F G H		34	A B C D E F G H
15	A B C D E F G H		35	A B C D E F G H
16	A B C D E F G H		36	A B C D E F G H
17	A B C D E F G H		37	A B C D E F G H
18	A B C D E F G H		38	A B C D E F G H
19	A B C D E F G H		39	A B C D E F G H
20	A B C D E F G H		40	A B C D E F G H

A-H 40 CAS

denote Print Limited 0121 520 5100

DP594/300

PAPER 4 LISTENING ANSWER SHEET

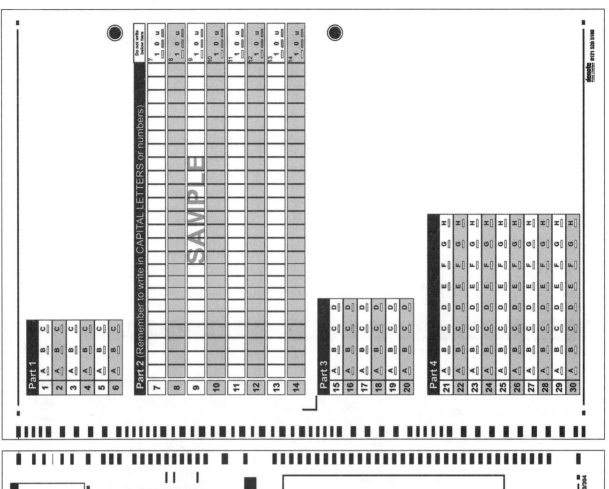

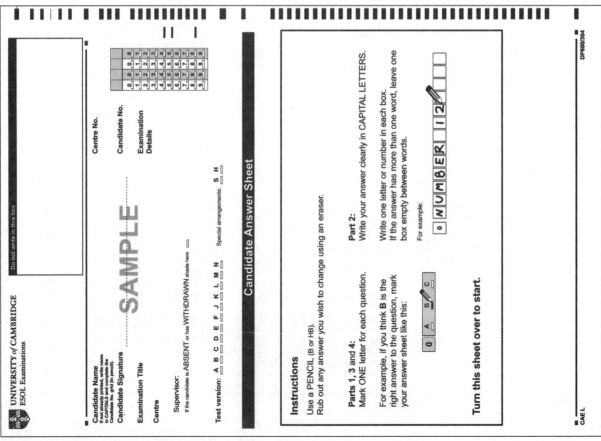

PAPER 3 USE OF ENGLISH ANSWER SHEET

UNIVERSITY of CAMBRIDGE
ESOL Examinations

Do not write in this box

Candidate Name
If not already printed, write name
in CAPITALS and complete the
Candidate No. grid (in pencil).

Candidate Signature

Examination Title

Centre

Supervisor:
If the candidate is ABSENT or has WITHDRAWN shade here

SAMPLE

Centre No.

Candidate No.

Examination Details

Instructions
Use a PENCIL (B or HB).
Rub out any answer you wish to change.

Part 1: Mark ONE letter for each question.

For example, if you think B is the right answer to the question, mark your answer sheet like this:

| 0 | A | B | C | D |

Parts 2, 3, 4 and **5:** Write your answer clearly in CAPITAL LETTERS.

For Parts 2, 3 and 4, write one letter in each box.

| 0 | E X A M P L E |

Part 1

1	A	B	C	D
2	A	B	C	D
3	A	B	C	D
4	A	B	C	D
5	A	B	C	D
6	A	B	C	D
7	A	B	C	D
8	A	B	C	D
9	A	B	C	D
10	A	B	C	D
11	A	B	C	D
12	A	B	C	D

Candidate Answer Sheet

Part 2

Do not write below here

13		13 1 0 u
14		14 1 0 u
15		15 1 0 u
16		16 1 0 u
17		17 1 0 u
18		18 1 0 u
19		19 1 0 u
20		20 1 0 u
21		21 1 0 u
22		22 1 0 u
23		23 1 0 u
24		24 1 0 u
25		25 1 0 u
26		26 1 0 u
27		27 1 0 u

Continues over ➡

CAE UoE

DP597/301

Part 3

		Do not write below here
28		28 1 0 u
29		29 1 0 u
30		30 1 0 u
31		31 1 0 u
32		32 1 0 u
33		33 1 0 u
34		34 1 0 u
35		35 1 0 u
36		36 1 0 u
37		37 1 0 u

SAMPLE

Part 4

		Do not write below here
38		38 1 0 u
39		39 1 0 u
40		40 1 0 u
41		41 1 0 u
42		42 1 0 u

Part 5

		Do not write below here
43		43 2 1 0 u
44		44 2 1 0 u
45		45 2 1 0 u
46		46 2 1 0 u
47		47 2 1 0 u
48		48 2 1 0 u
49		49 2 1 0 u
50		50 2 1 0 u

denote Print Limited 0121 520 5100

CD TRACK LISTING

CD1

01 Test One Part One instructions and Extract One instructions

02 Test One Part One Extract One (play twice)

03 Test One Part One Extract Two instructions

04 Test One Part One Extract Two (play twice)

05 Test One Part One Extract Three instructions

06 Test One Part One Extract Three (play twice)

07 Test One Part Two instructions

08 Test One Part Two (play twice)

09 Test One Part Three instructions

10 Test One Part Three (play twice)

11 Test One Part Four instructions

12 Test One Part Four (play twice)

13 Test Two Part One instructions and Extract One instructions

14 Test Two Part One Extract One (play twice)

15 Test Two Part One Extract Two instructions

16 Test Two Part One Extract Two (play twice)

17 Test Two Part One Extract Three instructions

18 Test Two Part One Extract Three (play twice)

19 Test Two Part Two instructions

20 Test Two Part Two (play twice)

21 Test Two Part Three instructions

22 Test Two Part Three (play twice)

23 Test Two Part Four instructions

24 Test Two Part Four (play twice)

CD2

01 Test Three Part One instructions and Extract One instructions

02 Test Three Part One Extract One (play twice)

03 Test Three Part One Extract Two instructions

04 Test Three Part One Extract Two (play twice)

05 Test Three Part One Extract Three instructions

06 Test Three Part One Extract Three (play twice)

07 Test Three Part Two instructions

08 Test Three Part Two (play twice)

09 Test Three Part Three instructions

10 Test Three Part Three (play twice)

11 Test Three Part Four instructions

12 Test Three Part Four (play twice)

13 Test Four Part One instructions and Extract One instructions

14 Test Four Part One Extract One (play twice)

15 Test Four Part One Extract Two instructions

16 Test Four Part One Extract Two (play twice)

17 Test Four Part One Extract Three instructions

18 Test Four Part One Extract Three (play twice)

19 Test Four Part Two instructions

20 Test Four Part Two (play twice)

21 Test Four Part Three instructions

22 Test Four Part Three (play twice)

23 Test Four Part Four instructions

24 Test Four Part Four (play twice)

25 Credits

KEY AND EXPLANATION

TEST ONE

p.7–10 PAPER 1 Part 1

Further practice and guidance (p.9–10)

Extract One

First paragraph: **A = 4 B = 2 C = 1 D = 3**

broad = wide/great

opinionated = expressing personal opinion

objective = based on facts and not personal opinions

impact = influence/effect

concern = involve/affect

first-hand knowledge = personal experience

Second paragraph: **A = 4 B = 3 C = 1 D = 2**

in person = to do something yourself

notification = announcement

restriction = limit

multiple = many

are expected = are obliged

Extract Two

First paragraph: **B** the purpose of sirens is usually to alert people to an approaching emergency vehicle. In the text, the fillers are sirens that alert people to important information (of significance).

Second paragraph: **1d 2e 3b 4a 5f 6c**

Extract Three

First paragraph: It refers to the option of communicating in Russian.

Second paragraph: They mean 'to be told about/to be informed about something' and 'the expression of feelings of sadness/the process of expressing great sadness because someone has died'. These phrases suggest that when the public are informed about the death of an animal species, they are very sad and consider this event to be very important news.
The use of *However* is used to show contrast. In this context, it suggests that the public reaction to animal extinction is very unlike their reaction to language extinction. In other words, the death of a language is not noticed and does not upset most people.

p.7–8 PAPER 1 Part 1 (Test)

1B 2A 3B 4D 5C 6A

p.11–12 PAPER 1 Part 2

7 C: The last sentence in C states *the kakapo also has a unique breeding system.* This is further explained in the next two sentences of the following text: *Males gather at an arena* *to compete for females. After mating, the females raise their young alone.* C also describes the unique features of the kakapo: its appearance, the noises it makes and the important fact that it can't fly. In the following paragraph, Don Merton says that these unique features/pecularities have made the kakapo *vulnerable*, in other words, easy to attack.

8 G: In the paragraph above 8, we read that before man arrived, the kakapo's only enemies were birds who found it difficult to find them as their green colour meant they could hide in the forest. G says that when men arrived *it was a different story*. In other words, the situation changed. They brought dogs and rats which killed kakapo. At the end of G, it says that people believed the kakapo was extinct in the 1960s. The text under 8 then shows that this belief was wrong: Merton found one bird that was still alive.

9 A: The text above 9 says that the team thought the kakapo were safe and then discovered they were still being killed in large numbers. The first two sentences in A say that the team then began to carry out a rescue operation by moving the kakapo to islands where there were no cats, stoats or possums. Unfortunately, there were rats on the new islands – but in the text under 9, it mentions that the team were trying to catch the rats with traps.

10 D: The last sentence of the text above 10 mentions that the team successfully moved the birds to Maud and Codfish Island where they were safe. D starts with *persuading the birds to breed was the next harder step.* This contrasts with the easy success of moving the birds. D also mentions the fact that the birds only breed when the rimu trees produce many seeds so that they have plenty to eat. The text under 10 mentions that the team try to find a diet/food that the birds like. The birds become healthier with the extra food, but still don't breed. The text mentions the rimu tree again, saying that the birds seem to be waiting for it to produce a lot of seed.

11 F: The text above 11 indicates that the birds will not breed until the rimu tree produces a lot of seed, so they have to let nature *take its course.* This means that they have to wait for the rimu trees to mast. The last sentence of F states that the team *recognized the fact that it was only the rimu tree that would turn things around* [change the situation]. The text under 11 begins with *Armed with this…knowledge. The fact* and *the knowledge* both refer to the understanding that kakapo breed according to good seed production.

12 B: The text above 12 mentions that the team are using electronic monitoring equipment. The last sentence of B says that the birds don't realize they are being watched by *electronic eyes.* B also says that the females look for a *mate* [a breeding partner] – and the text under 12 mentions the result – a large group of kakapo chicks.

p.13–16 PAPER 1 Part 3

Further practice and guidance (p.15–16)

13 A: No, only that they will find the advertisements absorbing. It doesn't necessarily mean they will buy products after having seen them.

B: The grammar is passive. It suggests that someone else, in this case the advertisers, will choose the advertisements for the viewers.

C: In this case, *medium* means a way of communicating a message. The *mediums* mentioned in the text are the fans' T-shirts which will receive and display digitized logos and the increasing use of TV to also display logos.

D: The text only mentions the Superbowl, and as record numbers of people are watching it, we cannot really say it is less popular or appreciated.

14 A: It refers to the way in which viewers are exposed to advertising. If someone is just a *casual observer* – someone who hasn't thought about how or why advertisements appear on the TV – he won't realize they have been specifically chosen for each individual.

B: *To target a group of people* is an advertising term which means 'to choose or focus on a specific group for promotion'. An *omnipresent* thing is 'everywhere' and you cannot avoid something which is *inescapable*. These words relate to the previous sentence as they refer to *the changes that are happening*.

C: The text doesn't mention viewers' reactions, but just mentions the fact that this technology will exist.

D: There is no mention of viewers feeling forced to purchase the disposable products; simply that the products are advertised.

15 A: *To condemn* means 'to express strong disapproval' and is negative. *Nifty* in this case means 'stylish' and is therefore positive.

B: If someone feels *indignant*, they feel that something isn't fair. The writer suggests the viewers will *tend to like advertising better*.

C: If something is *cost-effective*, it saves money. The text states that the advertiser will save money.

D: A *tailor* makes clothes to exactly fit and suit one person. The expression *tailor to somebody's tastes* means that you design something suitable for one person or company.

16 A: No, it just says these mediums will be *inadequate* [not enough].

B: *The rest of the world* refers to different media: art, entertainment and journalism.

C: It mentions that advertising has increased in music entertainment nowadays, not that it will become more important.

D: A *backlash* means 'a sudden adverse or negative reaction'. It suggests that people once liked having so many outlets, but they will change their minds and really dislike it. *Inevitable* means something will definitely happen.

17 A: Financial support refers to *direct subsidy* and someone 'aiming to make a profit' would have *commercial interests* in a project or venture.

B: He says *surely people…are capable of distinguishing between a commercial* [subjective] *message and an editorial* [truthful] *one*.

C: If something 'blurs', it is difficult to see it clearly eg when a camera is not in focus. In this context, the blurred or unclear line is the line that separates advertising and other forms of content [information

contained in journalistic writing/scenes in films/images in art etc].

D: Although he accepts that advertising has found its way into art, he does not see it as a dangerous thing since he believes people can recognize what is advertising and what is pure art.

18 A: No. He simply says that the park has a new name.

B: *Disturbing* means 'worrying'. It shows that the writer is critical of companies paying money to rename public places. The writer suggests that Boston Park is now called The Fleet Centre because a bank with the same name has paid for the change.

C: No. He simply provides them as examples of how companies rename public places to advertise themselves.

D: *Donation*. This contradicts the idea that advertising could be free.

19 A: *Vulnerable* means 'easily attacked'. There is no mention of any specific group which is most likely to be attacked by advertisers.

B: To *dispel* means 'to make something go away'. The writer has said in previous paragraphs that there will be far too much advertising in the future, so he is not trying to tell us that we have nothing to worry about.

C: The answer is in the last line of the final paragraph – *That's when advertising has gone too far: when it's become something we are, rather than something we see*.

D: No, he seems to disapprove of the amount of advertising that many companies use, but he does not say that any specific company is dishonest. He has also already mentioned that people are fully aware of what a commercial is, so there is no need for it to be exposed.

p.13–14 PAPER 1 Part 3 (Test)

13C   14B   15D   16D   17A   18B   19C

p.17–18 PAPER 1 Part 4

20   D: The answer comes from *Zirker's explanations are clear and sharp, although don't expect him to lead you by the hand*. This means 'don't expect him to make the explanations easy'.

21   A: The writer says that *I had her* [the author] *filed in a 'sentimental nature-lover…' category…a few years ago, I read my first Kingsolver* [book] *and ditched my ill-founded prejudice*. In other words, the author is saying that she had previously believed Barbara Kingsolver's books were too sentimental but recently she has discovered that this is not true.

22   C: The writer says…*others have often sketched out an answer. But in Zoo, Eric Baratay gives us an unprecedented, in-depth answer*. The writer is saying that other writers have written about zoos before, but Baratay is the first person to write about them in such detail.

23   D: The answer comes from *His story-meets-textbook approach mainly avoids confusing scientific equations*. The writer is saying that the author has chosen to combine a story-telling approach with an academic style which does not become too complicated.

24 C: The book presents a *grim* [depressing] *story*. There is a *wealth of statistics on the death rate in collections*.

25 B: The writer makes several mentions of how the book combines certainty and doubt: *This book gives us…a clear-eyed look at the subject's…uncertainties…The focus on uncertainty has the paradoxical effect of highlighting the areas in which seismologists are confident, which makes it easier to deal with the ambiguities.*

26 A: The writer mentions one of her first memories: *The pleasure of deciphering that first word (C-A-T, of course) remains with me to this day.* She is saying she can remember the first time she managed to read a word.

27 B: The writer compares earthquake predictions with car engines and repairs, suggesting that both provoke a feeling of uncertainty which leads to stress and anxiety: *Anyone who has ever driven an elderly…car knows the feeling: it's going to break down, but who knows when, where and what part of the system will fail? Predicting earthquakes is much the same.*

28 A: The writer says of Barbara Kingsolver: *Possessed of an analytical mind, she's capable of putting it all down with real passion* [enthusiasm]: *a rare find*.

29 C: The answer comes from *The text has been translated from the French and in places, not very successfully*. The writer also says that the book contains *appalling zoological errors* [factual mistakes about animals]. However, the writer also says that these few problems with style and content are *forgivable*.

30 D: The answer comes from *Up, down, in or out. If that's about as much attention as you pay the Sun, you're ignoring something incredible.* In other words, if you only think of the sun as coming up in the morning/going down at night, etc you are not thinking about all the other amazing facts about it.

31 C: The writer says that the book *neither apologizes for nor criticizes the modern zoo.*

32 B: The writer says that *her findings* [conclusions] *do not make easy reading*. This suggests that readers may not get all the answers they hoped to find. There is still a lot of uncertainty about earthquake prediction.

33 D: The writer says that the author *shows how solar research has progressed* [developed] *from inspired speculation* [guessing about the sun] *into a flourishing science*.

34 A: The answer comes from *'Small Wonder' is…a great place to set out from before you tackle her backlist*. The writer is saying that people should read *Small Wonder* before reading the books that the author has previously written.

p.19–22 PAPER 2 Part 1

Further practice and guidance (p.20–22)

Effect on target reader

a The editor of the newspaper where the review was published.

b You want to explain why the critic is wrong.

c You probably want the editor to print the letter so that other readers can see it and get a better impression of

the restaurant. For this reason, you need to remain polite in your letter, otherwise the editor will not print it.

Content

when the restaurant first opened (addressed in para 2)

information about the chef (para 3)

how you know the customers are happy (para 4)

why the owner was not there (para 5)

You also need to say clearly why you recommend the restaurant.

Organization and cohesion

a to explain who the writer is and their reason for writing.

b 'Regarding' introduces a new point.

c 'actually' and 'in fact' show or emphasize reality or truth.

Range

a 'to take issue with' means to disagree with something, or show that you intend to argue against it.

b 'comments' = 'remarks' 'unfair' = 'unjustified' 'opened' = established 'ask' = enquired

c completely, obviously, extremely, absolutely, truly

d (should+have+pp) should have checked (third conditional had+ pp/would + have + pp) had asked/ would have found out *and* had enquired/would have learnt

p.23–24 PAPER 2 Part 2

Further practice and guidance (p.24)

1 a The writer says in paragraph 2 that marriage does not help people to stay together forever. In paragraph 3, the writer says that children do not benefit from married parents – they benefit from good parents. In the final paragraph, the writer says there is no point in getting married (unless you are religious).

2 a a past situation/state that is no longer true = used to

b a trend that started recently and will probably continue into future = are choosing (present continuous)

c a situation/state that started in the past and is still true = has been (present perfect)

3 a central to this issue **b** It could be argued **c** To conclude **d** There is also the subject of…….to consider **e** in other words **f** It used to be the case that **g** Advocates **h** The question is whether **i** The point is that

p.25–26 PAPER 3 Part 1

1 D: *questioned* can be followed by *whether* and the open question; *argued* and *decided* and *suggested* are followed by the subject's point of view.

2   B: *agreed* can be followed by the preposition *on* and in this context could be rephrased as 'no one has ever agreed what the criteria are'. It is possible to use the formal term *think on* when it means *consider*, but this would contradict the first sentence of the text where it says people have been debating the meaning of beauty for years. You can *write on* a subject but it does not collocate with criteria. To *fix on* something means to choose someone or something after some consideration – but it would apply to one thing eg a place to visit, or a candidate for a job, rather than a whole set of criteria.

3   A: You can *judge* someone based on a set of criteria / guidelines / conditions. To *appreciate* something is to recognize its importance or value, and you would not need a set of criteria to do this. We use *view* in this way: She is *viewed* as beautiful by many people. You would *award* someone a prize (for their beauty) .

4   B: We use *according to* when we want to refer to the information from a text or to quote the ideas of another person. *Correspond to* means to be related or connected with something eg 'the instructions in the booklet do not seem to correspond to the TV we bought'. *Relate* and *correspond* can also be used in this way: 'Make sure your answers in the Writing Paper *relate/correspond* to the question.' *Connect* can also be used like this: 'My laptop isn't *connecting* to the Internet at the moment'.

5   A: *Accompanied by* can be used to show that two things / events happen or exist at the same time ie 'a person should have the right shaped face *accompanied by* [as well as] the right length of nose'. *Escorted* is used to describe people ie 'The President's bodyguard escorted [went with] him to his car.' Two things can be joined together ie 'you need stronger glue to *join* those bits of wood'. *Coupled* can be used like this: 'The heavy rain *coupled with* [together with] local deforestation caused terrible floods in the area.'

6   C: *to the human eye* is a fixed expression. We could say that symmetry is an important part of human *appearance*. *Sight* and *vision* refer to the abilty to see eg 'He has poor / good *vision/sight*.'

7   D: We can use *similarity* to say that two things share something in common; in this context, the two sides of a person's face. *Equality* is used in the context of having the same status, rights or opportunities. You could say 'so a face may seem beautiful because one side is a *reflection* of the other'. *Opposition* can sometimes be used in this way: 'There is great *opposition* [a big difference] between his idea of beauty and mine.'

8   B: We use *rate* in this way: to *rate something as* attractive / ugly / good / bad etc. We usually say: 'People *voted for* the younger candidate' or 'The students *voted to* go home early'. You can say 'Andrea was *selected* [chosen] as the winner of the competition'. The employees all felt *valued* [seen as important] by the company.

9   D: *universal agreement* is a collocation.

10   A: *constitutes* is used in this way: 'five papers *constitute* the CAE exam' – or you can rearrange this as: 'The CAE exam *comprises/contains/involves* five papers'.

11   D: an important *factor* means an important thing that has influence – in this context – on our decision about what makes someone beautiful. We use *reason* to explain our motivation for doing something eg 'Getting a good job is an important *reason* for me to learn English'. *Cause* (as a noun) is followed by of + a consequence eg 'No one is sure what the *cause* of the avalanche was'.

12   C: *regard* is the only verb in this group that can be followed by *as*. The other verbs take the form *to be + adj.*

p.27–29 PAPER 3 Part 2

Further practice and guidance (p.28–29)

1	13b	14a	15a	16c	17c	18a	19b	20c	21d
	22c	23d	24a	25a	26c	27b			

3	a	Despite
	b	Although
	c	However
	d	Whereas / Although / Even though
	e	whereas
	f	however
	g	Despite
	h	Nevertheless / However
	i	Despite

p.27 PAPER 3 Part 2 (Test)

13   few/no: *We make few/no demands* means 'we ask for little or for nothing' or 'we don't want to be treated differently to right-handed people'.

14   yet/but/though: In this sentence, these words are all synonyms. The writer says that he used to make a weak joke about being left-handed, *but* at the same time, he wants to be proud of it.

15   so: *so far* means 'until now'.

16   in: *in* is the preposition that precedes *circulation*.

17   to: *to the contrary* is the standard phrase.

18   is: we need *is* to form the present simple passive with *claimed*.

19   without: the writer is saying that there is also no proof that Einstein was left-handed.

20   in: the phrase *there is no truth* takes the preposition *in* followed by the object.

21   Despite: *despite* means the same as *although* but it is followed by a noun phrase. *Although* is followed by a whole clause.

22   by: *mean* ('intend' or 'have in mind') collocates with *by* in this context.

23   who: *who* is used to connect the verb *write* back to *those* ('people').

24   However: *however* is used to contrast this sentence with the previous one. It always requires a comma immediately afterwards when used as a conjunction.

25   what: (not how) this word can be used when referring forward, eg <u>What</u> you need is a good holiday. He didn't realize <u>what</u> was going to happen next.

26   even: *even so* means 'despite this', eg He worked really hard; even so, he didn't get the promotion.

27 **does:** *as does* means the same as 'so does'. Compare 'I live in Madrid as does my sister' to 'I live in Madrid. So does my sister.'

p.30–32 PAPER 3 Part 3

```
┌─────────────────────────────────────────────┐
```

Further practice and guidance (p.31–32)

A **a** residential (*adj*) describing an area in which most of the buildings are houses.   **b** resident (*n*) someone who lives in a particular place   **c** residence (*n*) (formal) a house or a place where someone lives.

B **a** visually (*adv*) in a way that is related to the appearance of something.   **b** visualize (*v*) to form a picture of someone or something in your mind.   **c** visible (*adj*) clearly seen/ obvious.

C **a** titled (*adj*) Lord/Lady etc.   **b** entitled (*v. passive*) to give a title to a book/song etc.

D **a** historian (*n*) someone who studies or writes about events in history.   **b** historic (*adj*) describing a past event that was significant and had great consequences.   **c** historically (*adv*) in a way that is connected with places, events or people from the past.

E **a** diversified (*in this case it is the past form of the verb but it can also be an adjective*) to develop into something different or to add to what you already do.   **b** diversely (*adv*) describing how something is treated or dealt with in different ways.   **c** diversity (*n*) the existence of a variety of people or things within a group or place.

F **a** informed (*in this case it is an adjective but it can also be the past form of the verb*) describing a choice or decision made on good information.   **b** misinform (*v*) to give someone the wrong/false information about something   **c** informative (*adj*) describing a person or thing that provides a lot of useful information.

F **a** perfectly (*adv*) in a way that could not be better.   **b** perfectionist (*n*) someone who always wants things to be done perfectly.   **c** perfection (*n*) a state in which someone or something is perfect or as good as they can be.

G **a** argumentative (*adj*) (negatively) describing a person who likes to argue.   **b** argument (*n*) an angry disagreement between two or more people.   **c** arguable (*adj*) used to say you are not completely certain if something is true or right.

H **a** unmissable (*adj*) used to praise something and recommend that other people experience it.   **b** missing (*adj*) used to describe someone who has disappeared and who others are looking for.

I **a** admittedly (*adv*) used to say that you admit something is true, although it makes your argument weaker.   **b** admission (*n*) the amount of money required to enter a place such as a gallery/museum etc.   **c** admittance (*n*) (formal) permission to enter a place or join something.

p.30 PAPER 3 Part 3 (Test)

28 resident   **29** visually   **30** entitled   **31** historically   **32** diversified   **33** informative   **34** perfectionist   **35** arguably   **36** unmissable   **37** admission

p.33 PAPER 3 Part 4

38 clear   **39** cut   **40** fix   **41** look   **42** notice

p.34 PAPER 3 Part 5

43 was under/had/got the impression that Sue

44 (his) having a/his reputation for being

45 no circumstances are you to/may you/can you/must you/should you

46 as if you did not (didn't) get/have

47 can't possibly have run

48 and I have a difference of

49 her not to pay/to pay no/give no attention to

50 there is little/not much chance of

p.35–37 PAPER 4 Part 1

```
┌─────────────────────────────────────────────┐
```

Further practice and guidance (p.36–37)

1 should be   **2** if they need ideas   **3** sort out this awful situation   **4** I can't see   **5** doesn't put most people off   **6** available to buy   **7** open-minded   **8** physical   **9** put off going   **10** trustworthy   **11** aware   **12** not sure   **13** for years   **14** warn   **15** aware of how close   **16** a warning

p.35 PAPER 4 Part 1 (Test)

1   **A:** The answer comes from *Kwabena had decided he wasn't going to wait around* [he wasn't waiting for government help]. *He says he wanted to come up with* [think of] *an idea that would sort out* [solve] *this awful situation in his lifetime.*

B: There is no mention of Kwabena going overseas – only that other similar projects exist there.

C: The speaker Richard says that it would be a good idea if governments sponsored/funded these projects, and not that they have given money to Kwabena.

2   **C:** Richard says *you can get bags made of bamboo or other fabrics but only a minority of people are using them, so I'd say* [in my opinion] *it's up to the supermarkets* [the supermarkets have a responsibility to] *to start promoting them a bit more actively – so that customers know they're available to buy instead.*

A: Richard doesn't think that making people pay 5 or 10 pence per bag will deter them from using them.

B: He doesn't believe the government will choose to ban plastic bags.

3   **B:** The answer comes from *I've always been fairly open-minded when it comes to hypnotherapy…at least when it comes to dealing with psychological problems.* In other words the woman is saying that she has always been willing to believe that hypnotherapy might be useful for treating psychological problems. This contradicts option A.

C: She doesn't say anything about the effect of hypnotherapy on its believers – only that she believed it might work.

4   A: The man thinks that many people do not trust hypnotists – *not trustworthy* – and the woman agrees with him *I think you're right*.

B: The woman insists that people are in control of themselves during hypnotherapy.

C: The man comments that people are *put off* [discouraged] by TV hypnotists – but not that they are disappointed with their own experience.

5   C: Fiona says *the hardest thing for me is being constantly alert to the risks because even though you do warn people about them, they just don't realize what could happen.*

A: is not possible because Fiona says the people on her tours have been going to the zoo for years.

B: She also says that people aren't sure what is going to happen on the tour – she doesn't say that the visitors insist on seeing certain animals

6   B: Fiona says *from that moment on I've always been doubly* [twice as] *aware of how close I am to an animal and what tools it has to get to me* [attack me with] *as well.*

A: she does not say that she doesn't want to work with chimpanzees again – only that she will be more careful in the future. She also says *he could have been a lot nastier…it was just a warning.* In other words, she admits the chimp did not treat her too badly.

C: Fiona knows why the incident occurred: she had been standing too close to the chimp's food.

p.38 PAPER 4 Part 2

7 scared   **8** interactive displays   **9** imagination
10 complete   **11** marine   **12** (volcanic) eruption
13 insulation   **14** donations

p.39 PAPER 4 Part 3

15   A: Peter is in the army when he meets a man from the navy: he asks: *'Where have you been?'* He [the navy man] said *'All over the world'* and yeah, *I liked the sound of that* [I thought that seemed interesting]. *The navy was for me* [I decided I would be suited to the navy]. *In the army the only option I had ahead of me was a few months in Singapore.* From this we can see that he wants to travel around the world, not just Singapore.

16   C: Peter starts by saying that the discipline and training is much harder in the army compared to the navy. He then says *However, I did have a hard mother and discipline was what she was all about* [discipline was what she believed in]. He says that she taught them to obey orders but also to be leaders, and to show others how to behave by giving a good example. He says *that's how you do it in the navy* – which means that the navy expect their officers to set a good example, too. He finally says *my mother set us on the right track in that respect* [my mother prepared us for this kind of behaviour] *and so the transition to the navy was easy.*

17   C: Peter explains that it is difficult to some young people to adjust to rules and regulations… *And taking care of themselves…Mum used to do your washing and your ironing…so a*

lot of these kids…don't even have these skills. In other words, he is saying that they have never had to be responsible for their own actions, lives and routines. He suggests they [school-leavers] need to be aware that *life in the navy is about self-discipline* [taking responsibility for yourself] *and that they're going to have to adjust to that. If you can achieve that, you'll do well.*

18   B: Peter says that older people from his hometown are curious about him, and that people his own age are jealous. He explains that he was the only person from his town to join the military and suggests that most people who stayed there have no sense of purpose and not much hope of a good future. He concludes by saying *So when I go home, it, er, reminds me of how far I've come, everything I've accomplished – and I get a lot of self-satisfaction out of that, to be honest.*

19   A: Peter says that the public often question why it is necessary to have a navy when their country is not at war. He thinks it would be useful to make the public aware of the other things that the navy do – for example, stopping illegal fishing vessels and drug smugglers.

20   D: Peter gives an example of how a fellow officer called Brendan left the navy after ten years' service. He applied for a job as a border control detective with the customs service, and was chosen over people with many more academic qualifications. Peter explains that *the skills that he* [Brendan] *attained* [got] *from the naval police were exactly in line with what they wanted* [were the same as what the customs department wanted]. *The guys from university had limited ability in communication and leadership but the customs people were confident* [sure] *he had everything they required, and that's why the application was successful.* In other words, the skills that Brendan got from the navy could be transferred [also used] in his new job.

p.40–42 PAPER 4 Part 4

Further practice and guidance (p.41–42)

Speaker 1

 1 foreign clients, remember names

 2 professional, position

 3 Have you met

 4 assistant

Speaker 2

 5 equipment

 6 lens

 7 offended, paying money, portrait

 8 business, recommendations

Speaker 3

 9 self-confidence

 10 department

 11 looking down on

 12 small

p.40 PAPER 4 Part 4 (Test)

Speaker 1:   **21E 26C**
The first speaker says *when I'm supposed to be showing foreign clients around* – this suggests he is in business. He also says *it* [this inability to remember names]*…doesn't exactly come across as professional for someone in my position* and mentions that he has an assistant. This suggests he is an important position in his company – in this case a manager. He says that he finds himself saying *Have you met?* which is the way to begin an introduction.

Speaker 2:   **22G 27B**
The second speaker is a photographer who takes pictures of children. She is saying that she is not always able to recognize whether a small baby is male or female so sometimes she says *Have you got a name yet for…?* and doesn't say 'him' or 'her'. She worries that this will offend the parents who will not recommend her to others. She mentions *equipment, the lens* and *portrait* which tell us that she is a photographer. She also says *They* [the parents] *feel offended and they're paying money to have their kid's portrait* [formal photograph] *taken. It's not exactly good for business or personal recommendations.*

Speaker 3:   **23F 28G**
The third speaker is talking about her inability to order from a foreign menu – she is embarrassed about making a mistake with pronunciation when ordering – or not exactly understanding what the dishes are. We can understand that she is an office worker from *we've gone out to eat after work*, and *I'm the new girl in the department*. We know that the other people in her department make her feel inferior from *I don't have much self-confidence in general…I really feel exposed* and *I'm fed up with them all looking down on me. It makes me feel really small* [inferior].

Speaker 4:   **24H 29F**
The fourth speaker starts by talking about his time at school. He then talks about his old classmate, Peter, who has organized a reunion of all the people in his class 20 years later. He finds the reunion very embarrassing because nobody knows what to say to each other. We can understand that the speaker is talking about school from *a couple of terms…I was in the same dormitory…everybody remembered hating the physics teacher.* The idea of an unnatural social situation comes from *nobody had much to say to anybody and the few conversations we had were utterly contrived* [unnaturally created/not genuine].

Speaker 5:   **25D 30H**
The fifth speaker is talking about a trip to Greece. He practised some Greek phrases on a restaurant owner but the owner laughed at him. He says that he wants to improve his Greek so that when he returns to Greece, other restaurant owners will be more impressed and more likely to give him a job. We know he is a chef from *my catering skills are alright.* We know he is trying to impress potential employers from *I thought it might make more of an impact if I could show I knew a bit of the language…showing my CV to a couple of restaurants… I want to be taken seriously* [I want people to recognize my ability] *there won't be many people prepared to take me on* [hire me] *unless I have some idea of the language.*

TEST TWO

p.48–49 PAPER 1 Part 1

1   **B:** The text informs us that applicants for this are assessed according to their income. This means that a person may get a Community Service Card depending on the level of their income [the amount of money they receive from work].

2   **C:** The text informs us that ACC only pay part [a share] of the fees, and that patients are *responsible for the balance* [the rest] *of the charge'*

3   **D:** The writer says that there is no identifiable condition called 'stress'. In other words, when we say we are 'stressed', we are actually experiencing feelings of nervousness, anger, tension etc, but we now use the word 'stress' to refer to *650 quite different things, including most human emotions.*

4   **A:** The writer suggests that it is better to face up to [recognize and admit there are] problems than try and escape from them. Ignoring problems makes the brain release chemicals that reduce the pain caused by stress but it prevents the immune system from working properly at the same time.

5   **B:** The writer suggests that because it is possible to buy many material things (such as cosmetic surgery), people believe they can *also buy something soothing for inside the head* – in other words – spending money can buy them real happiness and a superior life. It is also suggested that *commonsense* (in contrast to being unrealistic) will provide people with good skin/a good figure etc.

6   **C:** *To be manipulated* means to be controlled by others in a clever but unfair or dishonest way. The writer says that the people he observes *are bullied by an instructor*, that they are like *cattle being herded*: these are both images that show they are being controlled. The writer also says that people exercise and run because *they have been told it's the fast way*, in other words, that they are too willing to believe what other people tell them. In paragraph 1, the writer also says *If we can buy a lifestyle, can't we buy a life? A billion-dollar group of industries will tell you 'yes'* – but the writer says our commonsense should tell us that this is not true.

p.50–52 PAPER 1 Part 2

7   **E:** *There's less excuse for…explorers, scholars and philosophers who…were…more naïve.* Other people should have been able to recognize whether they were looking at real wool or not.

8   **D:** *too* suggests that the option must contain a similar description: *when the fruits ripened…to reveal tiny lambs.* The words referring to *tales* and *stories* are *in some versions*.

9 **B:** *he…had heard this from reliable sources.* Reliable sources means in this context 'people you can trust'.

10 **G:** *Still it eluded them* refers to *lamb* (singular) and travellers (plural). The word in the first line of that option which means 'to avoid being found' is *elude*. In the phrase *And so it went on*, the word *it* refers to the idea in option G that people who doubted the lamb-plant's existence were then persuaded it did exist. The idea continues in the text: *As soon as anyone voiced doubts … [there was] new 'evidence'.*

11 **C:** This option contains a 'singular' reference: *a curious object…a sort of toy animal.*

12 **A:** This option contains a reference to the case: *And so it was…for 180 years.* In other words, the case was closed for 180 years. The text under 12 also mentions 'Henry Lee' by introducing him as *a little known naturalist.*

p.53–54 PAPER 1 Part 3

13 **D:** The writer says that *if you think* [humans] *are the only creatures with a moral sense…you're in good company.* This simply means that many people believe this to be true. The writer is not saying he agrees. He also disagrees with *most experts* by saying *yet I'm convinced that many animals can distinguish right from wrong.* A *misconception* means 'a wrong belief which many people have'.

14 **A:** The writer says *Biologists have had real problems trying to explain why people are frequently inexplicably nice to each other…Perhaps we expect a payback somewhere down the line, or maybe our good deeds are directed only towards kin.* The word *inexplicably* means 'impossible to explain'. The use of *perhaps* and *maybe* also suggest a lack of certainty.

15 **C:** The writer states… *on the rare occasions when an animal says 'Let's play' and then beats up an unsuspecting animal, the culprit usually finds itself ostracized by its former playmates.* 'Let's play' suggests the animal wants to engage in non-aggressive social play. To 'beat up' in this context means 'to attack aggressively' – so the animal is not following the rules of social play. To be 'ostracized' means that an individual is ignored or excluded by others.

16 **D:** The writer says *If I'm right, morality evolved because it is adaptive. It helps many animals, including humans, to survive and flourish in their particular social environment.* In the writer's opinion, therefore, moral behaviour (morality) developed (evolved) in such a way that it would help people to survive.

17 **C:** 'This' refers back to 'play'.

18 **D:** The writer says that…*provided virtue is rewarded by a greater number of offspring, then any genes associated with good behaviour are bound to accumulate in subsequent generations.* A simpler way of saying this is if good behaviour results in a greater number of 'children', then any genes connected to good behaviour will probably increase in future generations.

19 **B:** The writer says *First, we didn't invent virtue – its origins are much more ancient than our own. Secondly, we should stop seeing ourselves as morally superior to other animals.* He is suggesting that people should not believe humans invented moral behaviour nor believe that we are morally better than animals.

p.55–58 PAPER 1 Part 4

Further practice and guidance (p.57–58)

1 c   **2** art/music/film etc   **3** a   **4** b
5 (example) modern dancing causes there to be less communication between people   **6** a   **7** b   **8** c   **9** b
10 'physical' refers to the body, 'psychological' refers to the mind.   **11** b   **12** b

p.55–56 PAPER 1 Part 4 (Test)

20 **E:** The answer comes from *On an average week, the entertainment guide…lists around 50 Latin dance nights… Meanwhile, traditional dance schools too have started to report significant attendance rises…*

21 **C:** The answer comes from *Cinema too has had an effect and we can expect the profile of the incredible Argentine style to skyrocket* [really go up/increase] *after several new releases* [new films].

22 **A:** The answer comes from *dancing is an innate celebration of physical existence, something automatic to us.*

23 **H:** The answer comes from…*DJ Vic Jones…fumed:* [said angrily] '…*I resent them gate-crashing and taking up all the dance floor. There is nothing worse than dancing round the floor and bumping into people doing a line dance. It stops your rhythm.*'

24 **G:** The answer comes from *clubbing, with its deafening music, solo dancing and heavy competitiveness, provides less and less social contact, and becomes an avoidance activity* [avoiding contact/communication with other people].

25 **B:** The answer comes from *More and more of us are returning home from foreign adventures…with glowing memories of cultures in which dance, including traditional forms, are a vital part of life.*

26 **G:** The answer comes from … *traditional dancing offers unparalleled opportunities to interact with a range of partners we would not normally encounter.*

27 **C:** The answer comes from *Yet for many years, the modern pop music played in British night clubs was the only kind the young generation would dance to, and formal ballroom dancing and Latin styles were perceived as embarrassingly old-fashioned and bizarre. These kinds of traditional dance were dismissed as something to be practised by old people in shiny, spangly outfits.*

28 **G:** The answer comes from *in a forum where your partner's skill, aptitude and passion for dancing count for far more than* [are more important than] *their age, gender and class.*

29 **A:** The answer comes from *Who really doesn't like dancing? Can even the most bad-tempered dance-floor-avoider last an entire lifetime without a…display at a wedding or a particularly good goal – or refrain from a secret shuffle around the privacy of their living room?* The writer is saying that even people who usually hate dancing will, at some point, be unable to stop themselves dancing.

30 **E:** *An evening's dancing is as good for you as a three-hour hike. It pumps blood up your legs, so it's good for your heart, and it helps posture and breathing.*

31 **F:** The answer comes from *Dance is also good therapy too, busting stress, promoting relaxation and…self-confidence and a sense of achievement.* The writer also says *All humans need tactile* *contact. The touch of another person affirms that we are real, that we are alive.*

32 B: The writer says that *for Britons, as a nation, our reputation as dancers has historically earned us no points and no recognition.*

33 D: The answer comes from *Lyndon Wainwright…lays the decline of social dancing squarely at the fast feet of the actor John Travolta.* The expression 'to lay something at somebody's feet' means to say that they are responsible. Wainwright is saying that John Travolta's character, Tony Manero, in the film *Saturday Night Fever* made people want to dance by themselves because he represented an *iconic…solitary figure.*

34 A: The answer comes from *Dance can take many forms: whether it comes as an impulsive* [spontaneous] *release of energy and emotion, or within a skilful display or within a skilful display of choreography after much rehearsal.*

p.59–60 PAPER 2 Part 1

Further practice and guidance (p.60)

Content

how to make friends/socialize

dealing with informal/colloquial language

learning about culture by watching TV

the behaviour of men and women

Effect on target reader

a Should you give a one-word answer or have a ten-minute conversation?

Why not invite some of your fellow students around for dinner? (a suggestion – using a question form)

What happens if you're having a chat and they start using colloquial language you don't understand?

b The whole first paragraph is a series of scenarios, and also the idea of people chatting and using colloquial language which a non-native speaker might find challenging.

Range and Accuracy

One thing you ~~will~~ **could** do is join a college sports team

so why not ~~to~~ invite some of your fellow students … ?

Don't be afraid **to** ask~~ing~~ for an explanation.

Watch**ing** the evening news will help you find

when you start~~ing~~ conversations

p.61–64 PAPER 2 Part 2

Further practice and guidance (p.62–64)

Reference

Content and effect on target reader

1 The reader needs to know that the applicant can work with a range of people from different countries eg

different age groups and nationalities , and that the applicant is interested in the history of the places that the tour company visits.

2 1 D   2 A   3 E   4 C   5 B

Further practice

1 as   **2** towards   **3** with   **4** in   **5** with   **6** to
7 with/in   **8** for   **9** in

Review

Describing the plot

1 present simple – *the heroine is Adrienne, pays little attention, has an imaginary friend, she shares her dreams, she can't stop, begins to wonder, moves in, the story unfolds, Adrienne seeks, this becomes, announces*

2 present continuous – [who is] *living, grieving,*

3 present perfect – *has passed away, has kept a secret*

Describing characters

1 weak   **2** likeable   **3** dull   **4** close
5 straightforward   **6** predictable   **7** impressive

p.65–68 PAPER 3 Part 1

Further practice and guidance (p.67–68)

1	**a** exact	**b** specialized	
	c detailed	**d** specific	
2	**a** suggest	**b** convey/suggest	
	c bear	**d** transfer	
3	**a** convinced	**b** determined	
	c converted	**d** persuaded/convinced	
4	**a** divided	**b** split	
	c detached	**d** separated	
5	**a** appear	**b** draw	
	c move	**d** approach	
6	**a** presented	**b** tempted	
	c demonstrated	**d** shown	
7	**a** view	**b** sight	
	c notice	**d** perception	
8	**a** expectations	**b** suspicions	
	c calculations	**d** estimates	
9	**a** assists	**b** informs	
	c enables	**d** facilitates	
10	**a** related	**b** connected	
	c descended	**d** evolved	
11	**a** fits	**b** ties	
	c corresponds	**d** complements	
12	**a** succession	**b** sequence	
	c system	**d** progression	

p.65–66 PAPER 3 Part 1 (Test)

1 A   2 B   3 D   4 C   5 D   6 C   7 D   8 D   9 C
10 A   11 A   12 B

p.69 PAPER 3 Part 2

13   by: is followed by *how* someone achieves/does something. Eg 'How do babies lie to their parents? By crying.' Notice the 'ing' form – this is often preceded by a preposition in the open cloze test.

14   in: *to be in pain* is a fixed expression.

15   so: is an adverb that intensifies 'badly' *the parents start giving the hugs the babies so badly desire* means 'desire so much'.

16   their: 'to do your best' means to try as hard as you can. We need *their* to refer to the plural babies.

17   far: 'to be far from the truth' means this is not the truth at all.

18   Like: In this context, *like* is a preposition, and means 'similar to'.

19   being: used to form part of the passive ie *chimpanzees hate being left alone* (by their parents).

20   who: we can use *who* as a relative pronoun to refer back to handlers and connect this to *have become their family*.

21   though/if: *Even though/if* means the same as 'although' in this context.

22   such: is followed by 'a' + (adj) noun. In this context, it means 'In a situation like this one'.

23   because/as/since: In this context, all these conjunctions are followed by an explanation of the previous clause/sentence/idea.

24   no: this forms part of the phrase 'no longer'. In this context, it means 'the handler cannot hear him anymore'.

25   over: *to have control* is followed by the preposition *over* + something/someone.

26   than: in this context, *rather than* means 'instead of'.

27   whether: *whether* is often preceded or followed by the verb 'depends'. Eg 'Are you going out?' 'It depends whether I've finished my work.' 'Whether this is an example of real lying depends on your interpretation of the chimpanzee's behaviour …'

p.70 PAPER 3 Part 3

28 mistakenly   29 worthless   30 irreplaceable
31 accompanied   32 likelihood   33 lessen
34 accessible   35 precautions   36 enable   37 presence

p.71–73 PAPER 3 Part 4

38 brought   39 read   40 fair   41 deal   42 face

p.74–76 PAPER 3 Part 5

43   why/how   it   was/could be   stolen so

44   has no intention of giving

45   made a change to learn something

46   though he   was/is   used to speaking

47   not trying to get   along/on

48   to take no

49   no matter how tough it   may/might

50   was not (wasn't) in the mood *or* was in no mood

p.77 PAPER 4 Part 1

1   B: The woman says *I actually felt cheated* [I thought I had been deceived and had not got what I deserved] *my husband had been enjoying a really expensive weekend, and I hadn't* [she regrets that she did not know the true price of the hotel room].

2   A: The man says *people should buy expensive wine if it really gives them additional pleasure* and the woman agrees by saying *And if paying $45 for wine makes you happy, why not?*

3   C: Petra says *I'm basically lazy and…the idea of running five or six times a week doesn't actually appeal,* [do not think this is enjoyable] *so I was more than pleased when I found out I didn't have to.* In other words, she does not want to train very hard by running regularly.

4   C: Petra explains that Sean *encourages people to work on improving their overall strength before they go anywhere near* [start to think about] *an actual long run – so I was doing tons of sit-ups and press-ups and weight-lifting* [examples of strength training] *– that kind of thing – before I did any kind of practice running at all.*

5   B: Laura says that she enjoyed school but admits that *there are children who shouldn't be there – it just doesn't suit their learning style.*

6   A: Bryan says that 'unschooling' *is a relatively recent trend* [it's a new development] *as far as educational theory goes and there's not been a proper study into how successful it actually is.* In other words, Bryan is saying that there is no proof yet about the success or failure of 'unschooling'.

p.78–79 PAPER 4 Part 2

Further practice and guidance (p.79)

Question 7: The gap requires a noun. It could also be adj+noun. Possible answers: stunts/live action/dangerous events etc.

Question 8: possible answers: food/equipment/accessories.

Question 9: It is a good idea to… It would be worth + ing … You should/ought to etc. The answer is probably not the name of a sport because question 9 already mentions *as well as the competitions.*

Question 10: The answer will either be a plural noun or a positive adjective. Both answers are likely to be positive because the question is referring to the fans' opinions.

Question 11: I'd say that was true … I'd go along with that…I think that's right etc. The adjective is going to be positive – again because the question is referring to the fans' opinion.

Question 12: Possible answers: a motor, an engine, different wheels, a sail etc.

Question 13: I recommend that you … In my opinion, you ought to … It would be a good idea to … etc. Possible answers: safety equipment/health risks/local conditions etc.

Question 14: Possible answers: ticket sales/television coverage/fans etc.

p.78 PAPER 4 Part 2 (Test)

7 (amazing) stunts   8 sportswear   9 music festival
10 heroes   11 unique   12 sail
13 (the) local conditions   14 publicity

p.80–83 PAPER 4 Part 3

Further practice and guidance (p.81–83)

15	1Bii	2Aiii	3Div	4Ci
16	1Ciii	2Ai	3Biv	4Dii
17	1Di	2Cii	3Aiv	4Biii
18	1Dii	2Biii	3Aiv	4Ci
19	1Biv	2Aiii	3Cii	4Di
20	1Biii	2Div	3Aii	4Ci

p.80 PAPER 4 Part 3 (Test)

15 B   16 A   17 C   18 C   19 D   20 B

p.84 PAPER 4 Part 4

Speaker 1:   21B   26C
The first speaker is talking about his favourite pop group when he was a teenager. He mentions his friend Simon, but does not say that Simon influenced him. We can understand that he is talking about a pop group/pop star from *they weren't that well known*…[then]…*they got pretty big* [became successful], *the* [music] *albums… The lead* [the main singer or guitar player] *was my absolute idol…*He adds *when things were really bad at home…my parents were rowing* [arguing and shouting]…*I'd turn the sound up…It was a way of escaping…a way of dealing* [managing/coping] *with all the bad stuff going on* [the bad things happening in my life].

Speaker 2:   22G   27A
The second speaker is talking about her interest in writing when she was a child. We know she is a writer from *I was quite a voracious reader* [I read a lot] *and I also had my own ideas for stories.* Her talent for writing is first referred to when she says *I suspected I could write.* We can guess she is talking about her teacher from *It was Mrs Shelly that gave me the push I needed* [she encouraged me]…*she read out one of my essays to the whole class.* By saying *Mrs* Shelly, we can tell that she had a formal relationship with the person who influenced her. An essay is a piece of writing you produce in school. When the speaker says *I reckon it was her who started me off* she is again referring to Mrs Shelly encouraging her to start writing and develop her talent.

Speaker 3:   23E   28D
The third speaker is talking about how his father was a very honest and direct man. We can understand that he is talking about his father from *Mum never got used to it. She'd be after* [she wanted] *some compliment…and he'd tell her straight out*

'No love, it's wrong on you'. We can understand that he wants to develop his father's qualities when he says *I'd like to think I take after him* [inherited his qualities/ personality] and *I've certainly made an effort to apply his honesty and directness in my work.*

Speaker 4:   24H   29F
The fourth speaker starts by talking about his life as a journalist now and how he often remembers his childhood friend, James. He says that James was a very interesting person and that it was James who originally intended to become a journalist. We can understand that he is describing a childhood friend from *I was a miserable teenager…James moved in next door and I was allowed to go round there* [to visit him]. We can understand that the speaker became interested in experiencing new things when he says *stories and photos from all around the world…were a real eye-opener* [they made me think about things I had never thought about before]…*James gave me the desire to go off exploring and discovering.*

Speaker 5:   25D   30B
The fifth speaker is talking about a TV star and the way he and his classmates used to copy the TV star's *moves* [the way he used to fight]. We can tell he is talking about a TV star from *It was on* [the programme appeared on the TV] *every Thursday night at 5 o'clock…I'd…grab the remote control.* We can understand that he got into trouble for behaving like the TV star from *I did this karate kick on a mate of mine and he ended up in hospital 'cos he'd fallen backwards and bashed* [hit] *his head on some stone steps….my parents were furious* [very angry]. *I had to stay in my room away from the television for a whole month* [I was forbidden to watch TV].

TEST THREE

p.87–88 PAPER 1 Part 1

1   B: The answer comes from *Cleverly, the programme makers … draw the audience in by keeping the excitement and mystery of the subject in focus* [as the aspect they are concentrating on].

2   A: The answer comes from *the program makers opt* [choose] *to include fragments* [pieces] *of interviews interrupted by generally redundant* [pointless] *narration that prevents the viewer from gaining a real sense of the memories that are being recalled… we are denied a chance to hear what they may have said in a more meditative fashion.*

3   B: The answer comes from *it wasn't until around the start of the 1980s that people's memories started to be about things, such as particular brand-name dolls like Barbie or the popular Scalextric racing cars.* In other words, the writer is saying that people thought they had to buy things in order to have fun. The writer suggests that before the 1980s, people were able to enjoy themselves without spending money.

4   A: The writer admits that things were difficult in the past (*cold houses, tough schooling, severe illnesses*) but says that they could manage these things because there was a sense of *everyone living through it together.* But today he says that children are isolated in their rooms and have unrestricted access to a computer which, he implies, can reveal many terrible things that elderly shoppers would never have seen when they were young.

5   D: The answer comes from *Whereas normally the human mind weeds out* [selects unwanted things] *irrelevant or out-of-date material and discards it* [throws it away], *clearly AJ's memory does not work in quite the same way.*

6   C: The answer comes from *while AJ's memory is impressive, it is not indiscriminate* [it does choose things carefully] *and could not be described as photographic. McGaugh's team asked AJ to close her eyes and describe what the researchers were wearing. She had no idea* [she couldn't remember what they were wearing].

p.89–92 PAPER 1 Part 2

> **Further practice and guidance (p.91–92)**
>
> 1 a   2 b   3 b   4 c   5 a   6 b   7 c   8 b   9 c
> 10 b   11 c   12 a   13 a   14 b   15 a

p.89–90 PAPER 1 Part 2 (Test)

7   G: The connection between the text above 7 and G is *this seemed more like a military operation* and *But that, however, was exactly what it was.* The writer is saying that in reality, this expedition was a real military operation. It also mentions in G that the writer was not a soldier and in the text below G, the writer says that Mark, the leader, would not be responsible for him – because he is a civilian, and not a soldier.

8   D: In the text above 8, Mark promises not to let the writer fall, in other words, he will keep him safe. D begins with *Despite that welcome reassurance.* To 'reassure someone' means to promise a person something in order to remove anxiety or fear.

9   F: In the text above 9, Mark explains all the reasons why climbing Mont Blanc is a dangerous challenge. F begins with *To add to my apprehension, it was this same route that had beaten me the last time around.* The writer suggests that travelling on the same route is an additional fear to others that Mark has already mentioned. F also connects to the text under 9: the writer says that the soldiers did not appear too fit. Then he says that *looks* [appearances] *can be deceptive.* He is saying that he was wrong about the fitness of the soldiers.

10   A: In the text above 10, the writer says that he had *turned back* or given up on the route up the Col two years ago. Option A begins with *This time…I was having better luck.* He is saying that he is having more success on the same route on this expedition. A also connects with the text under 10: the writer says that *everyone was suffering and slowing down.* The next piece of text begins with *Even digging snow pits for the tents was a real struggle.* Digging the snow pits was extremely difficult because everyone was suffering from exhaustion.

11   E: This paragraph finishes with the writer believing *at least the worst was over.* The text under 11 says *I couldn't have been more wrong* and continues *the descent made everything that had gone before seem easy.* The writer is admitting that he made a mistake – that the ascent to the top of the mountain had been easier than the descent to the bottom.

12   B: This paragraph begins with *It looked like the decision had been made for us.* This refers back to the previous text that mentions that the soldiers were forced to change direction because a large piece of ice was blocking their route. B finishes with the writer mentioning how easy it is to make a mistake. The text under 12 then says that he slipped and was unable to stop himself from falling.

p.93–94 PAPER 1 Part 3

13   D: The answer comes from *At one time the notion of a career on stage may have been frowned upon.* 'To frown upon something' means 'to disapprove of it'.

A: It was usual for comedians only to receive free drinks and sandwiches.

B: There is no mention of awards that were offered in the past.

C: The text only says that *stand-up comedian(s) would have to endure years on the circuit of small-time venues.* This means that comedians were forced to give many performances in places that only attracted a small audience. They did this as they hoped it would lead to a successful career, but this was not always the case.

14   B: The answer comes from *five comedy awards that are regarded in the industry as one long audition for lucrative TV work.* So, comedians take part in the festival in order to show their level of ability to TV producers or *a top agent.*

A: There is no mention of comedians wanting to 'revolutionize' comedy. The revolution which is mentioned refers to the growing interest in watching comedians.

C: Although the number of people watching comedy is growing, *a diverse audience* suggests 'people from different social or cultural backgrounds'. There is no mention of comedians hoping to be seen by a diverse audience.

D: There is no mention of a cash prize, only the possibility of future work in Melbourne or Montreal, where the comedians may receive a salary, not a prize.

15   A: The answer comes from *it's not all milk and honey for those seeking fame and fortune. Milk and honey* is a metaphor for the good things in life. The answer can also be found in *There are many, many comedians who have been around for years without a breakthrough.* This means they have tried for a long time to become successful, but have failed.

B: Although Burdett-Coutts refers to three cities where opportunities are limited, he does not say that comedians should not try to work there or in other cities. Perhaps some comedians will succeed.

C: Burdett-Coutts only says there are many comedians looking for success. He doesn't refer to how talented they may or may not be.

D: Burdett-Coutts maintains that *there's room for another comedy festival in a seemingly overcrowded market.* This means that he believes that the market is not really overcrowded and that another festival is possible.

16   A: *What you have these days is a concern with the comic's creative potential. They may think someone…has a talent that could be put to better use coming up with ideas for sketches in established TV shows or even for editing scripts.* This means that TV producers are looking for comedians who can write jokes for other people.

B: The text says *Not so long ago, TV producers would want to see someone up there performing live…* This is not the key because it refers to a past situation.

C: *and audience reaction was the bottom line.* This means that how the audiences responded to a comedian was the most important thing, but again, it is referring to a past situation.

D: The text says *Despite the risk of obscurity*. This means that there is a chance that the comedian will never become well known or successful. However, there is no reference to the comedian's attitude towards this.

17 C: Lisa says *It certainly helps in terms of knowing whether a joke is 'sayable' or if the timing's right when they go into writing or production*. This means that new comedians can test their material and their act on live audiences before later going on to work as writers.

A: The text states that if a new comedian wins an award, afterwards this will lead to work opportunities where he or she can practise their act.

B: Lisa believes *they are hardly an automatic guarantee of well-paid comedy life*. This means she thinks the awards do not necessarily lead to success.

D: There is no mention of this in the text. There is a reference to *the industry shop window* which means that TV producers and agents are able to see a lot of different comedians perform, but it does not refer to a choice that comedians make.

18 D: The answer comes from *I couldn't face starting over, doing try-out sessions…my heart sank at the thought*. Whelans had already had a successful career with a comedy partner. When this partnership finished, he did not want to start from the beginning again, trying to create a solo act. *I couldn't face* and *my heart sank* both refer to his lack of enthusiasm.

A: This is untrue. Whelans says that *there are hundreds of competent, blandish, slightly uninteresting stand-ups who I would be up against*. This suggests that he regards many other comedians as 'average' or having little talent. He did not want to waste time taking part in events in order to prove his ability.

B: Whelans says that people in the industry can earn a lot, but this is not the same as what his expectations were regarding his own salary when he became a writer.

C: The text says that his comedy act with a partner finished, but there is no reference as to why this happened. It does not say that Whelans found team work difficult.

19 C: The writer mentions both positive things eg *'lucrative broadcasting work'* (first paragraph) *'the openings for talented funny people are many and varied'* (fourth paragraph) and negative things eg *'There are many, many comedians who have been around for years without a breakthrough'*, *'overcrowded market'* (third paragraph) *'despite the risk of obscurity'* (fourth paragraph).

p.95–96 PAPER 1 Part 4

20 D: *I was over the moon to actually win something.*

21 C: *You've got to be aware of what is happening all the time, you can't switch off* [stop concentrating] *at any point during the trip.*

22 E: *I love caving but I wouldn't class* [consider] *myself as a* [real/professional] *caver.*

23 C: The answer comes from *I am now more involved in scheduling other drivers, so I don't spend as much time on the river as I did.*

24 B: *I just wanted to settle down and find a base.*

25 D: The photographer says, *And filing photos is not my strong point. It's the most tedious part…*

26 A: *The best aspect of the work is the quality of the students.* In other words, the students who he teaches are very capable and skilled.

27/28 B/E: (B) *without a guide it would be beyond most people's ability* [most people couldn't go climbing/trekking alone], *and it's rewarding to know they appreciate that fact*; (E) *Occasionally some people get scared stiff and I get a lot out of* [a lot of satisfaction] *helping someone overcome that.*

29 B: *To go through such training and have other people look at your work and get their input is invaluable.* The mountain guide is saying that he thinks the comments that more experienced guides make about his work/ability is very useful.

30 A: *but I am bothered* [annoyed] *by the endless meetings and things to do within the polytechnic system.*

31/32 C/D: (C) *For commercial driving it's learning as you go* [you learn through experience]; (D) *All my training for this career has been completely hands-on* [practical/not theoretical], *rather than through study.*

33/34 D/E: (D) *waiting on payment from people you work with is a frustration you have to put up with* [tolerate/accept]; (E) *I used to get really offended, but now I'm resigned to it* [I don't like it but I accept it].

p.97–99 PAPER 2 Part 1

Further practice and guidance (p.98–99)

Content

1 problems with the changing rooms + gym equipment/how to improve them **2** customers are happy with the staff/explain why the staff better this year **3** what problems are occurring in the caféteria **4** opening times **5** fees.

Expanded points

1 the showers were renovated only three years ago, changing rooms could be redecorated, cycling machines and mats should be replaced **2** training courses for staff have been effective **3** not many healthy options, so introduce salads **4** organize opening hours to suit college timetable **5** offer discounts for weekday afternoons

Effect on target reader

You are writing to someone in a senior position – someone who can influence your chances of promotion and pay rises, etc, therefore your suggestions need to be constructive, helpful and polite rather than negative and critical.

Organization

The report is divided into clear sections with the content points sensibly divided between each of them. You could also use subheadings in a report, for example:

Equipment and Changing Rooms:

The condition of these facilities was generally considered to be poor.

Range

1, 2, 5 are correct.

3 The correct form is *were renovated*. We need to use the past simple form of the passive because we know when the renovation took place ie 'three years ago'.

4 The correct form is *could be decorated*. Passive forms that begin with modal verbs require 'be' to refer to a future possibility or for making a suggestion eg 'John could be chosen as the next captain.' 'The building could be cleaned more regularly.'

6 The correct form is *is offered*. *Recommend/suggest/propose* are followed by the bare infinitive eg 'I recommend you pay the employees more next year.' Therefore, in the passive, a present form is used, not a future form of the passive.

Further practice

1b The structure *I wonder if* is a polite and tentative way of making a suggestion. The passive *might be held* is also less direct or more tentative than an active form.

2a The past continuous of *to hope, to think*, and *to wonder* can be used to make diplomatic or tentative suggestions in English.

3b *Would it be possible…?* is used for polite requests or suggestions.

4a *Perhaps* is a more formal way to say *Maybe*.

5b Using the passive makes the action more important, ie *It should be done…*. In an active sentence, ie *You should do it*, this can sound rather aggressive or accusatory.

6a *feel* can replace *think* when the speaker wants to make a tactful suggestion and avoid sounding too direct.

7b The second conditional, ie *If we did this, there would be…*makes the suggestion sound more tentative. The first conditional, ie *If we do this, there will be…*can sound too direct.

p.100–101 PAPER 2 Part 2

Further practice and guidance (p.101)

Effect on target reader

You would probably want to make your friend feel less nervous and more confident. You could achieve this by giving helpful advice and by reassuring your friend that interviews are not as frightening as some people imagine they are.

Content

A description of an interview that you have experienced (second paragraph) and advice about what to do and say in an interview (third paragraph).

Starting

c is the best answer. It can be used to start most letters which are responding to a friend's letter (unless your friend has told you about some very bad news).

a This is simply copying the question – which you should never do in Paper 2. It is also a strange way to start a letter.

b This is more suitable for a very formal letter.

Finishing

a Is the best answer. It is used to wish somebody luck.

b This is a common way to end many informal letters, but in the sample letter, there is no mention of a future arrangement.

c The writer of the sample letter is giving help, not receiving it.

Range

on top of = in addition to

it'll stand you in good stead = it'll help you prepare for the future and give you an advantage

started off = began

to figure out = to understand

in your case = in your situation

this goes without saying = I don't need to say this because it is obvious

just come out with = suddenly say

back it up = support

p.102–103 PAPER 3 Part 1

1   **C:** *committing* is the verb that usually collocates with *crime*.

2   **A:** if you are unable to *resist* something, you know that it is wrong but you do it anyway. In this context, the writer is saying that burglars cannot stop themselves from eating food they find in houses, even though this may slow them down. It is possible to *decline* or *refuse* food, but only when it is offered to you.

3   **D:** *premises* is preceded by the preposition on. *Premises* refers to both buildings and land that an organization, company or person owns. *Houses, locations* and *grounds* take the preposition *in* in this context. It is also unlikely that burglars would find food in *grounds* eg areas of land around a house.

4   **B:** *tendency* is the only abstract noun here which fits the structure *There is a ………………… to do something*. It means that in general, whenever burglars eat food in someone's house, they tend to leave some of it behind.

5   **C:** *hope* is the only abstract noun that fits the structure *in the ……………… of + ing*.

6   **A:** *commonplace* means 'not unusual'. *Regular* and *typical* would normally be followed by a noun, eg 'With DNA identification now a regular/typical part of an investigation…'

7   **D:** *to convict* a criminal means to 'prove and find them guilty in court'; *to be convicted this way* means to be found guilty using DNA identification techniques. The police or a lawyer would *accuse* a person of committing a crime *before* they obtained all the evidence.

8   **B:** we can use *reliability* to describe how well a test, process or method works, and if they work well all the time. The rest of the paragraph talks about how certain foods produce good DNA results, but other foods do not.

9   B: the expression *to limit yourself to something* means that you only allow yourself to use, take or do something in a small amount.

10   D: *remains* can refer to the part of a meal that is not eaten.

11   C: in this context, *virtually* means 'almost'; in other words, the chocolate was not at all helpful in providing DNA evidence. *'Hardly useless'* would be an unusual combination, but it would mean 'it is not useless at all'. The adverb *extremely* can only go with gradable adjectives.

12   A: *meaning* or *which meant that* is followed by a result or a consequence of an event, situation or action.

p.104 PAPER 3 Part 2

13   there: *there* introduces the clause that follows.

14   unless: the writer is saying that he doesn't believe there were any more ways that he could fall over *unless* another skier crashed into him – then that would be another way.

15   was/got: we need *was + pp* to form the passive, or *got + pp* as an example of the causative form when it is used to show that you were the victim of an accident.

16   what: we can use *what* to refer forward.

17   which: *which* refers back to the moment the writer's friend speaks.

18   other: the writer is saying that he put his skis under one arm and then put them under the other (arm).

19   Despite: *despite* is followed by a noun phrase.

20   with: *with no co-ordination* means 'without co-ordination'.

21   this: *this disability* refers back to the disability of having no co-ordination.

22   between: *difference* takes the preposition *between*.

23   an/the: *ability* is a noun and requires a determiner. We can use *an* to introduce an ability we haven't mentioned before, or *the* to emphasize the importance of this specific ability.

24   cannot: (not *can't* which would be counted as two words) the writer is saying that if you cannot learn to *snowplough*, (position your skis in a way that slows you down), you will not be able to stop.

25   it: *it* refers forward to the action of *turning my feet*.

26   did: *did* is used here for emphasis.

27   so: *so* goes in front of an adjective which is followed by a consequence, eg *It was so hot (that) all the plants died! The book was so expensive (that) I decided not to buy it.*

p.105 PAPER 3 Part 3

28 growth   **29** vacancies   **30** reliable   **31** proven
32 independently   **33** fluency   **34** preferably
35 satisfaction   **36** recruitment   **37** applicants.

p.106 PAPER 3 Part 4

38 land   **39** mind   **40** save   **41** deep   **42** place

p.107 PAPER 3 Part 5

43   no need to have

44   more to do with   his/a

45   it was (about/high) time (that) he took

46   recognized Takeshi due to

47   would rather   have/we had   gone

48   since they stopped seeing each

49   not have kept that information from

50   would   have/get   the rubbish taken

p.108 PAPER 4 Part 1

1   C: Marian says that…*people…look for anything that can connect you to them.* She then gives an example of how a stranger told her about a child she had given up for adoption because she thought that Marian had, too, because of a story she had written. Marian adds that the woman *thought I was someone who could relate to her* [understand her because they had similar experiences].

2   B: Marian implies that people are generally unhappy when she says *I think the world's become a rather depressing place for many people, and it's comforting for them to read about the misfortunes* [unhappy events/bad luck] *of others.*

3   A: The man says that when he was a child he never expected to receive gifts except on his birthday. He implies that by screaming, his son will usually persuade him to buy whatever he want, whenever he wants it. He adds *He's not the only one I've seen using that trick* – which suggests that it is common behaviour for young children.

4   C: The woman says that *we can't be bothered* [we do not want to make the effort – because]. *We can now buy a lot for little money. We've got used to buying inexpensive, easily replaceable things.*

5   A: Kesaia says that the Europeans *brought cotton with them, and this was welcomed with a great deal of enthusiasm. It was much easier to work with…*

6   B: Kesaia explains that some of the people who make tapa cloth *rely on it for survival – I mean the income it brings in, it can support a whole family.*

p.109 PAPER 4 Part 2

7 coffee shops   **8** Chinese   **9** cosmopolitan   **10** chains
11 loss   **12** delivery service   **13** supermarkets
14 calories

p.110 PAPER 4 Part 3

15   B: Callum says that *When people find out what you do, their response is always positive…they're always curious to learn more* [they want to know more]. *Most people are fairly ignorant* [they don't know much] *about geology, but when it comes to volcanoes, they don't hold back with the questions* [they don't limit the number of questions they ask].

16   A: Callum says that *it was on a field trip* [a research trip to a place of interest – in this context, a volcano] *that I saw my first eruption way down a crater. I was simultaneously quite terrified and quite amazed by the power of it all. I knew at that moment I would have to switch fields* [I instantly knew that I would have to change my area of study/change my career] *...that volcanoes would be a lifelong fascination* [that I would always be interested in volcanoes].

17   C: Callum talks about a time when he was flying over a volcano and it was suddenly too dark to see where they were going. He admits that the situation is *All my fault, I'm afraid. I should have known better ... I had this awful sense of responsibility for putting Jack* [the pilot] *into that position* [that dangerous situation].

18   A: Callum says that *I can't say I've got used to the reporters, though* [he still feels uncomfortable dealing with reporters]. *It can take a great effort on my part to remain patient* [I have to try very hard to be patient] *with them when a volcano's going off and I'd rather be monitoring the equipment.*

19   B: Callum says *something that students don't anticipate* [expect] *– that they'll need to be able to produce papers concerning their research findings, and that therefore a good command of written English is vital* [it is really important that they are able to write clearly and effectively].

20   D: Callum says that *The thing about volcanoes is that… you still never really know what's coming next. I like the element of surprise in my work, more so than having to work to a schedule which is what making a TV series seems to be all about.* In other words, he is saying that he is never sure what a volcano will do, which he likes, whereas you always know what you are doing when you follow the schedule of making a TV programme.

p.111–112 PAPER 4 Part 4

Further practice and guidance (p.112)

Speaker 1:   1T   2T   3F   4T   5T   6T   7F

Speaker 2:   8F   9T   10T   11F   12T

Speaker 3:   13T   14T   15T   16F

Speaker 4:   17F   18F   19T   20F

Speaker 5:   21F   22F   23T   24F

p.111 PAPER 4 Part 4 (Test)

Speaker 1:   **21E**   **26G**
The first speaker is talking about her lifestyle as a flight attendant. She says that when she was growing up, it was her dream to be a flight attendant, but now she doesn't find the job very satisfying. We can understand that she is a flight attendant from [I don't see] *much of the world except for hotel rooms…the hours are bad…jet lag…is the same old routine…* She also mentions that she has to deal with complaints when people are served with food they don't like. We can understand that she is disappointed from *It's all I wanted to be when I was growing up* and *If I'd known it was going to be like this…I would have chosen another career.*

Speaker 2:   **22G**   **27A**
The second speaker is talking about the problem of airplane delays and how this affects her job. She says that people

arrive at her hotel very late and that she has to work overtime. We can tell she is a hotel receptionist from…*we're still around to check them* [the guests] *in* [to the hotel] *when they arrive.* We can understand that she is irritated from *there's one thing that really winds me up* [irritates me] and *the most annoying thing is…*

Speaker 3:   **23H**   **28E**
The third speaker is talking about his work as a travel agent and describing the type of customers he has to deal with. He says that some customers are very decisive about the holiday they want, but others cannot make up their minds and take a long time to reach a decision. We can understand that he is a travel agent from *there's a lot more destinations we need to know about…you can get down every brochure, call up all the tour operators…and most people only get one holiday a year.* We can understand that he is accepting about the customers' indecision from *I don't blame them…You have to be patient…It's part of the job.*

Speaker 4:   **24C**   **29D**
The fourth speaker is talking about his future job working in Greece. We can understand that he is a tour guide from *I've got to start reading up on the history so…I know what I'm talking about* [he needs to be able to talk about Greek history to holidaymakers]. He also says *I've got about three weeks…before I'm having to explain it all…I can always refer to my notes.* We can understand that he is keen from *I've always been fascinated by the language, the customs…just the whole culture…I can't wait to go.*

Speaker 5:   **25F**   **30B**
The fifth speaker is a tourist who is talking about where the other people in his group want to go. His friends want to visit an art gallery and go sightseeing. He says *It's* [the art gallery] *about the last place on Earth I'd choose to go to* and *I'd rather just sit and have a drink…than…looking at a lot of old monuments.* He concludes that all statues look the same to him – *once you've seen one old statue, you've seen them all.* We can understand from this that he is unenthusiastic about art and sightseeing.

TEST FOUR

p.114–115 PAPER 1 Part 1

1   C: The answer comes from *it was involved in a collision* [a crash] *with an unmanned smaller vessel* [boat]. *As a result…the outer hull* [outer body] *sustained slight damage which will require at least two weeks to repair.* The text says that the boat was scheduled to have a service in early July. It passed its tests and should now be sailing again, but the accident with the smaller boat means that it is still not running.

2   D: The answer comes from *For customers with a currently valid monthly pass, a 10% discount will be granted when they are next renewed* [bought again]. Travellers do not have to travel at their regular time as there may be no room on the smaller Dolphin II. Travellers can't claim their money back from the place where they buy their tickets – instead they have to reclaim their money after they have reached their destination on the other side.

3   C: The answer comes from Andrew Sims's desire *not to overlook what's on your doorstep,* [what is local] *and to travel in a more leisurely way.*

4   D: The answer comes from *And today's trips are more like narratives in which the next page is yet to be written,* [no plans have been made] *and the traveller is the storyteller. The whole idea of 'If it's Tuesday, it must be Belize' is completely over.* The writer is saying that some people know exactly where they will be on every day of their holiday, but the new type of traveller rejects this kind of planning and prefers to be more flexible.

5   A: The answer comes from *it was only a matter of moments before he found his limbs* [arms and legs] *longing to break free of* [escape from] *the designated area. The resentful compromise of space* [he did not like having to share limited space].

6   B: The answer comes from *the confinement of his seat could well describe their interaction; there was his father's relentless attempt to shape him* [make Robbie behave in the way he wanted] *and Robbie's equally obstinate refusal to stay contained* [Robbie's rejection of his father's controlling behaviour and also his refusal to stay in his part of the seat].

p.116–117 PAPER 1 Part 2

7   D: In the text above 7, the writer says that she doubted the truth of what the doctor was saying. The doctor believed that baby talk is meaningless. Paragraph D begins with *it is science that is having second thoughts*. This means that scientists are starting to doubt the traditional theory too. D also includes *If they smile, it may well be because they recognize your voice. When they babble, they are probably not speaking nonsense.* This language for 'possibility' connects to the first line of the text under 7, *This is not just hopeful theorizing* [guessing].

8   G: The text above 8 mentions *the traditional understanding of early language development, which holds* [believes] *that babies must develop motor skills before they can…connect sounds to meanings*. Paragraph G begins with *Petitto and her team take a different view*. This means that they disagree with the traditional theory.

9   C: The text above 9 mentions the research done on three different groups of babies from France, England and Spain. Paragraph C starts with *The results showed uniformity in all cases*. This means that the results were the same in every case. There was no difference between how the French, English or Spanish babies were using their facial muscles to smile or produce sounds.

10   A: Most of the text above 10 is Petitto's explanation of how the brain controls facial muscles for different functions. Paragraph A begins with *What this tells us…. What* refers back to the explanation that has just been given. The text above 10 also mentions *smiling* and *babbling* [an attempt at speech]. There is a connection between these words and *a purely physical response* [smiling] and *an oral one* [babbling] in paragraph A. There is another connection between *the brain* in the final sentence of paragraph A and *that is not all it can do* in the text below.

11   E: The text above 11 states that [babies] *can tell the difference between happy features and sad features* [on a face]. Paragraph E begins with *This is borne out* [proven] *by the fact that they* [babies] *can imitate these same expressions* [happy/sad faces]. Paragraph E finishes by saying *This means they* [babies] *can learn how to use things just by watching people*. The text under 11 says *They can grasp* [understand] *simple arithmetic by using the same capacity* [ability]. This means that they can learn how to use things and understand simple maths because they watch people or things carefully.

12   F: Paragraph F finishes with *It appears that our brains all start out with the same approach to learning and development*. In the final piece of text it compares the brain of a baby and what it knows instinctively with a computer program. The writer then says that it depends what babies do with their brains and what they learn that leads to a difference between babies later on. In other words, everyone is born with the same potential for learning, but we develop according to how much stimulation the brain receives.

p.118–119 PAPER 1 Part 3

13   C: The answer comes from *another wave of anxiety* [worry] *arose over the title, the cover, the promotion* [how it was being marketed] *and a publicity blurb* [the description on the back of the book] *that would somehow describe it in 20 words or fewer* [she implies that 20 words is not enough]. She did not have to abandon the whole book but only 85 000 words. Nobody has misled her [given her the wrong information] about the book's likely success; she was only imagining what it would be like to be a successful author. She does not say that her writing ability is poorer than she believed, only that she was asked to make changes.

14   C: *'throwing down my pen forever'* is a metaphorical way of saying that the writer intends to stop writing as a career. *'To give it all up for good'* again suggests that the writer plans to give up [stop] writing permanently.

15   D: The answer comes from *I….smiled at passersby – because yes, they did pass me by* [walk past me]. *At last, someone came up. My heart skipped a beat* [I was hopeful they would buy the book]. The writer holds her book up hopefully even though the shopper is looking for cookery books and walks away. She is not reluctant to attend the book signing event because she says she is *on a high* – in other words, feeling very positive. There is very little interest shown in her book, whereas *amount of interest* suggests there was a good public reaction to it. The book was clearly displayed here, unlike other bookstores she had been to.

16   B: The answer comes from *you don't have to worry about facts getting in the way of* [preventing] *a good story. You can improve on real people, or merge several into one…anti-hero; you can embellish* [improve and add to] *a true story*. In other words, the writer is saying that there are no limits as to what you can say in fiction, unlike in newspapers where you should report factual information only. She does not suggest that fiction writers receive public admiration: getting published is not done for the fame. She says she sometimes finds it hard to begin writing fiction [*a new chapter*] – but does not refer to finding motivation to write news stories.

17   A: The writer explains that people lend her books to other people. This means that those people do not have to buy the book and so the writer loses financially. *You grind your teeth* suggests that the writer does not complain when people tell her this, but inwardly she feels annoyed and frustrated.

18   B: The answer comes from *writing on commission can be both professionally and financially rewarding* and *you need to write more than one…a year to make…a full time wage* but *you won't have any time left to write a novel*. She is not discouraging people from writing novels, just explaining the reality that you are unlikely to make a lot of money from it. She does not say what particular kind of commissioned book people should write, only that it is a good idea to choose subjects that interest them. She is very objective about the financial side of a writing career; there is no language in the text that suggests criticism of the publishing industry.

19   C: The writer draws a comparison between *the celebrity circuit* and *anonymous isolation*. A 'celebrity circuit' refers to all the events and parties that celebrities attend, whereas most writers are anonymous [unrecognized by the public] and pursue their career in isolation [alone].

p.120–121 PAPER 1 Part 4

20   C: *I was from the wrong class and went to the wrong university…You resign yourself to working at the local factory.* Sarah is saying that her social background and education would not help her career in the UK.

21   D: *People at work were far too competitive for my liking.* Lucy is saying that she didn't like the competetive behaviour of her colleagues.

22   B: *it would…have been harder to break into this kind of field… it may have taken longer in the US.* Jenny is stating that she has achieved success in New Zealand more quickly than would have been possible in the USA.

23   D: *Sometimes it bothers me that we're so remote – you can feel a bit cut of from…the rest of the world…*Lucy is saying that at times she is bothered/frustrated by the fact that New Zealand is a long distance from anywhere else and that she doesn't always know what is happening in other countries.

24   C: *if you want to do something here, you just go for it, which is an attitude I admire beyond belief.* Sarah is saying that New Zealanders are ambitious, and are not afraid of taking risks.

25   A: *she's mourning for a country she once called home…but I do miss it.* We usually use the verb 'mourn' when someone has died: *Everybody mourned* [felt and showed sadness] *when our great-grandfather died.* The writer suggests that Nicky thinks she has 'lost' her country.

26   D: *Another thing that impresses me is that you can leave your stuff in a café and it'll still be there…later. People are…trustworthy.* Lucy is saying that if a person accidentally leaves something somewhere, it will not be stolen. People are honest.

27   B: *'I'm from Alabama, but no, we didn't run around barefoot and my father didn't play the banjo!' she jokes, in anticipation of my preconceptions.* Jenny believes that the writer may imagine she is from a poor, uneducated background because of people's generally wrong ideas about life in Alabama.

28   A: *I just love the tranquillity and the fact you can lead a safe and ordinary life. Tranquil* corresponds to 'calm' and *ordinary life* corresponds to 'normality'.

29   A: *I have to take great heed of earthquakes, which isn't an issue in South Africa.* To take great heed of means 'to consider carefully'.

30   D: *He asked me to come back to New Zealand with him and I agreed, on the condition we'd eventually go back to London.* Lucy is saying that she only agreed to go to New Zealand if her boyfriend agreed to return to London one day.

31   C: *Being a foreigner certainly works in her favour… respondents tend to see me as impartial and open-minded and are… willing to share their lives with me.* Sarah says that because she's English and wasn't brought up in New Zealand, people feel that she can be more objective and fairer about local situations.

32   B: *opposing views are what make strategies, concepts and designs better.* Jenny feels that differences of opinion and discussion will finally lead to better results.

33   C: *I wish New Zealanders could see their country as I do. They don't think they're good enough on the global stage…they definitely are.* Sarah is suggesting that she sees many positive things about New Zealand that New Zealanders don't see for themselves.

34   D: *my…colleagues are…easy-going* [relaxed]. *A good atmosphere more than makes up for* [is more important than]… *salary.* Lucy is saying that she now enjoys working in a friendly, co-operative environment.

p.122–123 PAPER 2 Part 1

Further practice and guidance (p.123)

Effect on target reader

You need to state clearly what you think the target reader should do, or what choice they should make. Do not finish your proposal by saying 'Both of these options are good'.

Content

You should refer to the information from both texts, in order to inform your target reader fully. However, you need to decide which information is essential and must be mentioned, and which information can be left out of you proposal.

Appropriacy of register

1 h   **2** i   **3** f   **4** b   **5** g   **6** d   **7** a   **8** e   **9** c

p.124–127 PAPER 2 Part 2

Further practice and guidance (p.125–127)

Information sheets

Tips

- **T:** Use at least two or three subheadings.

- **F:** But avoid short sentences that do not show your range of grammatical structures and ability to link sentences, clauses and ideas together.

- **F:** It depends on the target reader and the subject of the information sheet.

- **F:** You can use the imperative when presenting useful advice and information: it sounds clear and direct.

Content

a   Buses: the sample answer mentions the route the most useful bus takes, how often it runs, and what you should do if you want the bus to stop.

b   Buying a car: where to look, how to be sure your car is safe. Driving: speed limits, seat belts, a traffic rule.

Range

1 relatively   **2** fairly   **3** regularly   **4** commonly
5 frequently   **6** reliable   **7** thorough   **8** vital

Letter of application

Content

In your answer you need to show that: you can work with children; you can help children with sports or something creative/artistic; you have already worked   successfully in a team.

Range

1 b 2 a 3 a 4 c 5 c 6 d 7 d 8 a 9 b 10 c 11 b 12 d

Further practice

1 **dealing**: In this sentence, *used to* is an adjective and preposition. It means the same as 'I am familiar with'. Remember that after a preposition, the verb takes the *-ing* form.

2 **have been**: We use the present perfect simple to show an activity or situation started in the past which continues up to the present.

3 **for**: *apply* takes the preposition *for*.

4 **worked**: You use the past simple to show a finished activity or situation in the past. You only use the past perfect *had worked* if the past simple also occurs in the same sentence, ie *Before I became a software analyst for TechSystems in March 2002, I had spent five years as a computer programmer*.

5 **with**: *familiar* takes the preposition *with*.

6 **from**: *graduate* takes the preposition *from* + university, or *in* + Maths/Science, etc.

7 **manner**: *telephone manner* is a fixed collocation.

8 **experience**: *experience* is used to show what you have achieved at work. *Experiences* refer to different things you have done in life (*I had some strange experiences when I was travelling round Europe!*).

9 **involve, liaising, setting**: *consist* requires the preposition *of*; *discussing* requires an object, eg problems/ideas; *to set up a meeting* means to organize it, to *make up* means to tell a story that isn't true.

p.129–130 PAPER 3 Part 1

1 **C**: *get along with* is a fixed expression and means 'to have a good relationship with'.

2 **C**: *ranged* is followed by *from*; *consisted* is followed by *in* or *of*; *covered* is followed by *with*.

3 **B**: *the management world* is a fixed expression.

4 **D**: *fooled by* means *tricked* and is the only option which makes sense here.

5 **A**: *management tool* is a fixed expression.

6 **C**: *eager* is the only option followed by the infinitive form and which makes sense here; *enthusiastic* and *excited* are followed by *about* and the *-ing* form.

7 **D**: *dedicating* is the only option which collocates with *themselves*.

8 **C**: *meet the demand* is a fixed expression.

9 **B**: *help* collocates with *from*; *assist* is followed by *with*; *aid* is followed by *in*; *support* is followed by *in*.

10 **C**: *to mean in practice* is a fixed expression.

11 **A**: *joining* is the only option which fits here; *participating* needs *in*; *entering* does not collocate with *session*.

12 **D**: firms cannot be *symbolized*, *demonstrated* or *illustrated*.

p.131 Paper 3 Part 2

13 **what**: this refers forward to *an alarming rate*.

14 **the**: *double the size of…*is a fixed expression.

15 **in**: *in place* means *in position* – ie to be put in place, to be held in place.

16 **either**: this is followed by a noun in the singular form. It means 'on both sides'.

17 **as**: *to be known* as means 'to be called by a particular name'.

18 **including**: is followed by some of the items found in the 'soup' eg footballs, kayaks and Lego.

19 **it**: *it* refers to the rubbish. Rubbish is an uncountable noun so you cannot use *them*.

20 **so**: is followed by an adjective + that + a consequence.

21 **are**: this is needed to form part of the present passive – *objects are found*.

22 **not**: the expression *not to mention* is used to add a comment that emphasizes the main idea of the previous sentence, or clauses.

23 **which/that**: these relative pronouns refer back to 'these creatures' and connects them to the following verb *mistake*.

24 **as/since/because**: in this context, all the options have the same function ie they are followed by the reason for the preceding situation/state etc.

25 **their**: *to work my/their/his way to* (somewhere) means to gradually move towards an area. We need to use *their* because it refers back to 'hundreds of millions of tiny pellets'.

26 **such**: *such as* is followed by an example/examples.

27 **long**: this forms part of the phrase '*It won't/didn't take long before...*'

p.132 PAPER 3 Part 3

1 advisable   2 voluntarily   3 extension   4 harden
5 overweight   6 reduction   7 resistance   8 updating
9 controversial   10 seasonal

p.133 PAPER 3 Part 4

38 form   39 work   40 strong   41 run   42 open

p.134 PAPER 3 Part 5

43 will hardly notice such

44 can't stand being lied

45 you mind giving me

46 made known his intention *or* made it known that he intends

47   on taking over from Paul

48   the possibility of rain in

49   leave John behind unless he

50   sooner had we escaped than

p.135 PAPER 4 PART 1

1   C: James says *not having one* [a TV] *lets me appreciate how addictive I did find it. Like if I went to a house and the TV was on, I'd find myself drawn* [really attracted] *to that, and drawn out of* [taken away from] *the conversation.*

2   A: James says that *I'd be willing to bet* [I am very sure] *that TV is coming to the end of its lifespan as the major form of entertainment. Eventually all digital media will go on to the Internet, so what'll be the point of having a TV?* In other words, James is saying 'Why do we need TV when, in the future, everything we watch or listen to will be available on the Internet?'

3   B: Martin says *that I think the image of the teaching profession in our society is pretty poor – no one wants to go to work and be disrespected. In the past and still in some cultures, people look up to* [respect] *teachers, but not here in the UK, not anymore.* In other words, Martin is saying that teachers do not have much status in society – their profession is not well respected by other peeople.

4   B: Martin mentions the argument to show that female staff respond to playground fights by reprimanding boys, but male staff leave them to find their own solution and a way to co-operate after they have finished fighting.

5   C: Shelley explains that *It* [applying to appear on the show] *was actually for a dare* [her friends had persuaded her to do something to prove she was brave] *…someone from the show rang me up and I'd got an interview, and when the others found out* [when my friends heard this news] *they wouldn't let me quit* [they wouldn't let me change my mind and not enter].

6   A: Shelley says that the tabloids get on her nerves [the low quality newspapers annoy her] because *I could be out doing the shopping and suddenly there's someone* [a reporter] *across the road taking your photo. Basically, it's quite intrusive,* [it invades my privacy] *but I guess that's what happens.*

p.136 PAPER 4 PART 2

7 ancestors   **8** climate change   **9** rope   **10** rats
11 crops   **12** seabirds   **13** disease(s)   **14** relevant

p.137 PAPER 4 PART 3

15   C: Toby explains that *I sort of chose it* [Madagascar]…. *mainly because the kind of work on the volunteer programme there looked like it was really going to stretch me* [challenge me] *and take me out of my comfort zone* [I would be in a situation I was not familiar with] *…like a test of character.*

16   D: Toby explains that *mum was all for it* [mum thought it was a good idea]. *Actually, she really got into it* [she became very enthusiastic about it] *by getting out books from the library and going online and I'd come home and she'd be telling me about the history and the culture, and that was quite handy* [useful] *really.*

17   C: Toby says that in the village *There was no running water and no sanitation, and that took quite a bit of getting used to* [that was difficult for me to adapt to].

18   B: Toby's wallet was stolen by a man he did not know well. Toby says that *I'd got used to the honesty of the people in Madagascar. It was sad to be reminded that not everyone is like that.* In other words, he is saying that it is a shame that not everyone is as honest as the people he had met in Madagascar.

19   D: Toby says that *The odd* [strange] *thing was my attitude towards England. After Madagascar, I could see the enormous gap in consumption between the UK and African countries and knew that if everyone in the world lived like a UK citizen then there'd be no resources left to use.* In other words, Toby is criticizing people in the UK for consuming and wasting too many resources.

20   A: Toby says *don't for a moment think you're superior* [to the people you are helping] *in some way. You need to recognize what you're gaining in return* [getting back] *from the people you're living with.*

p.138 PAPER 4 Part 4

Speaker 1:   21H   26D
We can tell that the speaker is talking about 'lack of open spaces' from the way she recalls her childhood in Cornwall: *the beach, the long walks in the countryside. You could walk and walk and not meet another living soul.* She compares this to: *where our kids are growing up, there's nowhere for them to really play or run about.….It's all concrete and not a bit of grass in sight.* In Task 2, option D is correct because she says *last week we made the decision to pack up* [pack our things and leave] *and head back* [return] *to Cornwall.*

Speaker 2:   22E   27E
We can tell the speaker is talking about inconsiderate neighbours when he says *You can hear it through the walls, really loud. And it's not just the sound – the walls, the floor, the bed, they actually vibrate because of how loud it is. We've asked them to turn it down and they do for a day or two and then it's back to square one* [it returns to the way it was originally]. In other words, he is saying that the neighbours' music is so loud that his wall and furniture shake. He asks them to make it quieter, but they only keep it quite for a few days. In Task 2, option E is correct because he says *I find I'm losing my temper* [becoming angry] *a lot – at work, with my wife, and it's not fair on them.*

Speaker 3:   23C   28A
We can tell that the speaker [a taxi driver] is talking about heavy traffic when he says *You could get from A to B* [you could travel from one place to your destination] *in 20 minutes… Now it takes twice as long. And you can see the passengers in the mirror, fuming because they're stuck in a jam* [traffic jam/heavy traffic] *and the fare's going up.* He also says *The government is talking about restricting access to the city centre – not letting private vehicles in – but I don't think that's practical* which means that he disagrees with the government's proposal to ban cars from the city centre. In Task 2, option A is correct because he says *I had a word with* [I talked to] *a mate of mine – I heard he was looking for some help* [he is looking for people to work] *on a construction site – and he said I could start* [start the job] *whenever I liked. I'm considering it* [thinking about it], *to tell you the truth.*

Speaker 4:   **24G**   **29C**

We can tell that the speaker is talking about pollution when she says *You hear a lot of complaints about air quality, – people can't breathe…but I still have to wear a mask on the bike because of the lethal fumes* [smoke/gases]. In Task 2, option C is correct because she says *I've stopped cycling…and it's having an effect on my weight and my general fitness, and I resent that* [dislike this/ think it is unfair].

Speaker 5:   **25A**   **30H**

We can tell that the speaker [a policeman] is talking about being alone when he says *It's a massive city with a huge population but you can still feel isolated* [alone/by yourself]. *I like my colleagues but it's not like we really socialize* [we don't often socialize] *after work*. In Task 2, option H is correct because he says *The odd thing is, I've actually got used to it* [I don't mind it anymore]. *I'm quite fond of my own company* [I like being by myself] *these days, so I'll probably stick at* [continue doing] *the job for a while longer.*

LISTENING SCRIPTS

TEST ONE Part 1

Extract One

Interviewer: Richard, can you give us an example of what people in other countries are doing in terms of recycling?

Richard: Absolutely. Erm, well, 60 tonnes of plastic packaging are dumped on the streets of Accra, the capital city of Ghana, every day. But recently a businessman called Kwabena Osei Bonsu set up a company called Trashy Bags to do something about it. He pays people to collect plastic bags and these are stitched together to make new ones. This kind of venture should be sponsored by governments, and there are plenty of similar projects occurring in other countries if they need ideas. But Kwabena had decided he wasn't going to wait around. He says he wanted to come up with an idea that would sort out this awful situation in his lifetime.

Interviewer: I believe that in Britain, though, you'd like to stop the use of plastic bags completely?

Richard: Well, yes – they are an absolute environmental disaster but I can't see our government going as far as banning them. I know that some supermarkets are charging customers 5 or 10 pence per bag, but such a small charge doesn't put most people off. Actually, you can get bags made of bamboo or other fabrics but only a minority of people are using them, so I'd say it's up to the supermarkets to start promoting them a bit more actively – so that customers know they're available to buy instead.

Extract Two

Man: You've just had a few sessions of hypnotherapy, haven't you? I have to say, I didn't think you were into that kind of thing.

Woman: You thought I was the skeptical type? Well I've never been a believer in most alternative therapies but I've always been fairly open-minded when it comes to hypnotherapy…at least when it came to dealing with psychological problems. I mean, before I experienced hypnotism for myself, I didn't think it would work for actual physical symptoms. I went along because I wanted to quit smoking, but Dr Grey helped me overcome my back pain, too.

Man: I guess a lot of people see celebrity hypnotists on TV embarrassing people they've hypnotized – making them do ridiculous things. And I think the result of that is that people are put off going to see genuine hypnotherapists – because they think anyone who practises hypnotism is not trustworthy.

Woman: I think you're right, but people should know that hypnotherapy is a serious profession. And if the idea of being under someone else's control makes you nervous, I can tell you it's not like that. You're always aware of what's going on.

Extract Three

Interviewer: Erm, Fiona, how is it working with visitors to the zoo?

Fiona: The public? Generally they're fantastic. Maybe they're a little bit quiet to start with because they're not sure what they're going to do but soon after we've met the rhinos or we've started doing the monkeys they normally open up and they're all 'Oh, this is fantastic'. They start asking questions and they know a lot about the animals anyway because they've been going to the zoo for years. But the hardest thing for me is being constantly alert to the risks because even though you do warn people about them, they just don't realize what could happen. I mean even the cheetahs look so docile and so cuddly.

Interviewer: Have you ever had an incident yourself?

Fiona: No, not exactly, but I did get a bit too close to the bars of the chimpanzee enclosure once, and the chimps had branches with them to try and get food from beyond the bars, and one of the male chimps basically just reached through the bars with his branch and poked me in the ribs and it was basically a 'Get back! That's my food!' and from that moment on I've always been doubly aware of how close I am to an animal and what tools it has to get to me as well. He could have been a lot nastier, though, than he was. It was just a warning.

TEST ONE Part 2

I've been working in the museum for, er, well it's almost twenty years now, and I can tell you that people come along for many different reasons. For some, it's the desire for knowledge, for others, they just want to be entertained on a rainy day. But with the dinosaurs, it's plain old fear. They enjoy being scared, and there's nothing like a 30-foot monster towering over your head to do that, regardless of your age. The first thing the kids do when they run into the exhibition is seek out the interactive displays. I suppose in this age of technology, young people have got used to information being presented on a screen – one brief, bright image after another. But here – nothing moves. You look, usually up – you read, and hopefully you feel something. And I think that the exhibition can help with certain aspects of a child's development.

It's my opinion that you require imagination to appreciate an exhibition like this – you have to be able to fill in the missing pieces for yourself. This is something that is often neglected in mainstream education. Often I have to tell people that we simply don't have all the information yet… even about the more famous dinosaurs like Tyrannosaurus Rex. Dinosaur research is incredibly challenging because so few fossilized skeletons have been found. Did you know that only two of the T-Rex skeletons that scientists base their work on are actually complete? That's not much to go on. What you see in most museums are models based around a few recovered bones – just reconstructions.

You see, the fossilization process requires particular conditions – the creature needs to be buried quickly – then gradual sedimentation needs to occur – and the body has to lie undisturbed. That's why the environments in which fossils are generally discovered tend to be marine ones, rather than geographical areas that have remained comparatively dry. One of the challenges of showing a dinosaur exhibition is that you need to keep up with new theories and decide which ones are credible. Some interesting findings have come out of China in the last decade – which I'll explain in a moment. It's still generally accepted in the scientific community that dinosaurs disappeared following the event of a giant meteor crashing into Earth – which led to significant climate change. But not all dinosaurs succumbed to the cold. It was an enormous volcanic eruption that wiped out many of these creatures in China. They were instantly buried alive – and thus preserved – because there was no oxygen to help in the process of decay. And what interests scientists the most about the Chinese dinosaurs is that they appear to have been covered in feathers. It's possible that they were used for display or defence, but the general opinion is that they were used for insulation. Bird feathers have all these functions, too, of course, but whether birds have directly descended from dinosaurs is still a matter of great debate.

I have to admit that I am rather proud of the exhibition, and the feedback we receive is always positive. But – there's even more we could do to make it a better experience for visitors – and for this reason, their donations are always welcome. In fact, the recent discoveries in China mean that some of our displays will need adapting so that the appearance...

TEST ONE Part 3

Interviewer: As you may have observed from its recent television campaign, the navy is keen to recruit young men and women. With us today we have Chief Petty Officer Peter Martin, who has kindly agreed to share some of his experiences with us. Peter, what was behind your decision to join the navy?

Peter: Well it goes back to where I came from – I knew there were better opportunities out there compared to what was in my hometown. There was nothing there for me except a lifetime of unemployment and messing about. I joined the army and whilst in the army I bumped into a navy guy and I asked him, you know, 'How long have you been in the navy?' He said 'Just two years,' and I said 'Where have you been?' He said 'All over the world' and yeah, I liked the sound of that. The navy was for me. In the army the only option I had ahead of me was a few months in Singapore – so it was an easy decision to transfer – and I've never regretted it.

Interviewer: Was the transition easy – I mean from the army to the navy?

Peter: Oh yeah. Once I was in, well the difference between the army and the navy is the discipline – it's er, how shall

I say – it's that the training in the army's intensive. I did the basic training in the navy – I found it a breeze, I could do that with my eyes closed. However, I did have a hard mother and discipline was what she was all about. If you're raising six boys, and they're all competing for your attention, that's how it has to be. But it wasn't just about obeying orders – it was about leadership. What I mean by that is that my mother led from the front, always showed us by example how to behave. And that's how you do it in the navy. So, yeah, my mother set us on the right track in that respect, and so the transition to the navy was easy. You know, at one stage I was managing 110 people, when I was, er, a petty officer, and I managed that amazingly well. I thought I'd get myself into trouble but no, it went well.

Interviewer: So you adapted, but what about the new recruits, how do they find it?

Peter: Well, some of these new recruits plan on coming for a good time not a long time. When I joined I walked in and said 'this is me for twenty years'. These guys, they can't handle leaving home, that security, er… adjusting to a structured military organization…where rules and regulations are put on them. And taking care of themselves…a big thing when you're coming from school. Mum used to do your washing and your ironing… all that stuff…so a lot of these kids come and don't even have these skills. So – I think it's important for, um, kids leaving school and thinking seriously about the military… they need to be aware that life in the navy is about self-discipline and that they're going to have to adjust to that. If you can achieve that, you'll do well. The other big factor they should remember is that you get friends for life, whether you like it or not, basically…it's the camaraderie that keeps you going at times.

Interviewer: And when you go back to your hometown? What kind of a reaction do you get from people when you go back home?

Peter: Yeah, well, I think it's more jealousy. A lot of them can't see past the front gate, I mean, they've got no desire to find out what's going on in the world beyond the edge of town, and that's all my generation I'm talking about. However, the older people down there welcome you in for a cup of tea to talk about where you've been, what you've done, what you've achieved and just er…because they've never been anywhere else either, but they're curious. I was the unusual one – I was the only one from my year…I think I was the first one from my actual town to join the military. If I'd stayed there, it would just have been a matter of time before I ended up the same way as my old mates – pretty aimless really…So when I go home, it, er, reminds me of how far I've come, everything I've accomplished – and I get a lot of self-satisfaction out of that, to be honest.

Interviewer: How do you think the public perceive the navy?

Peter: It's generally naivety…all they hear is how much money we're pumping into this and that, when things have gone wrong, guys having accidents – they only see what the media feeds them. And a lot of people see that it's not war time, so why do we need a navy? I think more publicity's going to help. We've just done a documentary on the officer training school – more stuff like that would be beneficial to the navy, such as boardings – it would be good to document a boarding – when the navy goes aboard illegal fishing vessels in our own waters or deals with smugglers in international waters – stopping drugs getting into the country. That kind of stuff should be in the public eye…so they know we're doing a good job.

Interviewer: And what about life after the navy? Can the navy prepare you for returning to civilian life?

Peter: Yeah, definitely, I'll give you an example. My mate Brendan, we joined together. He was in the navy for ten years with the naval police, and then he left and went into a position with the customs service – a border control detective. The requirements for that position were that you had a Master's degree, but he went in there with just his basic skills from the navy and he got selected against 500 people that applied, and they all had university qualifications. You name it, they had it. But the skills that he attained from the naval police were exactly in line with what they wanted. The guys from university had limited ability in communication and leadership but the customs people were confident he had everything they required, and that's why the application was successful. I think this kind of thing is something else that makes the navy a good prospect for young people who…

TEST ONE Part 4

1   The thing I hate…and I always used to get myself into this situation – fortunately I've got a strategy now – but when I'm supposed to be showing foreign clients round, I can never remember names. My mind just goes blank. It's pretty poor, really. I mean, it doesn't exactly come across as professional for someone in my position. I'm supposed to be setting an example but I'd find myself saying things like 'Have you met…?' and hoped people would get on with it themselves. I became really aware that I was getting a reputation for it. My assistant actually suggested I rehearse the whole thing with her beforehand so that's what I do now. We actually role-play the whole thing. I'd be lost without her.

2   Well, I'm not exactly the maternal type. Maybe that's got something to do with it. They come along and I'm setting up the equipment and they're beaming with pride and of course you're expected to make all the right noises and comments, but it's not really me. I often can't tell which are boys and which are girls. And recently I've found myself in this situation a couple of times. I've managed to come out with 'What's his name, then?' or 'Have you got a name yet for…?' and then my voice just trails off and I just hide behind the lens. And they've noticed, of course. They feel offended and they're paying money to have their kid's portrait taken. It's not exactly good for business or personal recommendations.

3   I don't have much self-confidence in general but I really feel exposed when we've gone out to eat after work. It's usually the others who decide because, you know,

I'm the new girl in the department and I haven't been in the area long either, and it's always somewhere posh and foreign. I usually get one of them to order or I just say 'the same' so I don't have to repeat it. I wish I'd studied foreign languages at school. They all seem to know exactly what they're ordering, or they pretend they do. I think I'm going to get a phrase book – one that shows you the meaning and the pronunciation nice and clearly. I'm fed up with them all looking down on me. It makes me feel really small at times.

4   I didn't spend a lot of time there, a couple of terms I think. My father was working as a foreign correspondent so we were always relocating. But I was in the same dormitory as Peter Hayward and we got on from the absolute start. Really nice guy, Peter, and we've always kept in contact. It was his idea…in fact, I think he organized the whole thing. I really didn't want to go – I knew exactly what it'd be like – but he went on and on and eventually I gave in. And when I turned up, it was worse than I could possibly have imagined. Nobody had much to say to anybody and the few conversations we had were utterly contrived. What do you expect after a gap of 20-odd years? Nothing in common except most of us had ended up in banking and everybody remembered hating the physics teacher.

5   My brother was working on the island as a diving instructor. It's a good lifestyle. My grandmother was Greek and used to make us repeat certain phrases but I can hardly remember a thing, so I flicked through this pocket dictionary on the way over just to have a few ideas. Anyway, my brother took me to meet some people and I was speaking to one owner in English but I thought it might make more of an impact if I could show I knew a bit of the language. I came out with a couple of phrases I'd memorized…or thought I had. Obviously not well enough judging by his face. He just collapsed laughing. I'm going out there again in a month's time and showing my CV to a couple of restaurants. At least my catering skills are alright…but first I'm going to get myself some private tuition…I mean, I want to be taken seriously. There won't be many people prepared to take me on unless I have some idea of the language.

TEST TWO Part 1

Extract One

Man: How did your anniversary weekend go, Jennifer?

Woman: Well, you know, Tom and I went to a hotel I found on the Internet – and we had a perfectly nice time there. But when it was over and I went to pay, I realized I hadn't looked closely enough at the price. It wasn't for the two of us – it was per person. I went back to our suddenly twice-as-expensive room and I had to confess to my husband. But actually he'd known the price all along and said not to worry and that we could afford it. But that wasn't the point. I actually felt cheated out of a better experience. My husband had been enjoying a really expensive weekend, and I hadn't.

Man: Well, researchers at Stanford University wouldn't be surprised at that. They asked people to try a wine marked with a $5 price tag and then one with a $45 price tag. And of course they preferred the more expensive one – even though the wine came from the same $5 bottle. In a sense, I suppose people should buy expensive wine if it really gives them additional pleasure. And they did the same experiment with painkillers – with the same results.

Woman: Yes, I'd say people will pay more for anything, whether it's a fast car or a packet of potato chips, if they think it's better quality. And if paying $45 for wine makes you happy, why not? But don't you think some of these experiments are misleading, though? I mean, the way they're set up?

Extract Two

Interviewer: Erm, Petra, you've been in training for the marathon for twelve weeks now. What advice would you give would-be runners?

Petra: Well – for a start, if you've never done a race before, like me, you have to go and get yourself a good fitness trainer. It helps keep up the motivation, and if you want to avoid painful blisters and swollen ankles and that kind of thing, you're best off finding someone who knows what they're doing and can work out the right training plan for you. Look, I'm the first to admit that I'm basically lazy and that the idea of running five or six times a week doesn't actually appeal, so I was more than pleased when I found out I didn't have to. I suppose I wanted a short cut to being a marathon runner!

Interviewer: Can you explain what you mean by that?

Petra: Yes. My fitness trainer, Sean Deacon, he's very much against people wearing themselves out before they even get to the day of the marathon. He encourages people to work on improving their overall strength before they go anywhere near an actual long run – so I was doing tons of sit-ups and press-ups and weight-lifting – that kind of thing – before I did any kind of practice running at all. I've heard other runners say you've got to train the way you feel best, by instinct almost, but that wouldn't have worked for me.

Extract Three

Bryan: What do you think of the idea of being educated at home, or 'unschooling', as it's been called?

Laura: Yes, I think 'unschooling' was first used by the American educator, John Holt. He rather saw schools as prisons – where children were bored and weren't in charge of their own development. Personally, I loved school. It was a traditional education but we had the chance to be creative through drama and story-writing and for me, it was beneficial. I mean, of course there are children who shouldn't be there – it just doesn't suit their learning style. And I think employers are often just as impressed with personal skills as with actual qualifications nowadays, so you don't need a formal education as much as you used to but...

Bryan: I can see the benefits. You get lots of individual attention and you get to interact with your family members or others in the community. I believe things like museum trips and studying things in your environment play a big part. But it's a relatively recent trend as far as educational theory goes and there's not been a proper study into how successful it actually is. Also, I can't imagine it'll really catch on with many parents.

Laura: No, a lot of us like some time away from the kids!

TEST TWO Part 2

On this week's *Sports Review* we're taking a look at one of the biggest extreme sports festivals in Europe – The National Adventure Sports Show. If you're not entirely sure what an extreme sport is, you'll be able to see for yourself when the three-day event is televised this weekend. Everything kicks off on Friday afternoon, when the cream of the Continent's skateboarders, BMX riders, snowboarders and all manner of other athletes will turn up to compete, give interviews and sign autographs. For their fans, the amazing stunts will be the biggest attraction of the day.

If you're under 30 and a fan, you'll probably already know that the Sports Show is, for many, the highlight of the extreme sports calendar. The event has grown dramatically since it started in 1999, and this year 40000 people are expected. The success of the show seems to be due to a combination of factors. First, there's the fact that it's not only the biggest exhibition of its type – you can buy or just gaze enviously at the huge range of sportswear on sale, and order the latest equipment on display – but it also provides the setting for a number of major national and international extreme sport competitions, and, on top of all that, there's a massive music festival as well, which is well worth a look.

A lot of the young competitors I met this week while they were practising say the Sports Show in Britain is one of their favourites – one of the best in the world. And the fans were equally enthusiastic. They're not ashamed to admit that these people are heroes in their eyes, and that here's a chance to mix with them, and bring along their own bike or board and have a go themselves. It's these kinds of opportunities, they say, that makes the atmosphere at the show unique, and I have to go along with that.

One of the main aims of the show, according to the organizers, is to introduce new sports from abroad, some more successfully so than others. They told me that last year, apparently, an enthusiast from Holland had attached a sail to his skates and was managing speeds of up to 70 kilometres per hour. Unfortunately for him, they said, the wind died on the second day and that was the end of that. I guess an engine would have been more reliable! So, for anyone planning on introducing a new sport this weekend, bear in mind the local conditions – are they going to work for you or not?

Anyway, if you needed further proof of the event's success, you only have to look at how much more publicity it's getting these days. A few years ago, it was on TV for a mere ten minutes after most people had gone to bed. Now it's promoted by a major organization and if you prefer to watch sport from the comfort of your own home, the whole event is being screened by Channel 4.

TEST TWO Part 3

Interviewer: Sandra, I have to tell you that my kids have been reading your books for years. They're the kind of pictures that completely capture a child's imagination. Do you get as much delight out of producing them?

Sandra: Thank you Mark. Well, yes, certainly I do. But don't think I'm illustrating all the time. I work freelance and freelance work tends to be really great from the point of view of, erm, if you like a variety in your life about what you do and when, particularly with children's illustration, because you have intensive bursts and then you have periods of time when you haven't got any work coming in. But when it does, meeting the deadline is the hardest part. When a book's being produced, the illustrator is the last person to do their bit and by that stage often the restriction of time means that you resort to a similar style – one you know you can do fast, but you have to accept that. But yes, it's ideal for a mother at home with small children which was my situation when I started. You can work any time of the night or day.

Interviewer: How did you get into illustrating children's books? Did you do a particular course that trains you for it?

Sandra: Not really. I did a three-year graphic design degree when I left secondary school and learned all sorts of things, and while I was at college, I also worked for an advertising agency. I've always believed that you try and work in the situation you're heading for while you're training because that's a really good way of networking with people and making contacts, and finding out what the real world's like, so from that perspective it was great. I did lots of ads for the Vogel's bread company and at any one time in my flat I would have all these varieties of bread in my kitchen, and I would be using black charcoal pencil on quite rough paper and it would give a beautiful texture when you did realistic drawings of the bread, but I had to hurry up and draw it before it went mouldy. It was quite time-consuming, what with all the tiny seeds and crusty edges, but the company wanted very realistic pictures. I lost count of how many buns and loaves I had to draw, but, erm, realistic illustration gives me immense satisfaction, so I didn't mind. And then, um, I didn't start doing children's books until I had children and needed to work from home.

Interviewer: How does the actual process work? Do you and the writer ever meet up?

Sandra: No. The editor and the writer have worked on the script of the story together. Then I get a phone call and the editor says 'It's due in this amount of time. Are you interested?' and I always say 'Yes'. Then you receive what we call the 'layout' in the post – that's basically big sheets of white paper with an outline of the book on it, and the actual story positioned on the page where the editor wants to see it. And then they will give you a brief, which is a page-by-page idea of what they want to see from the artist. And I'm lucky in that I've developed a relationship with a few editors in different companies now, so that that brief can be quite flexible when I receive it, because they understand that I've been doing this long enough to know the relationship that's got to happen between the picture and the word, particularly in emergent readers, that's little children who are learning to read. They need a very strong picture–word relationship, and consistent pictures. You can't have a drawing of someone on one page wearing a certain sort of clothing and then change it on the next – that just wouldn't work.

Interviewer: Yes, I know from my own children that repetition and familiarity are important in books. But, erm, when you know you've got work, what's the next step?

Sandra: Well, it usually starts with me reading through the story and I immediately see it in my mind – I have an immediate idea about the central character and often if it's not an animal or cartoon idea, if it's actually a child or an adult, I try to think of someone I know and I base the character on that person. Especially if it needs to be realistic, I might then go out and take a lot of photos of that person, if they agree, to sort of help me get some idea about facial expression and that sort of thing. I used my neighbour in my last book and she thought it was hilarious. My eldest son James has appeared through his life in many of my books. The poor child has had to pose doing all sorts of things because children are quite tricky to draw and it's really helpful if you actually have their little bodies and hands to see how they work – they tend to hold themselves and stand differently to adults.

Interviewer: Have you ever used your own children to get some erm, feedback on your work?

Sandra: No, not like that. When they were younger they used to look at the pictures a lot – they've always been part of their lives. Me illustrating at home has always been part of what they know. I think the best spin-off has been that they've both been exposed to books constantly, and I have a deep belief in reading to children right from the word go. And, um, James and Andrew were barely 6, and they were thoroughly enjoying all sorts of books by that stage, I mean, they had a reading ability way beyond some of their friends at the same age. It's all about the contact you have with your child and I think that children are missing out on that more and more, perhaps with everybody being busy, but books are a wonderful way to curl up and get together.

Interviewer: And for any young person who would like a career in illustration. How should they go about it?

Sandra: Well, you need to build up a portfolio, lots of examples of your work, to show to publishers. It's really good to show a range of ethnic backgrounds, the fact that you can draw people and animals, perhaps that you can cartoon; versatility is the key to getting work. And when I started out, I just went round lots of different children's publishers and met the editor. I suppose you could send in your CV first, but I tended to ring and make an appointment and go and see them because I believe that it's always best to go and speak to somebody. They get a better idea about the person they're dealing with. And if you really want to get on, you have to market yourself really well. You need to generate your own work and put your face in front of people at overseas conferences, that sort of thing. The great majority of our most successful contemporary artists are trained teachers, and they've worked in that profession while they've consolidated their art career – so it's always handy to have something else up your sleeve.

TEST TWO Part 4

1   When I was a kid, well, a teenager I suppose, they weren't that well known, not at the start, although, you know, they got pretty big afterwards. But me and my mate Simon, we were really into them and I used to go round to his house when we knew they'd be on and we'd be glued to the TV set for the whole performance. I had a Saturday job just so I could buy the albums…the T-shirts, posters, magazines, you name it. The lead was my absolute idol. And when things were really bad at home – when my parents were rowing over money or whatever – I'd turn the sound up and switch off to the world. It was a way of escaping…a way of dealing with all the bad stuff going on.

2   It was about the only thing I was interested in. I wasn't much good at anything else. I still can't add up and I've got no brain for anything scientific. But at that age I was quite a voracious reader and I also had my own ideas for stories. I suspected I could write but I was too shy to show anyone. Certainly not my mum. She's never read a book in her life unless you count cookery books. It was Mrs Shelly that gave me the push I needed. She read out one of my essays to the whole class. It was one of the proudest moments I ever had the whole time I was there. I reckon it was her who started me off. In fact, when I first got published, it was Mrs Shelly I dedicated it to.

3   There's one thing I can say for him, he was honest. He said what he thought with no hesitation – just 'this is how I see it'. He was the same with everyone. Friends, strangers, the men he worked with, his bosses. Not everyone liked that but at least they knew where they stood. Mum never got used to it. She'd be after some compliment about her new dress or her new hair-do, and he'd tell her straight out. 'No love, it's wrong on you.' It was a bit much at times, but I'd like to think I take after him in that way. I've certainly made an effort to apply his honesty and directness in my work. When you're in government, the public need to trust you. If you even slip up once, you'll never get that trust back.

4   Sometimes, when the paper has sent me overseas on an assignment, and it could be in the middle of gunfire or I'm just sitting next to my broken-down jeep, I have this sudden flashback to the first time we met. I was a miserable teenager with no interests to speak of, really.

And I was probably going to be following my dad into the factory. Then James moved in next door and I was allowed to go round there. He was interested in just about everything – his room was full of unfinished science projects and weird pets, but what I really liked were his books – full of stories and photos from all round the world. They were a real eye-opener. My parents, I don't think, had ever seen the value of learning for its own sake, but suddenly James gave me the desire to go off exploring and discovering. Now I think about it, he was the one who wanted to be a reporter but it turned out to be me instead.

5   He was brilliant. It didn't matter how many bad guys there were, they were no match for him. It was on every Thursday night at 5 o'clock. My dad would collect me from school and as soon as I got out of the car I'd run in and grab the remote control off my sister. All the kids in my class loved him, too! As soon as the bell went, all of us – well, not the girls of course – we'd all rush into the playground and do all the moves on each other. One day I did this karate kick on a mate of mine and he ended up in hospital 'cos he'd fallen backwards and bashed his head on some stone steps. I think my mate thought it was quite cool, actually, but my parents were furious. I had to stay in my room away from the television for a whole month. I suppose it didn't do my homework any harm, though.

TEST THREE Part 1

Extract One

Interviewer: Marian, is there ever an autobiographical element to your work?

Marian: Definitely not. But people seem desperate to believe it and look for anything that can connect you to them. A woman came up to me recently while I was in Brighton and asked if I'd ever tried to make contact with the child I've given away for adoption. I had to tell her that I'd never had a child, and she looked – at first – astounded – and then rather angry with me, as if I'd lied to her. And I realized she'd wanted to exchange stories – that she'd given away a child, and thought I was someone who could relate to her.

Interviewer: There seems to be a growing interest in autobiographies of people who've had absolutely terrible lives…

Marian: True, and many of them are bestsellers. I think the world's become a rather depressing place for many people, and it's comforting for them to read about the misfortunes of others…not that that's a good thing, mind you, but it's probably not a trend that's likely to go away. For once I don't blame the publishers – they're only responding to a demand.

Extract Two

Man: I think you'll laugh at this. I was shopping with my five year old – we were in a rush as always but – of course

– he insisted on looking at the toys. Now I looked at toys when I was a kid but I never thought my mum would actually buy anything. It was 'look, don't touch' and 'wait for your birthday'. Anyway, I can see my son pointing at this plastic truck in its big bright box, and he's going to scream if he doesn't get it. He's not the only one I've seen using that trick. Anyway, you know what, we get home and it's broken after ten minutes.

Woman: Yes, that sounds familiar. And I'm pretty sure – like most consumers – you didn't bother going back to the store.

Man: You're right. Why do people put up with substandard products nowadays?

Woman: Well, Paul, people are usually entitled to a refund if they want one, as long as they've got proof of payment. But the simple fact of the matter is that we can't be bothered. We can now buy a lot for little money. We've got used to buying inexpensive, easily replaceable things. But that's an expensive way to do things in the long run.

Extract Three

Interviewer: Kesaia, where do these beautiful cloths come from?

Kesaia: These here, from Hawaii, these from Fiji, and here...these ones, from Tonga and Samoa. The pieces are quite old but nicely preserved. One of the reasons why we don't see so many examples from the more recent past is that the craft of tapa-making nearly died out in some of these places, especially in Hawaii, what with the arrival of the Europeans and their effect on society. You see, they brought cotton with them, and this was welcomed with a great deal of enthusiasm. It was much easier to work with, see. And of course, the European missionaries did not like the way tapa cloth was worn in religious ceremonies. Not at all.

Interviewer: But I believe there's a bit of a revival of this craft going on?

Kesaia: That's true – to an extent. In Fiji, for example, some women I know are making tapa again. They learnt the skill from their grandmothers and now they're teaching their daughters. They rely on it for survival – I mean the income it brings in, it can support a whole family. In the main, it's sold to local people, rather than holiday-makers. I'm glad that it's one cultural tradition that isn't going to die out.

TEST THREE Part 2

What's the number one takeaway food in Britain? Hhmm, I'll let you know in a while – but first – let's look at the picture a few years ago. It was then that the Restaurant Association carried out its first ever study conducted solely into the restaurant business...um, I'll just point out that coffee shops weren't included in that. It reported that we were eating – approximately – a staggering 1.7 billion restaurant meals a year – that's about 30 meals per person apparently.

The study also revealed that Britons had developed a preference for Chinese food, over our old favourite, Indian curry. And by comparison, far more meals were being eaten in Italian restaurants than in what the study called cosmopolitan restaurants, that's a category that includes fusion cuisine – the kind of food that takes something from the menu of one country and combines it with another's. I'm sure you know what I'm talking about. And while we tend to think of restaurants as small family businesses, the study revealed that as many as 40 per cent of restaurants belong to chains – that is – they're all owned by the same corporate group. That's higher than I would have guessed.

Another thing the report suggested and which is still very much the case, is that while the restaurant industry is growing, this doesn't necessarily mean all is well. More than 30 per cent of restaurants this year reported a loss. I suppose it's to be expected. There's a lot of competition and you need more than a marketing plan and a chef.

Anyway – what is the current number one takeaway food? It may or may not surprise you to know that it's sushi, or at least our British version of this Japanese cuisine. Sushi first arrived on Britain's tables sometime in the 1980s when it appeared as party food at exclusive business gatherings. Then the interest in sushi really took off when some sushi restaurants began providing a delivery service: this allowed middle managers to get their healthy lunch without actually moving from their desks.

Not all developments have been positive ones, though. The expansion of the sushi industry and the food's growing popularity meant that the supermarkets were forced to notice the trend...and they rapidly began stocking their shelves with chilled blocks of rice, seaweed and tuna. If I sound less than enthusiastic – it's because I've had the pleasure of eating real sushi in Japan. Hhmm, anyway, sushi is not without its critics. There is some debate about how many calories can be found in sushi.... perhaps not as few as the health-conscious among you would prefer...for example...

TEST THREE Part 3

Interviewer: Today I have with me Callum Gray, volcanologist and recently the presenter of Channel Two's excellent series *Living with Volcanoes*. Callum, the media and the public reaction to the series has been extremely positive, hasn't it?

Callum: So far, yes, it's all good. But to be honest, the subject matter makes it easy. What person hasn't drawn a volcano when they were little? And the presenting part was fun...I mean I'm always happy to go on about my work. When people find out what you do, their response is always positive...they're always curious to learn more. Most people are fairly ignorant about geology, but when it comes to volcanoes, they don't hold back with the questions. It's not one of those jobs you mention and people instantly stop listening. They assume your job is risky, that you must be some kind of heroic figure...which is definitely not always the case! There's an awful lot of sitting in your chair, analysing endless streams of data – that kind of thing.

Interviewer: So, if it wasn't the danger, what drew you to becoming a volcanologist in the first place?

Callum: Well you know, I think, my father was a geologist, and you might think it was in the blood, but dad's preoccupation was with fossils mainly. We were expected to go along on the expeditions and I wasn't entirely disinterested but I was more eager to see if there was anyone around to play with. I suppose I did take after dad in that I took a geology degree. In fact, it was on a field trip that I saw my first eruption way down a crater. I was simultaneously quite terrified and quite amazed by the power of it all. I knew at that moment I would have to switch fields...that volcanoes would be a lifelong fascination. It's a real shame that my father didn't live to see the series.

Interviewer: There was one episode in the series when you were in Hawaii – in a helicopter flying over a huge volcanic crater. I heard you say something to the pilot about it going better than last time?

Callum: In the episode you saw, the volcano was quiet, but Jack – he was the pilot – and I – we'd been there a few years earlier, and at that time, when we were flying over the crater, I suspected it might be the end. There was an eruption in progress and I wanted to check the lava flows one more time but it was just before dusk already. All my fault, I'm afraid. I should have known better. We were over the crater when the clouds suddenly came in and we were just flying blind. We could easily have flown into the side of the hill or into the fountain. Neither of us spoke while he was trying to get us out but I had this awful sense of responsibility for putting Jack into that position. We finally got back to camp and it was only then that I felt rather shaky and incredibly relieved, of course.

Interviewer: I suppose it's the kind of job where mistakes can be fatal. It must be rather difficult to get things right all the time.

Callum: Well we don't. That's the thing with volcanoes – you're always learning. But we do have an enormous responsibility to get things as near to right as possible – for example we have to evaluate the damage a lava flow could potentially cause...which direction it's taking. You don't want to evacuate a town unless it's really necessary. I'd like to think that's something I have the experience and confidence to manage now; that, and being able to talk to the local communities whose houses and property might be destroyed. I can't say I've got used to the reporters, though. It can take a great effort on my part to remain patient with them when a volcano's going off and I'd rather be monitoring the equipment. The other thing you gain with experience is knowing that you have to remain alert to the many hazards that an active volcano poses. It's not just an eruption that can get you – you need to be careful where you step – the ground can be extremely hot!

Interviewer: For those listeners that don't know, Callum also manages to fit in a couple of terms of lecturing a year.

Callum, do you think the TV series'll mean there'll be an upturn in the number of students taking volcanology?

Callum: I don't know about that. I think any student seriously considering volcanology as a career will probably have done their research and will be aware of the competitive nature of the job – that there's not enough volcanoes to go around! Even if you get work, it could be months after an eruption occurred. I suppose the TV series may give some viewers the impression that we're always outdoors, but in fact a great deal of work is done at a computer analysing data, and we're often off at conferences, too. Actually, that's something that students don't anticipate – that they'll need to be able to produce papers concerning their research findings, and that therefore a good command of written English is vital.

Interviewer: I see. Well Callum, we're almost out of time but I hear that you're about to set off for Iceland. Will you miss the TV work while you're back working in the field?

Callum: Working on the programme has been a great learning curve and the series gave me the freedom to travel to some incredible countries I hadn't yet been to, but no, I'll be happy to be back doing what I do best – peering into craters, taking rock samples...all that. The thing about volcanoes is that, despite all the research and the knowledge we've gained, you still never really know what's coming next. I like the element of surprise in my work, more so than having to work to a schedule which is what making a TV series seems to be all about.

TEST THREE Part 4

1 It's hard work, you know. People still have this image that it's a glamorous lifestyle but it's not. I was the same. It's all I wanted to be when I was growing up. Never wanted to be anything else. And here I am. Not exactly seeing much of the world except for hotel rooms and if I'm lucky, the hotel swimming pool. The hours are bad. It's not the jet lag – you get used to that. But it's trying to have a social life when all your friends have regular jobs… or at least jobs with normal working hours. And a lot of the job, well most of it, is the same old routine every time. And you always have to keep a smile on your face, even if you're absolutely fed up and there's four or five people all complaining that they ordered a vegetarian meal and where is it? If I'd known it was going to be like this, I guess I would have chosen another career instead.

2 On the whole, I quite like what I do, but there's one thing that really winds me up. Delayed night flights. They have this chain effect. Of course it starts with the people waiting in the airport, you know, they're really excited about their holiday, and then they find out they've got to wait another five or six hours. By the time they get over here, they're exhausted and in a bad mood and they take it out on you. What they don't realize is that we've had to work longer shifts so we're still around to check them in when they arrive. And the most annoying thing is that we often find out at the last minute. You think you're finishing at 8.30 and then one of the couriers calls from the airport and tells you it's going to be another three hours before they all arrive.

3   I've been in the job for quite a while now. There's been a lot of changes, mostly to do with the technology side and there's a lot more destinations we need to know about – but the customers don't change. There are certain types. Some of them come in knowing exactly where they want to go and then it's simply a matter of finding something at the right price and time. Then there's the other type who you can spend hours and hours with and still they're hesitating about it. You can get down every brochure, call up all the tour operators – and still they're saying, 'Maybe…I'm not sure…can we think about it?' I don't blame them. It's a lot of money to pay out and most people only get one holiday a year. You have to be patient with them. It's part of the job.

4   This year I'm off to Greece. I've never even been there myself before, so it's going to be a bit of a challenge. I've got to start reading up on the history so I sound like I know what I'm talking about. Before I was working in St Lucia and Antigua – really different – so this really is a big jump. But I'm looking forward to it. I've always been fascinated by the language, the customs…just the whole culture. Yeah, I've got a lot to learn and I've got about three weeks to make a start before I'm having to explain it all but I can't wait to go! I can always refer to my notes or ask one of the others if I get stuck.

5   You know where we're off tomorrow? An art gallery. It's about the last place on Earth I'd choose to go but then, you see, it isn't my choice. That's the problem when you go with a group of people…they're all different. It was supposed to be just the three of us at first and then…I don't know…it ended up there's eight. It's impossible. I don't know. Maybe I'll go off and do my own thing, but then you get accused of being anti-social. And the day after, they want to drive around and go sightseeing. I tried to tell them about the traffic but they won't listen. I'd rather just sit and have a drink than be driving round looking at a lot of old monuments. I mean, once you've seen one old statue you've seen them all.

TEST FOUR Part 1

Extract One

Interviewer: I recently heard you say that you never watch TV. Is that right?

James: Yep. I threw it out a while back. I'm not saying there aren't any good things about it, but the negatives outweigh the positives in terms of what it does to society. It encourages us to be passive, so although I haven't taken a particularly moral step to not have a TV, I'm happy to do without it. TV's all about programming people to buy certain things – far more so than it used to be – and it makes us become more materialistic – not a great value, I think. And not having one lets me appreciate how addictive I did find it. Like if I went to a house and the TV

was on, I'd find myself drawn to that, and drawn out of the conversation.

Interviewer: Don't your friends find your lack of a television set a bit weird?

James: Honestly – a lot of my mates don't have one either. I'd be willing to bet that TV is coming to the end of its lifespan as the major form of entertainment. Eventually all digital media will go on to the Internet, so what'll be the point of having a TV? That's not to say that everything on the Net is or will be of superior quality to what we get now on the TV – but at least you can ignore the advertising on the Net.

Extract Two

Interviewer: Martin Greenwood – why do we need this campaign to get more male teachers into secondary schools?

Martin: Look at the ratios. For every ten female teachers, there's one male and that's been the case for too long. The government has made progress in offering better financial incentives, but the number of young men currently enrolled on teacher training courses is still depressingly low. I think the image of the teaching profession in our society is pretty poor – no one wants to go to work and be disrespected. In the past and still in some cultures, people look up to teachers, but not here in the UK, not any more.

Interviewer: But surely it's the quality of the teacher that counts, not the gender?

Martin: Look, let me give you an example. I was observing a playground recently and a couple of young boys got into a bit of a fight – not too serious – just some pushing around. One of the female staff went running over and told them both off for being violent, but a male teacher would have known they had to sort things out for themselves. They know that boys fight and then get on with things.

Extract Three

Interviewer: It's been – what – er, two months since you won the show, Shelley. Have you spent all the prize money yet?

Shelley: Yeah, that soon went. It wasn't a lot in the first place. That's not why I did it. It was actually for a dare. I said I'd have a go at getting in if my friends Sandra and Jasmine did. You know, you have to send in a video – you talking about yourself, that kind of thing – but I never thought I'd hear back. And then someone from the show rang me up and I'd got an interview, and when the others found out, even though they hadn't got on to the show, they wouldn't let me quit. They liked the idea of having a famous mate.

Interviewer: And are you still seeing those same people, or have you moved up in the world?

Shelley: No, nothing's changed there. We still hang out together. But I do feel like a new member of the royal family sometimes. Well, it's not like I'm getting into exclusive restaurants for free, but it's the tabloids that get on my nerves. I could be out doing the shopping and suddenly there's someone across the road taking your photo. Basically, it's quite intrusive, but I guess that's what happens.

TEST FOUR Part 2

Most people have heard of Easter Island. We know it for its huge stone statues – or – to be exact – its stone heads – that were built and erected along the coastline. Anyone looking at them cannot fail to be impressed by the incredible carving…these images of power and mystery. Who or what do they represent? Going by the art in other Polynesian cultures, most archaeologists conclude that what we're seeing are the ancestors of the people who made them.

But once you've got past admiring the statues, you have to ask yourself, how did they get there? You see, Easter Island has no trees, and in pre-industrial societies, you can't move heavy objects without them. Well, we know that there were trees, that there were once millions of palms across the island. There are researchers who claim that climate change was responsible for their disappearance, but I'm not convinced we have the evidence for that yet. There's no dispute that many trees were used in the construction and transportation of the stone heads. Not only did they provide wood, but also the bark of the palm trees could be used to make rope. You need both of these things for creating the kind of machine that could move several tons of stone, and of course the people needed wood for housing and fuel, too.

But was man responsible for the loss of all the trees? Another theory has been put forward and the evidence comes from the shells of palm seeds. There's not one shell that hasn't been found without toothmarks…all from the teeth of rats. They probably arrived on the island by boat – hiding in the canoes of the Polynesian settlers. So, it's been seriously suggested that they simply ate all the seeds and that's why the trees disappeared. Once all the trees were gone – for whatever reason – there was nothing to stop harsh winds from sweeping across the island and destroying the crops that the people had planted.

What else could they eat? Well, we know from the thousands of bones that have been found that great colonies of seabirds used to inhabit the island – but they soon became the main part of the islanders' diet and eventually all died out. Worse was to come.

When the Europeans arrived, they introduced diseases that had previously been unknown on the island and the native population naturally had no immunity. This is one of the absolutely tragic situations where local people were absolutely defenceless and could do little to save themselves. We really can't say yet with certainty what got rid of all the trees – but they did go – and this deforestation largely contributed to the downfall of Easter Island. And I believe that what occurred there in the past is relevant now, in our own, modern world. That destruction was a small-scale version of the environmental devastation happening around the globe. It is essential that we learn lessons from the past in order to protect the future.

TEST FOUR Part 3

Interviewer: It's that time of year again when thousands of students are about to take their final exams…but then what? Will they begin their search for a well-paid job or will they choose to take a year off before entering the labour market? I'd like to welcome Toby Burrow to the studio, who is here to talk about the year he spent doing voluntary work in Madagascar.

Toby: Hi Andrea. First of all, before I say anything that might come across as a bit negative, I completely recommend Madagascar. In fact, I just saw in the paper today that there's a documentary on it tonight so any interested students should have a look. I sort of chose it partly because it was so far away from England and exotic, but mainly because the kind of work on the volunteer programme there looked like it was really going to stretch me and take me out of my comfort zone…like a test of character. And it wasn't like anyone could give me any advice. The students I knew from the year before us had gone off travelling, but only on a backpacker's tour.

Interviewer: I'm sure that many parents are anxious when their children announce that they're going off to distant lands. How did yours react?

Toby: Honestly, they were fine about it. I suppose dad tried to talk me out of it at first. He thought I should be getting on with finding a secure job…that kind of thing, but mum was all for it. I think she would have loved to have travelled herself but she missed out on that by having me and my sisters. Actually, she really got into it by getting out books from the library and going online and I'd come home and she'd be telling me about the history and the culture, and that was quite handy, really. The only thing I had to prepare for was getting all my vaccinations done and taking a course of malaria tablets.

Interviewer: And when you arrived in Madagascar, was it what you expected?

Toby: Sort of. The organization which was running the volunteer programme had been quite clear about the teaching work I'd be doing. But I admit I'd led a sheltered life up to then and living in the village was quite an eye-opener. There was no running water and no sanitation, and that took quite a bit of getting used to. I didn't mind so much the fact that I was sleeping in a room with the other volunteers. Coming from a large family, I'm used to sharing my living space. And in fact, I actually need background noise to get off to sleep, otherwise I can't help but feel rather lonely.

Interviewer: Was there any time that you wanted to come running home?

Toby: No, I can't say there was. I remember I once went off sailing for a day. There were six of us – all from Europe – some mates from the programme and some guy I didn't know who worked for a hotel in the city. When we got back to shore I found that my wallet had disappeared... someone had obviously taken it. I felt that I couldn't directly accuse anyone so I ended up saying nothing. A few days later, I heard that the hotel guy had been arrested for stealing other stuff...and eventually I got my...um.. empty...wallet back. I realized that – whereas in England I was always careful about not leaving my stuff around – I'd got used to the honesty of the people in Madagascar. It was sad to be reminded that not everyone is like that.

Interviewer: And after all that, when you finally got home, did it take long to readjust to – if you like – normal life?

Toby: In a sense. There were many things I missed about Madagascar, although I knew that part of my life was definitely over. The odd thing was my attitude towards England. After Madagascar, I could see the enormous gap in consumption between the UK and African countries and knew that if everyone in the world lived like a UK citizen then there'd be no resources left to use. It was good seeing my family. It's a selfish thing, but even though you've changed, you don't want anyone else to, and I liked the familiarity of home, but I didn't immediately get in touch with my friends from university. Being in Madagascar was a life-changing experience and when I got back I felt rather disconnected to people I'd known previously – at least initially.

Interviewer: And now you can speak from experience, what should prospective gap-year travellers know?

Toby: That's a hard one to answer because your experience is what you make it, and very much to do with the kind of person you are. Some graduates just go off and have fun for a year and if that's what you're into, fine. There's hardly a moral obligation to do charity work. But if you do volunteer, for example, to do something for a local community, don't for a moment think you're superior in some way. You need to recognize what you're gaining in return from the people you're living with. I'd also avoid signing up for a project with a friend because that way you won't make the effort to get to know new people, and make sure you choose a reputable company to go with, otherwise you'll just end up miserable and probably out of pocket.

TEST FOUR Part 4

1   We came up here from Cornwall when I was a kid, when I was about 10 years old. So I was old enough to remember what it was like – the beach, the long walks in the countryside. You could walk and walk and not meet another living soul. But, you see, where our kids are growing up, there's nowhere for them to really play or run about. When they built these flats, I don't think they had kids in mind. It's all concrete and not a bit of grass in sight. Anyway, just last week we made the decision to pack up and head back to Cornwall. The money won't be as good but at least we won't be squashed up like rats in a cage.

2   It drives me absolutely crazy. And the worse thing is, I find I'm losing my temper a lot – at work, with my wife, and it's not fair on them. It's not their fault. You see, I work nights, so I really, really do need my sleep during the day. I get home about 8am – and I see my wife for about 30 minutes before she goes off to work, and then I'll get to sleep about 11am. I'm just about in a really deep sleep when it starts. You can hear it through the walls, really loud. And it's not just the sound – the walls, the floor, the bed, they actually vibrate because of how loud it is. We've asked them to turn it down and they do for a day or two and then it's back to square one. I'd be happy to move, only we just bought the place 18 months ago.

3   It wasn't as bad as this when I started out. You could get from A to B in 20 minutes, no problem. Now it takes twice as long. And you can see the passengers in the mirror – they're sitting there in the back, fuming because they're stuck in a jam and the fare's going up. I'm not saying I know what the solution is. The government is talking about restricting access to the city centre – not letting private vehicles in – but I don't think that's practical. The public transport's already overcrowded. The other day I had a word with a mate of mine – I heard he was looking for some help on a construction site – and he said I could start whenever I liked. I'm considering it, to tell you the truth.

4   There's no need for it. People are just lazy. Our society has just become completely reliant on the private car, and it's not necessary. You hear a lot of complaints about air quality – people can't breathe – but they're not prepared to do anything about it. I live in a village and the traffic isn't that bad, to be honest, but I still have to wear a mask on the bike because of the lethal fumes some vehicles chuck out; it's just unbearable. It's got to the point where I've kind of given up. I mean, I've stopped cycling during the week and it's having an effect on my weight and my general fitness, and I resent that.

5   When I was stationed in the village, all I had to deal with was a few bicycle thefts and lost dogs. So when they told me I was being transferred to the city, I was certainly pleased about it, but...to be honest...I found that life here isn't all it's cracked up to be. It's a massive city with a huge population but you can still feel isolated. I like my colleagues but it's not like we really socialize after work. Maybe it's my fault – I'm often really exhausted and just go home. The odd thing is, I've actually got used to it. I'm quite fond of my own company these days, so I'll probably stick at the job for a while longer.